W9-AFK-583

The

Americans

Contributors

Alfred Owen Aldrich
Paul M. Angle
Elliott Arnold
Herman Ausubel
Bernard Bailyn
Whitfield J. Bell, Jr.
Ray Allen Billington
Carl Bode
Claude G. Bowers
Irving Brant
Carl Bridenbaugh
Roger Burlingame
Robert Cantwell
Bruce Catton
Thomas C. Cochran
Alfred Crofts
George Dangerfield
Philip Davidson
Adele deLeeuw
O. M. Dickerson
Richard M. Dorson
Edward Ellsberg
James Thomas Flexner
Alfred Frankenstein
Frank Freidel
John A. Garraty
Virginia C. Gildersleeve
Walter Havighurst
Robert Selph Henry
John D. Hicks
Robert S. Holzman
Howard Mumford Jones
Waldemar Kaempffert
Madison Kuhn
Oliver W. Larkin
Irving A. Leonard
Jay Leyda
Dumas Malone
Kemp Malone
Nathan Miller
Richard B. Morris
Frank Luther Mott
Allan Nevins
Donald Culross Peattie
Nathaniel Peffer
Dexter Perkins
Charles van Ravenswaay
Robert E. Riegel
Max Savelle
Arthur M. Schlesinger, Jr.
Charles Coleman Sellers
Odell Shepard
Clarence ver Steeg
Boyd B. Stutler
Benjamin P. Thomas
Paul A. Varg
Charles Vevier
Thomas J. Wertenbaker
T. Harry Williams
George F. Willison
Charles M. Wiltse
Carl Wittke
Louis B. Wright

The

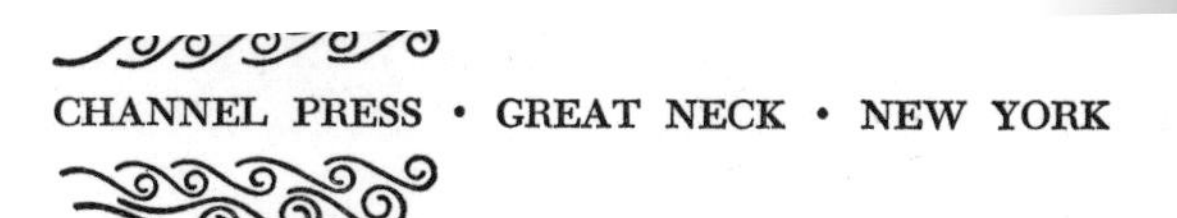
CHANNEL PRESS · GREAT NECK · NEW YORK

Unforgettable Americans

Edited by John A. Garraty
Developed as a project of the
Society of American Historians
by Allan Nevins

First printing

Library of Congress
Catalog Card Number: 60-15694

Printed in the United States of America

Designer: Ernst Reichl

PREFACE

A LITTLE more than a century ago Emerson published *Representative Men*, which of all his books—save the first and second series of essays—has probably had the most readers and widest influence. Each of the figures whom it treated belonged to the Old World, without a single American, and all but one were thinkers, men of intellect and not of action. His one great doer was Napoleon, a bizarre choice that would have been condemned by Emerson's friend, William B. Channing; for it is hard to call Napoleon a representative of any one force, and he was far from a model or illustrator of great virtues. But Emerson used the word "representative" in a special sense. He was thinking of men who on a fairly heroic scale represented some of the prime categories of human achievement: the poet, the philosopher, the prophet. And it seems clear that he, like Carlyle in *Heroes and Hero-Worship*, a book with a clearer thesis, wished to lead men to think about some of the problems of individuality and leadership.

These problems are endless. What are the qualities of human excellence that make a man great? How can they be identified? While a majority of the world calls Francis Drake a great hero, a minority term him a pirate, and people quarrel violently about the merits of Cromwell and Jefferson. What are the traits of a successful man, and how can success be measured? Is history shaped as much as Carlyle thought it was by strong men, and had Carlyle any evidence for his assertion that right makes might? Or is history shaped, as Karl Marx taught, by social and economic forces? Does the crisis do anything to create the leader, and if so, how much? Or is the leader rather controlled by events, as Linclon frankly stated he had been?

It is to be hoped that the present collection of studies will induce readers to ask themselves not dissimilar questions. In this book we meet men and women representative in a humbler and more practical sense than that implied by Emerson. The sketches all present "Americans." Among them the men and women of intellect are few compared with the men of action. No figure supremely great in spirit and mind, no Spinoza or Shakespeare, appears, for America has not yet produced one. Many people will read these scores of studies for the color and drama of the lives, for their sharp contrasts, and for the way in which they mirror different facets of our history. But the approach to them should not be on a merely factual and episodic plane. They raise philosophic inquiries which deserve thought.

How does this great group of personages differ—essentially—from an equal group of Englishmen, or Frenchmen, for the same span of time? Do they show any common denominator of national character? Do they bear out the frequent assertion that the prevailing tone of American life has been materialistic, and that our typical men are those who have explored wildernesses, led armies, built iron mills, or made mechanical inventions? Are those of our famous men who can justly be denominated great as few as a first glance at this list would suggest? Why do we find so few thinkers—thinkers on an abstract plane—and why still fewer skeptics?

One reassuring fact seems to be demonstrated by this volume. It has been said by Tocqueville, Bryce, and other acute observers that our democracy reduces culture to a monotonous, even commonplace, level, and irons out distinction; the exceptional man, the genius and the radical dissenter, is obliterated by our passion for conformity. No doubt this is too often true. Since our civilization became above all a business civilization, this old reproach has taken a new form. The organization man, we are told, in the church, in education, in the legal profession and engineering, and in most other callings, has replaced the hardy individualist; and most of all this is true in our great corporations. Nevertheless, the men and women here described are nearly all bold individualists, and many of them are aggressive rebels (Tom Paine, Mary Emerson, Edgar Allan Poe, Wilhelm Weitling,

Ignatius Donnelly, for example). They prove that if some forces in American life make for conformity and the cult of the average, other forces—the pioneer impulse, the vital role of innovation in our economy, the stimulating clash of Old World cultures poured into our melting pot—have made for variety and

and that it is often achieved at the expense of the integrity that is essential to greatness. Many a famous man is petty or mean; comparatively few are without the flaws that make us deny Andrew Jackson, or Charles Sumner, or Mark Hanna, for example, a title to greatness. Character, it must always be insisted, is more important than intellect or talent, and high distinction without character is worthless. But this volume by no means supports the thesis that Americans overvalue success. It rather bears out our claim that one of the more prominent American traits has always been a self-forgetting idealism, and that the man who cherishes a vision outside himself has been a more typical figure than the self-seeker. In this fact lies a great deal of such inspiration as this book may give its readers.

ALLAN NEVINS

Huntington Library
San Marino, California
October, 1960

TABLE OF CONTENTS

PUBLISHER'S NOTE

In 1951, in answer to a request from the Society of American Historians for assistance in bringing about wider acceptance of history in the mass media, Carl Haverlin—president of Broadcast Music, Inc.—originated "The American Story," a series of radio scripts telling the story of the United States. Each written by an authority in special areas of history, these papers (in the words of Allan Nevins) "were heard by audiences which certainly aggregated millions of people. No other series of narratives and essays on the American past ever had so extensive a currency."

In 1956, sixty of the papers were collected in book form, edited by the distinguished historian, Earl Schenck Miers, and published by Channel Press under the title "The American Story." That volume also reached a vast audience—through regular book channels, through distribution by major book clubs, and as a result of publication abroad by foreign publishers and by the United States Information Agency. "The American Story" is now being used as a textbook in high schools and colleges across the nation.

To continue the telling of this nation's past, Broadcast Music, Inc., and the Society of American Historians developed and made available to broadcasters an additional group of essays relating our history in terms not of events but of the lives of significant Americans. As Director of Special Projects of Broadcast Music, Inc., Mr. Russell Sanjek has had over-all responsibility for this radio project. The Society of American Historians and Channel Press take this opportunity to acknowledge Mr. Sanjek's important contribution to this country's knowledge of its heritage.

INTRODUCTION

ANYONE who looks about himself in America today cannot help but be impressed by the burgeoning population of the country and the ever-increasing wealth and complexity of our civilization. Progress—quantitative, if not necessarily qualitative—seems built into the system. Each decade the census shows that increasing millions of Americans have produced more goods, are enjoying more leisure time, spend—and save—more money than ever before. Minor swings of the business cycle cannot obscure the trend.

Until recently Americans have been much too complacent about this situation. But fortunately, events of late have disabused us of most of our comforting but dangerous misconceptions about ourselves. It is now apparent that while we top them statistically, other nations do not always look up to us. Furthermore, Russia's sputniks drove home to us the fact that the United States has no monopoly of scientific brains and technical know-how. As a people, Americans are beginning to develop a healthy dissatisfaction with their own accomplishments. A great newspaper and a magazine with a huge circulation recently combined to sponsor a reexamination of American objectives by some of the top thinkers and doers of the day. Everywhere people are questioning previously "accepted" attitudes toward government, toward foreign relations, toward our educational system. Only good can come of this.

In any such examination it is useful to turn to the past, to seek in the study of earlier times some help in understanding contemporary problems. Nearly two thousand years ago Plutarch wrote that his study of the lives of "Noble Grecians and Romans" served "as a sort of looking-glass, in which I may see how to adjust and adorn my own life." Sensitive students ever since have followed the great Boeotian's example. In the Middle Ages men read the lives of saints so to be inspired by their piety and self-sacrifice, and in the eighteenth century Samuel Johnson wrote: "Biography is, of the various kinds of narrative writing, that which is . . . most easily applied to the purposes of life."

Thus we follow a well-beaten path in searching the past for help in grappling with our own problems. And the huge reservoir of history is at our disposal. Even if the field is confined to Americans, the number of examples that could theoretically be studied is vast. It is easy to be impressed by our 180,000,000 that will soon be 200,000,000 and then still more. Instead, think of the persons who have lived and died in America since the time of Columbus. These, after all, are the men and women who have made us what we are, and who have provided the potential that we are in the process of fashioning into the future.

Yet which among these millions of ghosts should be raised for consideration? In answering this question one comes up against a startling fact that must have a healthy deflating effect upon our vanity about the human race and its accomplishments. For the choice is not nearly so wide as a purely statistical view would suggest.

In his fact-filled *Encyclopedia of American History,* Richard B. Morris has included brief lives of three hundred "Notable Americans." Morris admits that many outstanding names had to be left out because of the limited space at his disposal, but the point is that he *was* able to include most of the really outstanding American statesmen, soldiers, professional men, religious leaders, scientists, artists, adventurers, and businessmen in his group. In the comprehensive *Dictionary of American Biography,* where importance was the only standard of selection, only 14,870 biographies are included. Even conceding that a few worthy names may well have slipped through the editorial net, it remains true that there have been only 15,000-odd persons whose contributions to American civilization have been prominent enough to merit recording in this authoritative work.

Much, of course, might be learned from the study of less important people than those included in dictionaries and encyclopedias. Dr. Johnson believed it would be profitable to read the life of any man, that of a humble farmer as much so as that of a great prince. But without questioning the goodness and dignity of "ordinary" people, they are not suitable subjects for our purposes. By and large their stories have been buried with

[illegible] This relative handful are the unforgettable Americans.

In his Preface, Allan Nevins suggests that the fact that such people have lived as are described in the following pages gives the lie to the belief that the United States is a nation of conformists. I am not so sure. Certainly most of the men whose stories you are about to read were original, forceful, and independent people, but they are rare birds. Their existence should make us proud not of ourselves, but of the fact that in thousands of ways we share the heritage and benefit from the labors of these few. My intention, in other words, is to remind the reader that while he may not have heard of all of these Americans and may therefore question their right to be called *unforgettable*, among the millions of American souls they are the super-elite who rose enough above the mass to be remembered at all.

They should not, however, inspire the reader to blind hero worship, for Allan Nevins is certainly right in saying that these are not great men. Nevertheless, as we *talk about* thinking and acting creatively and constructively in the face of the challenges and crises of today, we should remember that in their times and subject to their very human limitations, each of them —William Brewster sending his Pilgrims to the New World, Peter Harrison designing a Newport synagogue, De Witt Clinton planning the "Big Ditch," Jonathan Letterman organizing his field hospitals, Henry George theorizing about the value of land, Walter Chrysler solving problems of mass production—faced his particular challenges and crises in a way that later generations have not been able to forget. Yes, even Bill Williams making a way of life in the wild Rockies, and poor Sam Patch going over Niagara.

Having gone to such length to show that unforgettable Americans are in short supply, it remains to be pointed out that their rarity is relative. A single volume can deal only with a few of them. But this sample, I believe, is fairly representative, although not chosen in a very scientific manner. It has been determined by the interests of the distinguished authors, who were asked to write about men and women who interested them and whose lives might reasonably be expected to interest others. For any one of our subjects another name might easily be substituted: Roger Williams for John Wise, de Tocqueville for Crèvecoeur, Susan B. Anthony for Elizabeth Cady Stanton, John Roebling for James Eads, and so on. It does not matter. The range covered here should be wide enough to satisfy all tastes and provide enjoyment and stimulation to every reader.

Amerigo Vespucci and Henry Hudson

... and Sebastian Cabot, Martin Frobisher, and Sir Walter Raleigh in the service of the English crown—all these and many more ranged over vast stretches of the western sea in Columbus' pioneering wake.

A truly fabulous company they were. Willingly they underwent incredible privations, braving alike Caribbean hurricanes and chill nor'easters off the bleak shores of Newfoundland. They picked their way through shifting sandbars along the pestilential Mosquito Coast of Honduras and amid the jagged, hull-crunching ice floes of Arctic waters. Treacherous natives and strange diseases threatened their lives while toredo worms riddled the unprotected hulls of their frail vessels. To face thirst, scurvy, and the terrors of the unknown on an unmapped ocean thousands of miles from home was their common destiny.

And for what? Wealth and fame of course, for by and large they were an ambitious, ruthless, and greedy lot. Proud Columbus risked losing the support of Ferdinand and Isabella rather than compromise his grandiose claims to personal hegemony over the "Ocean Sea." He and others after him stole from the guileless, enslaved the defenseless, and slaughtered innocents by the countless thousands in hope of filling their coffers with gold and pearls. They sought a short route to the wealth of the Orient, the mythical, always-around-the-next-headland "Strait of Anian," and in search of it they mapped thousands of miles of coast and explored harbors and inlets without number. They planned to win princedoms for themselves and their descendants; they conquered immense regions and hopefully founded many cities.

But more highminded motives drove them too. Like the mountain climber who must top Everest simply "because it is there," the explorer was impelled by the spirit of adventure. As young men today dream of setting foot on the moon, so in the fifteenth and sixteenth and seventeenth centuries these intrepid sailors dreamed of lands where civilized men had not yet trod. If these distant places were paradises where gold lay about like rubble, so much the better. These men had a sense of historic mission; they felt an obligation to bring the word of God to the heathen; they were sure that some obscure destiny controlled their fates. Columbus believed himself the God-chosen agent of discovery. He saw visions. At one desperate moment on his last voyage he heard a celestial voice saying: "Fear not, but trust, all these tribulations are recorded on marble, and not without cause." Sir Humphrey Gilbert, the English explorer, in his last moments on the Golden Hind, *shouted above the roar of the wind and sea to his men: "We are as near Heaven by sea as by land!" Gilbert, indeed, perfectly typified the mixed motives of the explorer who, he once wrote, seeks "to make himselfe rich, and the world happie." Will the astronauts of tomorrow do as well in these respects as their sixteenth-century forebears?*

Our particular explorers are representative rather than typical. The name of Amerigo Vespucci, as every schoolboy knows, was attached to North and South America at the whim of an obscure geographer. But as Irving A. Leonard makes clear, Vespucci would be remembered because of his own voyages in any case. Hudson's true importance has always been widely recognized. Richard B. Morris reminds us of his epic explorations, and gives us also a vivid portrait of the man himself.

Irving A. Leonard is Professor of Spanish American History and Literature at the University of Michigan. A former Guggenheim and Fulbright Fellow, he has written extensively on various aspects of Hispanic culture. His most recent book is Baroque Times in Old Mexico. *Richard B. Morris is Gouverneur Morris Professor of History at Columbia University. He edited the* Encyclopedia of American History *and is co-editor of the New American Nation series. Of his many books, his* Government and Labor in Early America *is outstanding.*

". . . tidings of a vast new continent"

IRVING A. LEONARD

land after its discoverer . . . So let it be called America, since both Europe and Asia bear names in feminine form."

So pleasing to the eye and ear was this new word that the public everywhere promptly adopted it and would have no other. Some years later another geographer extended this name to our northern continent where, much later, the inhabitants of these United States appropriated the term "American" for their own exclusive use. Succeeding generations have seen in all this a great injustice to Christopher Columbus who, it was claimed, was cheated of his rightful distinction by a boastful adventurer, a publicity-seeking fellow-Italian.

Who was this Amerigo Vespucci, then? And how was it that his name rather than that of Columbus was given to the "New World" of the Western Hemisphere?

The well-to-do Vespucci family had long resided in Florence, a great artistic city of Italy, and there some of its members had held high office. The year 1454 saw the birth of a son who was baptized Amerigo. An uncle, a clergyman, took charge of his early education, introducing him to the practical sciences as well as to the literary arts then more highly esteemed. So readily did young Amerigo master mathematics, geography, and astronomy that his father decided upon a business career for him. Amerigo's enthusiasm for geography and navigation admirably fitted him for work in foreign trade, and soon he became an executive of the powerful banking house and trading firm of the Medicis.

In the 1480's Spain beckoned as a land of great business opportunities, for a war to expel the Moors from that peninsula was creating a large demand for imports. Religious persecution was forcing Jewish merchants and money-lenders to leave the country, and Italian businessmen, especially Florentines, were warmly welcomed. The commercial interests of the Medicis expanded enormously, and soon required the services of a resident manager in Spain. To this position Amerigo Vespucci was appointed, and the historic year of 1492 found him established at Seville, the gateway to the Ocean Sea where Christopher Columbus was embarking upon unprecedented discoveries.

Soon Vespucci had obtained an exclusive contract with the Spanish crown to supply the many expeditions sailing to the distant Indies. The success of the Portuguese route around the continent of Africa to the wealth of the East was spurring the Spaniards to a feverish effort to find a rival way directly westward. So keen was this competition of Portugal and Spain for the treasures of the Orient that it held the sharp threat of war, and already the Pope, seeking to appease his two most powerful supporters, was dividing the globe between them. To prevent trespass of their respective spheres both nations agreed upon a line of demarcation in 1494.

This was the situation when Columbus set out on his later quests of a westward route to Asia, and Amerigo aided him in preparing his voyages. But Columbus remained the stubborn visionary and touchy dreamer. Obsessed by medieval myths, he persistently closed his mind to the realities of his own achievements. To him the islands discovered lay off the coast of Asia, and he would never admit that Cuba was other than a projection of the Asiatic mainland. To him it was a part of the Kingdom of Cathay, and to this effect he obliged every member of his crew to take an oath before a notary. His *Mondo Novo* or New World was not a separate continent but a previously unknown eastward reach of Asia which he had discovered. And he was convinced that the fresh waters in the Gulf of Paria on the northern shores of South America issued from the Terrestrial Paradise. "The more I reason on this subject," he wrote, "the more satisfied I become that the Terrestrial Paradise is situated in the spot I have described." Though the supporting evidence that his successive voyages supplied grew more meager, he clung with undiminished tenacity to his extravagant fancies, and with them he died.

Amerigo Vespucci, the shrewd, hardheaded businessman, began to lose confidence in his Genoese countryman.

The Spanish drive to find a westward route to the Indian

ocean, he felt, required a more practical-minded leader. When Columbus kept returning from his voyages without looking south for a possible strait leading to those waters, and with his fanciful notions of geography unchanged, Amerigo determined upon a personal inspection. Thus he embarked upon at least two and probably four voyages across the Atlantic

[illegible] to pun on the word "ambrosia" by naming this region "Land of Saint Ambrose."

Stalled by contrary winds and currents, Amerigo turned north without finding the elusive strait. After beating about the Caribbean islands and the Bahamas for months, he returned to Spain, having sailed along the mainland of the Western Hemisphere a distance many times greater than Columbus had done. This experience had transformed Amerigo completely from an acquisitive merchant into an inquisitive scholar. His mathematical and navigational hobbies had had full play during the long months at sea, and he had spent much time working out a method of determining longitude by observations of the moon. The mariners of the time had crude ways of ascertaining latitude, or the distance north or south of the Equator. They could never be sure of their position, however, without also calculating their longitude, or the distance from a north-south meridian. For the latter they depended upon intelligent guessing called "dead reckoning." Amerigo developed a practical means of finding longitude by lunar observations, thus providing one of the great achievements of the Age of Discovery.

But the Florentine merchant-scholar was haunted by the unsolved mystery of the westward strait, and he decided upon further explorations. To avoid friction between Portugal and Spain because of the line of demarcation, Amerigo took service under the Portuguese monarch, who was eager to learn the exact nature of his new possessions in the west. As an Italian engaged in international trade Amerigo was free to exchange masters without implication of treason or disloyalty. These later journeyings carried him thousands of miles along the South American coast, enabling him to establish the boundary between Portuguese and Spanish territories there. He passed the mouth of the River Plate and coasted Patagonia, but before he could anticipate Magellan's discovery of the long sought strait he was forced to turn back. Now, however, he was certain of the fact that the dream-ridden Columbus would not face—the off-shore islands and mainland discovered were not the coast of Asia *but a completely new and hitherto unknown continent.*

This astounding revelation created a furore throughout Europe that Columbus' discovery of ten years before had not aroused. The Genoese sailor had claimed to have reached the vicinity of Cathay and the domains of the Grand Khan in Asia by a westward course—realms which were already dimly known to Europeans. But Amerigo now brought tidings of a vast new continent, a "New World" beyond the dark seas, the existence of which was unsuspected.

He had reported his findings to his employers, the Medicis in Italy, and in garbled form these letters soon found their way into print. They circulated rapidly, and all over Europe excitement ran high as fevered imaginations speculated on the strange nature of an enormously expanded globe and its alluring possibilities. Little wonder, then, that Waldseemüller, the enthusiastic map-maker in Lorraine, roughed out the vague outlines of a new continent on the chart he was tracing! And it was but natural that he should exalt the new hero by placing his name on the new land.

Was there not, indeed, a certain justice in this? Had not Columbus, who had traversed scarcely two hundred miles of the South American coast, obstinately denied the existence of a land barrier to Asia? And had not Amerigo Vespucci, after probably as many voyages as Columbus, during which he had journeyed thousands of miles along those distant shores, reached his conclusion soberly and by open-minded observations? There is, indeed, no clear evidence that Amerigo sought at any time to have his name attached to the new continent, but the professor of geography in Lorraine had invented far better than he knew, and the ear-pleasing name of "America" was destined to remain forever.

Amerigo's last years were spent as Pilot Major of the House of Trade which the Spanish crown established to supervise its great shipping activities. Here he trained navigators in the most advanced nautical sciences and collected the ship-logs and charts which they brought back from voyages of discovery. In this fashion he came to have a knowledge of the lands and waters of the New World far exceeding that of anyone of his day. Perhaps there was a prophetic aptness in bestowing the name of this enterprising and capable

RICHARD B. MORRIS

HENRY HUDSON's is a tale of great discoveries, of hair-breadth escapes, of romantic voyages undertaken in ice-bound waters and under terrific hardships. All this he packed into five brief years of brilliant explorations in the service of the English and the Dutch, until he prematurely perished by treachery and amid the scene of his triumphs. In Canada Hudson's memory is perpetuated in the title of a great trading corporation, the Hudson's Bay Company. In America his name is affixed to one of our most majestic rivers. From the capes of the Delaware to the ice-bound Arctic our continent has associations connected with the name of Henry Hudson.

Hudson enters upon the stage of history on the 19th of April, 1607, when, as a captain in the employ of the Muscovy Company, an English firm engaged in trading with Russia, he set out to search for a passage to Japan and China via the North Pole. At this time the English, the Dutch, and the French saw the more southerly routes to Asia blocked to them. The Cape of Good Hope route was controlled by the Portuguese; the routes to the Orient via the Straits of Magellan or the Isthmus of Panama were dominated by the Spaniards. Hence the northern nations hoped to establish trade with the fabled lands of the East by discovering a Northeast passage along the north coast of Russia or a Northwest passage across or above North America to the

Orient. To find the latter a long line of explorers, beginning with John Cabot in 1497 and including Verrazano, Cartier, Frobisher, Davis, and Weymouth, had traversed the eastern coastline of North America, reconnoitered along its bays and inlets, and even penetrated the great St. Lawrence River.

With a little crew of but ten men and a boy Henry Hudson, on his first expedition, skirted eastern Greenland. He reached the ice barrier and then turned east to Spitzbergen, where ice barred the way further. The Muscovy Company now felt that he might have a better chance of circumventing the ice by going along the northern coast of Russia to the Kara Sea and so to the East. This was the route of Hudson's second voyage of 1608. In addition to sighting the usual walruses, whales, bears, and Arctic birds, Hudson's party claimed to have seen something else, which the explorer dutifully recorded in his journal under date of June 15, 1608. The entry for that date reads:

> This morning, one of our company looking overboard, saw a mermaid, and calling up some of the company to see her, one more came up, and by that time she was come close to the ship's side, looking earnestly on the men. A little after, a sea came and overturned her: from the navel upward, her back and breasts were like a woman's, as they say that saw her. Her body as big as one of us, her skin very white, and long hairs hanging down behind of color black. In her going down they saw her tail which was like the tail of a porpoise and speckled like a mackerel.

The "mermaid" was more likely a seal, which the overheated imaginations of the crew transfigured into something more glamorous. On this voyage the sinister presence of Robert Juet, the mate, is first felt, and so is the weakness and indecision of Hudson as a disciplinarian. Failing to get through the barrier, Hudson was forced by a mutiny of the crew to turn home instead of trying further alternative routes.

What is especially noteworthy about these two expeditions is the fact that they were justified in Hudson's mind by the notion of an open polar sea, a theory which later investigators adopted and finally confirmed. Hudson's error, and that of other explorers who followed him, was his persistent belief that beyond the frigid waters there would be found a warmer, ice-free area, open to navigation. It took a more modern type of transportation to prove the soundness of Hudson's basic objectives. The polar route used by airplanes to traverse from west to east has proven to be practicable, and, of course, much the shortest.

By now Hudson had a fabulous reputation, and the Dutch East India Company, likewise concerned with finding a Northeast passage for their traders, hired him to undertake a voyage for

Hudson River had first been seen by Verrazano in 1524, circumstances did not permit that Florentine explorer to linger in the area more than a few hours. It was Hudson's distinction to make the second great entry into North America, the first having been made by Jacques Cartier who sailed up the St. Lawrence River in 1535.

On September 3rd Hudson and his *Half Moon* company found themselves inside Sandy Hook. "This is a very good land to fall with, and a pleasant land to see," a journal of the voyage records. Indians came to their ship with tobacco and other articles of trade. But in the course of relations between the two people, a member of the *Half Moon*'s crew was killed. Proceeding cautiously now, Hudson entered what is now the Upper Bay on September 11th, and then for the next eleven days sailed the *Half Moon* up the beautiful valley, whose magnificent forests were changing to their brilliant fall coloring. Surviving accounts of the voyage tell us about the richness of the country, how it abounded in fish, fur, game, and Indian crops. Hudson was able to navigate the *Half Moon* for some one hundred and fifty miles upstream, beyond the present site of Albany. Another twenty-five miles was explored in small boats.

Significantly, at the very moment in late September when Hudson's crew was probing north of Albany, Samuel de Champlain, the greatest French explorer of North America, was only a relatively few miles away on the lake which now bears his name. Hudson had not found a strait across the North American continent, but he and his crew returned with reports of fine farmlands in the broad valley. More immediately important, they brought information that the Indians possessed "beaver skins and otter skins which we bought for beads, knives, and hatchets." It was this fur trade which impelled the Dutch to return to the river the next year and to pursue what proved to be a lucrative business, shortly to lead to the permanent settlement of the Hudson Valley.

The English were now determined to keep Hudson in their service. He was sent once more on a voyage. This, his fourth and last, was to find a northern way through to the west, possibly to penetrate Davis Strait, which John Davis had discovered some twenty years before. Starting out in April, 1610, in the ship *Discovery*, Hudson reached the strait which now bears his name on June 25th. Because of the prevailing early summer fog and the prevalence of icebergs, he paused before trying to penetrate the strait and did not enter Hudson's Bay until August 3rd, the last date recorded in his journal. By now his crew was thoroughly frightened and demoralized. The bleak, rocky lands looming up out of the fog had given them a sense of unknown terrors. But Hudson, heedless, pushed ahead south, coming at last to the marshy, desolate shore of James Bay. There, despite a dangerously disgruntled crew, he explored still further until frost closed in on him and he was forced to beach the *Discovery* near the southeastern limits of the waters.

Officers and men passed a dreadful winter waiting until ice conditions should permit them to sail again. In June, 1611, Hudson felt that he could now continue exploring the western shore of the bay. But his crew had had more than enough. Smoldering fears and hates broke into open mutiny, and the crew, led by Robert Juet, Henry Greene, and William Wilson, set Hudson, his son, and six officers adrift in a little shallop. That was on June 23rd. But unlike Captain Bligh of the mutinous ship *Bounty*, Hudson was never heard from again.

Retribution descended upon most of the mutineers. The majority either starved to death or were killed by Eskimos. Eight finally reached England. Seven years later, four of these went through the motions of a trial for the murder of Hudson. In one of the strangest verdicts in history, they were acquitted. They were felt to be too valuable to kill, for they had seen new waters and looked upon new lands known only to Hudson, a dead man. This knowledge was more precious than justice.

In 1632 Captain Thomas James, exploring the Hudson Bay area, found relics in James Bay of what may well have been Hudson's marooned party. James's report provided the raw material for Coleridge's *Rime of the Ancient Mariner:*

> And through the drifts the snowy cliffs
> Did send a dismal sheen:

William Brewster

When the average American thinks of the beginnings of his country he tends to call to mind a bleak New England coastline and the landing of the Pilgrims on Plymouth Rock. Of course even casual students of our history know that the Virginia colony was more than a decade old when the Pilgrims made their famous landfall. Indeed, it was to Virginia that they had intended to migrate when the Mayflower *weighed anchor in old Plymouth and turned her prow toward the New World. And even in New England the Pilgrims were never very important numerically; they were soon engulfed by the larger and more dynamic Puritan commonwealth of Massachusetts Bay.*

However, the popular conception of the Pilgrims as the true Founders is accurate in spirit. Although their settlement never amounted to much so far as material things go, the Pilgrims possessed fundamental qualities of courage, determination, idealism, and practical piety without which the hardships of life in the American wilderness could not have been endured and surmounted. These qualities of mind and heart were so well demonstrated by the Pilgrims that they have come to symbolize the struggles of all the early settlers, and also their ultimate triumph. They are qualities as important in our "mature" civilization as they were when the country was young.

Grim New England, with its thin soil and cruel winters, provided a fit testing ground for all the Pilgrim virtues. Too often, however, we forget that these plain but dedicated men had already suffered adversities that had tested their temper thoroughly. George F. Willison, author of Saints and Strangers *and other works dealing with the Pilgrims, here uses the life of William Brewster to describe how the members of an obscure congregation of separatists from the town of Scrooby, in England, prepared to meet their destiny.*

". . . a civilized man"

GEORGE F. WILLISON

tarianism of every kind. Brewster had qualities of heart, mind, and spirit that the whole democratic world might well strive to achieve in larger measure.

At a time of fierce and often brutal ideological strife, with fanatics on both sides calling for the blood of their opponents, Brewster remained a civilized man, a man of good sense, a man of good will. Though passionately devoted to the cause of religious freedom, to what he and his brothers called the right to liberty of conscience, he believed in persuasion, not force, in bringing men to see what he regarded as the errors of their ways.

Brewster was more a man of the world than any of the Pilgrims, though one of the least worldly among them. Before boarding the *Mayflower* for her historic voyage he had been many things: a university student at a time when not one in scores had any schooling at all, a secretary to one of Queen Elizabeth's most trusted ambassadors, the bailiff or general manager of a huge semi-feudal estate, a postmaster, a tavern keeper, a private tutor. He had also been a printer and publisher of religious books denounced by the authorities as "seditious," forcing him to run for his life and lie in hiding for a while, a fugitive from the law.

In Pilgrim history Brewster has been overshadowed by Governor William Bradford, who directed the infant Plymouth colony for almost forty years. Bradford was one of the really towering figures of seventeenth-century New England. It is not taking anything away from him to say that he was, in a meaningful sense, Brewster's creation. Early left an orphan, young Bradford was virtually adopted by Brewster, who taught him his letters, his philosophy, the ways of the world, the powers and pleasures of a well-furnished mind, and the secrets of the often wayward human heart.

William Brewster was born about 1566; just when or where is not known. He grew up as a lad in a great manor house at Scrooby in central England, where his father had charge of an extensive lordship consisting of villages and thousands of acres of farm lands, all owned by the Church of England. In 1580 young Brewster rode off on horseback to enter the University of Cambridge. It was here, in a Pilgrim phrase, that he was "first seasoned with the seeds of grace and virtue," meaning that he had become one of the Puritans demanding radical reforms in the Church, in order to restore it to its original simplicity in Christ's day, to its "ancient purity."

Before graduation young Brewster went up to London to enter the service of one of the most powerful men in the realm, Sir William Davison, principal secretary of state. The dazzling brilliance of the court of Queen Elizabeth was a revelation to the country youth from Scrooby. He might perhaps have stayed there all his life if Davison had not suddenly fallen into disfavor and been jailed in the Tower of London. His master in disgrace, his own career in the great world ruined, Brewster, now a man in the middle twenties, returned to the lonely countryside at Scrooby, where he soon succeeded his father as postmaster, tavern keeper, local magistrate, and bailiff of the manor. These offices made him relatively well-to-do, but Brewster was more interested in other things. He did his best to fill the pulpits in the villages round about with "godly and religious" preachers—meaning Puritan preachers, who were finding more and more fault with the Church of England, the only authorized church. Everybody had to belong by law and under threats of the direst penalties—many thousands had been jailed and scores had been hanged or burned for refusing to comply.

Determined to crush all criticism and opposition, the Anglican bishops launched a savage offensive against the Puritans, silencing more and more of their preachers. Brewster and his friends stood this patiently for more than fifteen years, but in 1606 they decided that as the "Lord's free people" they had a God-given right to withdraw from the Church of England. They would set up their own tenets of belief, choose their own pastor in a democratic manner, and worship as they pleased. This was treason as then defined.

Led by Brewster, the congregation began to meet secretly, as it had to do, usually at Brewster's expense in the great Scrooby manor house, which belonged to the Church of England. The illegal meetings had scarcely begun when authorities struck. Brewster was twice jailed, but escaped harm. Harassed on all

to Leyden. While the Dutch were friendly, these exiles from the English midlands had a very hard time earning bread and butter. They had been brought up as farmers and now, not knowing the Dutch language or the ways of the country, had to take what jobs they could get—the least skilled and worst paid—in weaving, metal, leather, and other handicraft trades.

Brewster had a particularly hard time of it, having exhausted all his means in helping his poorer brethren across. Older than most, he could not do the heavy rough work, so falling back upon his university training he set up as a private tutor, teaching English to students at Leyden University. Then he went into a more interesting business.

The Brewsters had taken a small house in the old quarter of the city, on a dark narrow lane called the "Stincksteeg," or Stink Alley. An extension of the house ran through the "Koorsteeg," or Choir Alley. In this extension Brewster set up a printing shop, a book publishing house now famed as the Pilgrim Press, as active as any in its day.

In 1617 the press issued four books, all non-controversial and bearing the imprint of the house. But these signed copies were a blind to cover other activities, for it was Brewster's purpose to publish books that could not be printed in England because of the iron censorship there. Manuscripts were smuggled out of England, put into type by Brewster, and printed copies smuggled back, often in French wine vats, to be sold and circulated surreptitiously throughout the kingdom.

All went well for several years until one of these books—a sharp criticism of King James' religious policies—fell into the hands of the English authorities, who denounced it as an "atrocious and seditious libel." There was a great hue and cry, with King James personally demanding the apprehension of Brewster and forcing the Dutch authorities to cooperate. The print shop was raided, the type carted off, the door nailed up. But they failed to catch Brewster. Taking to his heels at the first alarm he went into hiding for almost two years, not being reported again until the *Mayflower* was well out to sea.

It was fortunate for Brewster that he escaped, for he might well have suffered the fate of another so-called "seditious" publisher of that day who was sentenced to pay a fine of 100,000 pounds, to be whipped and pilloried, to have his ears sliced off and his nose split, and to have "SS" (stirrer of sedition) branded upon his forehead, and then be thrown into jail for life. We have come a long way since that time in our fight against censorship and for the right to liberty of conscience.

As the *Mayflower* reached our shores, mutiny threatened. To preserve order the Pilgrim leaders drew up the celebrated Mayflower Compact, under which they established their own free, democratic commonwealth. As the only university man on board, and as one who had some familiarity with documents and phrases of law, it was probably Brewster who drafted the Compact, one of our great charters of liberty with its promise of government under "just & equall lawes."

During the early years at Plymouth, Brewster, now almost sixty, did his share of the hard work in building the town and hoeing in the fields. And every Sabbath, as ruling elder, he preached to the Pilgrims and led them in prayer. It is a curious fact that there was no minister on the *Mayflower* and, except for a brief unfortunate period, none at Plymouth for nine years. Though a layman, Brewster headed the Pilgrim brethren in laying the firm foundations of what became the Congregational Church, performing all the offices but baptism and communion, and giving eminent satisfaction. Though never in public office at Plymouth, Brewster had a commanding influence in councils of state. Governor Bradford, as he himself tells us, always relied heavily upon his judgment.

In his later life, after the death of his wife and almost all of his family, Brewster spent more and more time in his library—a remarkable one for that day, containing some 400 volumes, larger than the library John Harvard left as principal endowment of the famous university that bears his name.

Brewster remained Plymouth's most respected and beloved leader down to 1643 when, nearing eighty, he "died in his bed, in peace," mourned by everybody.

As Brewster was a very literate man, dealing in so many ways with the "Word," it is curious that we have not a line written

Richard Bourne

Unlike most American settlers, the Pilgrims enjoyed harmonious and mutually beneficial relations with the Indians. It was they who established friendly contacts with the Wampanoag chief, Massassoit, signing a treaty that assured all the New England colonies half a century of precious peace; and it was Samoset and Squanto, local braves, who guided and tutored the Pilgrims in the ways of wilderness life. Squanto's instructions in the arts of fishing and the planting of Indian corn probably saved the Plymouth colony from extinction during the first winters.

Fortune played a part in this development, for Massassoit was by nature a peace-loving man and his people, superstitiously attributing a recent plague to the murder of two or three white fishermen, feared that an attack on the new settlers would bring a further visitation of the disease. But the Pilgrims, by their fairness, simple good sense, and lack of aggressive instincts, contributed their full share to the work of preserving good relations. In this they were thoroughly atypical.

In the following chapter Virginia C. Gildersleeve, former dean of Barnard College and delegate to the 1945 San Francisco Conference which drew up the Charter of the U.N., discusses the career of one early settler at Plymouth, Richard Bourne. His warm and intelligent understanding of the Indians played a key role in saving all New England when, after Massassoit's death, Metacomet (King Philip) broke the long peace.

". . . the wisdom of one man"

VIRGINIA C. GILDERSLEEVE

RICHARD BOURNE, preacher-apostle to the Indians, the White Sachem of Mashpee on Cape Cod—few Americans have ever heard of him, yet perhaps we may owe to him in no small measure the nature of our great country as it exists today. We are English speaking, lovers of freedom, our laws and our government derived in good part from ideas brought to the American wilderness by a few humble men and women who clung precariously to the edge of a savage continent: one hundred and two Pilgrims, half of them dead the

and influence in England. Trained as a lawyer at the Inns of Court in London, his legal ability was at once in demand. New colonists were continually arriving. Many deeds had to be drawn up for the purchase of land from the Indians. To do this, he realized he must learn the language of the Wampanoag Indians. This he did promptly and well.

So, too, did certain of the ministers. They had come to America with missionary zeal, anxious to save the souls of the heathen who were thought to be the spawn of Lucifer, or the descendants of Cain. The poor puzzled Indians, listening to brimstone sermons, found them hard to take, whereas the good lawyer who refused to let them be cheated of their lands, who clearly believed in justice for Red Men as well as White Men, seemed to them an interpreter they could trust. Eager to get some grasp of the new civilization that confronted them, Indian leaders asked Richard Bourne to expound not only the White Man's laws but the White Man's religion. Hard put to it to make the Pilgrim faith understandable, Richard sought parallels in Indian tradition, and found in their stories of gods and miracles and heroes similarity to some of the famous Biblical tales, like Noah and the Flood, and Jonah and the Whale. Skillfully he adapted Indian stories into their Christian counterparts. From these resemblances he built up a curious Indian faith, not altogether Christian, yet certainly not heathen.

Now many of the Praying Indians, as such converts were called, were hangers-on at the outskirts of the White Men's villages. Not so Richard Bourne's Praying Braves. He had purchased a large tract of salt meadows and forests at the shoulder of Cape Cod, the great arm of land that reaches into the sea south of Plymouth. This land he shared with his Indian converts. As more and more Indians sold or traded the sites of their villages, Richard realized that a time would come when natives who thought a bead or a kettle more valuable than many acres would be without hunting lands and homes. He appealed to the General Court for new grants until his lands extended in a belt completely across the entrance to the long peninsula of Cape Cod. Then he petitioned the Court to set aside a grant adjoining his own, for the permanent use of Christian Indians.

Incredulous outcry greeted this idea. It was "madness," men said, to encourage Indians to group together. Besides, the land that this White Sachem wanted for his Redskins was agricultural land suitable for new settlers. Quietly, forcefully, Richard pleaded his case before the Court. The goodmen shook their heads in bewilderment, but they granted him a partial victory. Sixteen square miles of territory was set aside to belong, as the old deed puts it, "to the South Sea Indians and their children forever."

There was feasting and dancing when Richard rode back to Bourneland. That night a hundred pine torches were struck into the ground forming a fiery circle. Inside the circle the Indians began to build their own church. Richard had taught them Christian doctrine and reading and writing. Now he taught them how to build with tools.

Gradually his army of Praying Braves grew in numbers. It was said to contain between five and ten thousand skilled bowmen and spearmen, ready to die for their "little father," the White Sachem. Richard also acquired a reputation for magic. Squaws brought their sick babies to him for healing, so he sent to England for medical books and prescribed cures. In 1649 famine desolated the country. Richard fed his Praying Braves and their families with corn purchased at his own expense. Legal adviser, judge, teacher, doctor, nurse, architect, in later life he also became an ordained minister.

He had preached for some years to his fellow colonists in the little village of Sandwich, standing humbly, as became a "secular," on the stair below the top step of the pulpit. At first the goodmen eyed him askance, doubting, half-hostile. In time they became his loyal supporters and friends. The powerful preacher-rulers of the Massachusetts Bay and Plymouth colonies disputed among themselves about his ordination. "Better regularize this strange man's position" was apparently the consensus of opinion. "Many Christian souls are in his charge. As a minister of God he will no longer be able to partake in heathen practices."

John Cotton and John Eliot journeyed to the Kingdom of Mashpee to ordain Richard Bourne. In fact, to the ordination came all of the leading men of the colony, including Governor Thomas Prince, Richard's

Less than five years after Richard's ordination Indian tocsins sounded their call for all-out war against the white invaders. King Philip's War, it was called, a fight to the finish between colonists and redskins, one or the other to survive and rule. Indian runners carried to all Wampanoags and their allied tribes a summons to join Philip in his stronghold some miles west of Bourneland where the final battles would be joined. Bonfires flared. Warpaint gleamed. There were freshly sharpened spears, newly feathered arrows and stolen firewater and guns. Then down the length of the Cape came a disorganized horde of savages planning to attack the hard-pressed Puritan forces from the rear. To do this it was necessary for them to cross through the Mashpee Kingdom or the lands of Richard Bourne. They had expected to gather well-armed recruits from the Praying Braves of Mashpee. It never occurred to them that they might not be given safe conduct through Indian territory. Instead they found their way blocked, across the entire Cape, by well-ordered companies of trained spearmen and bowmen, while expert sharpshooters were hidden in the trees. The yelling bands launched a few feel-out skirmishes, then realized that, to reach the army of the colonists, they must first fight their way through Richard's Praying Braves. Group by group, they straggled back to their homes.

Almost all military strategists agree that had King Philip won over even a small number of Richard's Praying Braves, or had these permitted the Cape Indians to pass through their territory to attack from the east while the colonists were battling Philip in the west, the Puritan forces would have been disastrously defeated. Horror and massacre would have followed, possibly even the complete destruction of the Plymouth and Boston settlements. For a long time there would have been little heart for renewed English colonization in that area. Without Plymouth and Boston, without a strong New England in the early days, should we have been quite the same Americans that we are? I doubt it: possibly neither better nor worse, but different. Conceivably Dutchmen or Frenchmen or the colonists of the South might have dominated our early tradition, have set the pattern of our ways.

In the thankfulness of a victory in which every white man capable of carrying a gun had done his utmost, the colonists made no special hero of Richard Bourne. After all, Richard had donned no sword. He had stayed at home and never struck a blow. Not long afterwards he disappeared. No one knows how he died or where his bones lie buried. The Mashpee Indians claimed that he had been murdered by a band of embittered warriors of Philip. Tradition says that his Praying Braves found his mutilated body and buried it secretly in the floor under the altar of their church. And now even the memory of the White Sachem of Mashpee lies buried in dusty archives.

Yet seldom have Americans owed so much to the wisdom of one man.

John Wise and Cotton Mather

Bay were outspoken materialists. Witness the case of the blunt sailor who stood up in church after his minister had remarked that religion was the "main end" of colonization and said: "Sir, you are mistaken. . . . Our main end was to catch fish."

Nevertheless, most of the settlers took their religion very seriously. Perhaps it was not always their "main end" in coming to America, but it was a vital part of nearly everyone's existence. More important, the founders and developers of the Bay colony were ardent Puritans and they set the tone for the whole settlement. Disgusted with the failure of the Anglican Church to wipe out all of what they considered the evils of Roman Catholicism, and frustrated in their own efforts to "purify" the Church in England, they had come to the New World to establish a religious Utopia. They constructed their society on theocratic lines. Ties between church and state were very close—civil authorities enforced moral law and, in turn, the church laid down the framework within which the civil government functioned. Thus the Puritan minister was the arbiter of constitutional as well as religious controversies and the real master of society. Even the sturdy fisherman who stated his true reason for coming to New England so boldly was speaking, it will be noticed, in church.

However, religious orthodoxy was very difficult to maintain, fundamentally because the Puritan philosophy placed on each individual the responsibility for understanding the word of God as recorded in the Bible. Since men could not always agree about the meaning of Biblical texts, angry arguments often developed. Fortunately America was large enough to accommodate many beliefs. Dissenters like Roger Williams and Thomas Hooker could take their followers to Rhode Island and Connecticut and worship as they pleased. But even among those who remained in Massachusetts different points of view developed. Probably this was inevitable, for there were logical contradictions within the Puritan approach to religion. Man must understand for himself. (This accounts for the Puritan stress on education. Harvard College, for example, was founded when the colony was only six years old.) But man can only "know" salvation if he has felt "God's grace." This was an emotional, inspirational, non-rational experience, and no amount of intellectual effort could take its place. Eventually these conflicting lines of philosophy led to highly intellectual Unitarianism on the one hand and to the emotionally oriented evangelical sects on the other, but for decades they existed together within the same creed, a constant source of soul-searching and discord.

There was also a conflict between the democratic and authoritarian sides of Puritanism. This can be seen clearly in the careers of John Wise and Cotton Mather. Professor Clarence L. ver Steeg of the Northwestern University History Department, whose biography of Robert Morris won the Beveridge prize of the American Historical Association, explains Wise's democratic philosophy; and Max Savelle, Professor of History at the University of Washington and author of Seeds of Liberty *and many other books, describes the views of Cotton Mather. Keep in mind, in reading the following pages, that Mather and Wise were contemporaries, that they lived and worked within a few miles of each other, and that they were ministers of the same Puritan church.*

". . . eloquent spokesman for representative government"

CLARENCE VER STEEG

To a stranger in Massachusetts it would be surprising enough to see the Reverend John Wise, minister of Chebacco Parish, engage in a wrestling match with a hefty and skilled challenger from a neighboring town. In view of such decidedly unclerical conduct a stranger would be positively shocked to learn that this minister was much more clever with his pen than he was with his muscles. The truth was that the words of John Wise were destined to be read by future generations of Americans because he appealed to enduring values. Man's liberties served as his text.

John Wise was born in 1652, the son of an

student whose "hunt" had taken place in the yard of one of the local villagers. Most of John's time, however, was spent with his books, and, as was the case with most of his fellow students, he trained for the ministry. After serving several churches, John Wise took charge of the Chebacco parish near Ipswich in 1680, just seven years after graduating from Harvard. He served the Chebacco parish for nearly half a century.

The personality of the Reverend John Wise was direct and compelling, and his mind was fresh and creative. Friends who admired his athletic prowess were equally taken with his Sunday sermons and his weekday lectures. We are told that he was a delightful companion around the fireside, where his conversation was full of good sense, punctuated with wit and warm good humor—qualities that carried over into his writing. Wonderful indeed was his combination of spiritual power and secular wisdom.

This combination came in handy when John Wise served as chaplain to the militia forces of Massachusetts on an expedition to subdue the French at Quebec; for it was generally recognized that this man could minister to the soul and still endure the hardships of the flesh. He served his countrymen well. Although the expedition ended in disappointment and frustration, it proved to be something of a personal triumph for Wise.

Such achievements made John Wise a recognized figure in Massachusetts; but these are *not* the reasons for which we remember him today. Rather it is John Wise the eloquent spokesman for representative government that we cherish.

Two episodes in the career of John Wise dramatize his overwhelming concern for man's fundamental liberties. The first took place in the 1680's. The English Crown had revoked the charters of several New England colonies, including that of Massachusetts Bay, and set up what it called the Dominion of New England. Although there were many features of the Dominion that annoyed the colonists, the most infamous was the lack of a colonial assembly. For more than 50 years the voters in each colony had elected representatives to an assembly which, in turn, acted on questions that affected colonial welfare. Without an assembly, the colonists were without a voice in their own affairs.

This was especially important when it came to taxes. Before the time of the Dominion, taxes were levied by the colonial assembly, speaking for the great body of freemen. Under the reorganized government, Edmund Andros, who had been appointed Governor of the Dominion of New England by the Crown, could arbitrarily levy and collect taxes without consulting anyone.

This procedure aroused the resentment of freemen throughout Massachusetts. When Andros tried to collect taxes in the Ipswich district, he encountered fierce opposition led by the Reverend John Wise. Wise contended that it was a basic right of Englishmen to have a voice in taxing themselves, and that Andros exceeded his authority in collecting taxes which had *not* been levied by the colonial assembly. John Wise told the people to stand by what he called their "privileges"—in this case the right to tax themselves. Wise's plea, protesting the action of Andros, was one of the earliest cries in America of "no taxation without representation."

Because of his opposition, John Wise, together with several other leaders in the community, was placed in jail by Governor Andros. Eventually Andros and the Dominion of New England were overthrown, and Wise was released. More important, the principle that freemen had an inherent right to elect representatives to take part in managing colonial affairs, particularly in the matter of taxation, was firmly planted in the minds of many colonials. Some seven decades later this principle moved men to Revolution.

A second episode involved the churches of New England. There was a movement afoot to bring the New England churches into a greater unity. Although this appeared desirable at first glance, John Wise saw in it an attempt to dictate to the individual churches. To Wise it was a challenge to the independence of each church congregation, and he published a long pamphlet in

1717 entitled "A Vindication of the Government of New England Churches." It was a pamphlet that roamed far beyond the boundaries of church government; it probed the basis of human liberty and examined the foundations of civil government.

Although Wise leaned upon ideas expressed by European [illegible]

[illegible] was to carry out the wishes of the people. "The end of all good government," Wise wrote, "is to cultivate humanity, and promote the happiness of all, and the good of every man is all his rights, his life, liberty, estate, honor . . . without injury or abuse done to any." How much these phrases remind us of the Declaration of Independence! In fact, Wise was strongly advocating democratic, representative government as the touchstone of liberty fifty years before independence and a century before democracy became a central theme in the story of the American people.

It is no wonder that later generations of Americans recognized the wisdom of John Wise. When the colonies girded themselves for the American Revolution many decades later, Wise's pamphlet was reprinted, and many a patriot applauded his observation that "the Prince who strives to subvert the Fundamental Laws of the Society, is the traytor and the rebel, and not the people, who endeavour to preserve and defend their own."

In more recent times, when individual liberty and democratic government have been wiped out in areas abroad and placed under severe strain at home, John Wise and his writings have been read anew. This is entirely right and proper; John Wise's sermons on individual rights and freedoms, on equality, and on democratic government looked beyond the narrow confines of his own day. They looked toward today—and tomorrow; for John Wise preached from a timeless text: "Man was born free."

". . . one of the first articulate Americans"

MAX SAVELLE

COTTON MATHER is probably the most maligned individual in all American history. We are accustomed to think of him as a vain, stiff-necked, dogmatic, intolerant, and meddlesome Puritan; the man who was chiefly responsible for the Salem witch-hunt of 1692 and its judicial murder of a number of innocent men, women, and children. It is true, of course, that Mather was a Puritan and that from our point of view he was all that is charged against him, though he was only indirectly responsible for the witchcraft hysteria. But we of the twentieth century must try to be objective, and to study history and individuals in terms of the times and the society of the period in which the individuals lived. The fact is that Mather was one of the three most brilliant and influential Americans of the eighteenth century before the Revolution, the others being Jonathan Edwards and Benjamin Franklin.

Basically conservative in his religion, Mather, whose life spanned the years from 1663 to 1727, was a typical—and probably the greatest—intellectual leader of his own generation. Raised in the home of one of the most distinguished Puritan leaders of the seventeenth century and educated at Harvard, he was a strange mixture of conservatism and liberalism. As a conservative, he devoted his life to the preservation of the ideals of the Puritan utopia of his grandfathers' generation in an age that had moved on beyond them. He preached anywhere from three to seven or eight sermons a week, and many of these were printed and circulated all over the English colonies; many were reprinted in England and a considerable number were published in German, French, and Spanish.

The Puritanism that Mather preached was originally derived from Calvinism. But the New England religion of Cotton Mather's grandfathers and their generation had already softened the rigid doctrines of strict Calvinism, and had moved a long way towards a theology of various "covenants," or contracts, between men and God which gave men a somewhat more dignified role in the scheme of salvation than Calvin himself would ever have done. Puritanism, of course, was not all ugly, as we are apt to regard it. But the thing to stress about Puritanism is not that it negatively tended toward the suppression of individual moral freedom and responsibility, but rather that it was a utopian ideal. The happiness of the individual who could lose himself completely in his utter dependence upon God's will was thought to be the

most human beings. But this was the ideal for the elect—for those whom God had chosen for salvation. Outside the pale of these were the unsaved, the unregenerate, who were predestined to sin and to eternal hell-fire. Since these could never do good because their eyes were closed by sin, they must be supervised by the chosen of God—the "elect"; and this thought caused Mather and his colleagues to sponsor a sort of "snooping committee" for keeping sinners in line. This Puritan "big-brotherism" was unquestionably one of the ugly sides of Puritanism. But we must not let it blind us to the much more significant Puritan ideal —that of bringing into existence a society that would function truly according to the wishes of God.

In his effort to set up the God-directed utopia, the Puritan's guide was the Bible. But everybody believed that Satan was at work to frustrate the work of the utopia, and that his most subversive agents were witches. And the Bible itself said: "Thou shalt not suffer a witch to live." Thus there was nothing new in Cotton Mather's belief in and fear of witches. That fear was almost as old as human society itself. He indirectly helped to precipitate the witchcraft hysteria of 1692 by writing about his own study of the case of a little girl he thought was bewitched—a study undertaken partly in the interest of science—and a description of the cases of some persons already on trial at Salem. But he cautioned the judges to be lenient and to observe strictly the laws of evidence. Later he condemned some of the executions as miscarriages of justice.

In his deep conviction that all human existence took place, as it were, under the scrutiny of God, Mather saw religious meaning, for good or evil, in every human activity. He organized many clubs and societies for the practical promotion of God's work among men. Some of those "do good" societies took it upon themselves to supervise the morals of their fellow-citizens, as "snooping committees" and gossip mongers. Yet some engaged in charitable and educational work, and did much real good.

Much more important in the long run than his social Christianity was Mather's work as a scientist. Even his interest in witchcraft was largely a scientific one. He was also deeply interested in botany, physics, and astronomy, and his writings on medical subjects were of genuine significance. It was Cotton Mather who, when most citizens and medical men were against him, prevailed upon Dr. Zabdiel Boylston to introduce inoculation against smallpox into the colonies. His great interest in science and his writings on scientific subjects led to his election, in 1713, as a Fellow of the Royal Society of England.

Curiously enough, despite the orthodoxy of his Puritan views, he saw in science only a wonderful way of discovering the complexity and the majesty of the ways of God in the natural universe. In fact, he went so far in the direction of accepting the natural laws of nature and man's capacity to know them that, for all his orthodoxy, he has been spoken of as a sort of bridge in the intellectual history of America between the rejection of reason by the old Calvinists and the thoroughgoing rationalism of the eighteenth century.

Since Cotton Mather was a scientist, philosopher, poet, educator, and historian as well as a preacher, his writings were many and varied. Indeed, it is probably safe to say that for sheer volume of output or number of printed items, no other American writer has ever rivalled him. He published, in all, nearly five hundred separate works. He had genuine literary gifts, but in the style of his own day. It is probably true that the quality of his writing was superior to that of any other American down to his own time, with the notable exception of his contemporary, Edward Taylor, the Puritan poet.

He wrote a number of historical works, the greatest of which was the *Magnalia Christi Americana,* which was a sort of history and collection of biographical studies of the founding of the New England colonies and the great leaders in the Puritan migration. He firmly believed that this migration had been inspired by God. In this work, as in others, Mather's patriotism emerges very clearly. He is an American—one of the first articulate Americans. Nor is his loyalty to America merely a religious loyalty to God's purposes; it is also a loyalty to the new nation arising about him in the wilderness.

In Mather's personal life there was much tragedy. He was married three times—two of his wives died; the third went insane. Of his fifteen children, nine died in childhood, and only two survived him.

... too strict discipline and an over-indulgence of his fatherly love. As he said: "I will wholly avoid, that harsh, fierce, crabbed usage of the children, that would make them tremble, and abhor to come into my Presence. I will so use them, that they shall fear to offend me, and yet mightily Love to see me, and be glad of my coming home, if I have been abroad at any time." He resolved to avoid corporal punishment except for "great offenses," and he would never strike his child in anger. "The Slavish, Raving, Fighting way of Education too commonly used," he wrote, "I look upon it, as a considerable article in the Wrath and Curse of God, upon a miserable World."

When we try objectively to place Cotton Mather in his proper place in the long perspective of American history, we find unquestionably that he was the most distinguished American of his generation. Some of his personal traits make him unattractive to the twentieth century, to be sure; but we must not permit this feeling to obscure the much more important fact that in the history of religion in America, of science, of literature, of politics, of education, and of the growth of a national self-consciousness, Cotton Mather made contributions not rivalled by those of any other American of his time.

He was a tragic figure because, conservative and orthodox in his outlook, he tried to stem the tides of progress. Paradoxically enough, despite his efforts to hold back the tides of his time, his most brilliant contributions to the culture of America were precisely those which helped to move that progress forward!

William Byrd II

Much has been said and written about the marvelous generation of Virginians that flourished during the era of the American Revolution. During the three decades between 1725 and 1755, when the whole colony possesssed perhaps a hundred thousand persons exclusive of slaves, Virginia produced such giants as George Washington, Thomas Jefferson, James Madison, Patrick Henry, John Marshall, George Wythe, James Monroe, George Mason, and a host of others of only slightly lesser stature. Aside from their distinction as statesmen, lawyers, and political thinkers, these men have also attracted attention because of the incredible variety of their other interests. To point out that Washington was an expert surveyor and a scientific farmer, Jefferson an architect, violinist, and amateur scientist, Wythe an outstanding classical scholar as well as a brilliant lawyer, is but to illustrate the wonderful versatility of a whole generation. Would that we could fully understand the circumstances that produced such men!

That it was not merely chance seems sure. For this lush flowering of genius was not without precedent in Virginia. The generation that fathered the Revolutionary giants was itself full of amazing talents, and drawn from an even tinier population. Robert Carter of Corotoman, who died in the year of Washington's birth, was a man of wide learning, rector of William and Mary College, possessor of a large library, and a shrewd businessman, although his main occupation was that of planter and the manager of 300,000 acres. Robert Beverley was another planter who experimented with the cultivation of the grape, held local office, and wrote a charming and highly original history of Virginia. And there were others like William Fitzhugh and Richard Lee (progenitor of a dozen famous soldiers, statesmen, and civic leaders).

Perhaps the most versatile Virginian of that generation was William Byrd II. Louis B. Wright, Director of the Folger Library, gives us here a sketch of his fascinating career, which demonstrates clearly Byrd's right to be called an unforgettable American. Dr. Wright, a prolific and imaginative student of colonial life, has edited William Byrd's diaries and written many books, the most recent of which is The Cultural Life of the American Colonies, *a volume in the New American Nation series.*

of old Colonel William Byrd, one of the wealthiest planters and Indian traders in the colony, who had died the previous December. It was hoped that the heir to all the Byrd estates would take a Virginia wife, settle down at Westover, and become a man of substance and influence in the colony.

This second William Byrd, thirty-one years old, had received an education in England, had travelled on the Continent and learned the secrets of trade in Holland. He had been a member of the Middle Temple, and had been admitted to the English bar ten years before. He had also been elected to the House of Burgesses in 1696, and was clearly a coming man, now that he had inherited the family plantations along the James and a substantial credit with bankers and merchants in London and Bristol. Furthermore, Byrd was a polished cavalier, the familiar friend of titled folk in England, and was on easy terms with people of note in the English world of fashion. He had had his fling in the restless whirlpool of London society and was now ready to become a bigger frog in a smaller pond, though he did not sever his ties with London. A year after his return to Virginia he chose as his wife Lucy Parke, daughter of Daniel Parke, the rakish governor of the Leeward Islands. Two years later he was elected to the Council of State, that exclusive little clique of aristocratic planters who really controlled Virginia. Byrd was on his way to colonial success.

A man with Byrd's training was useful as diplomatic agent for the colony in England, and he served on three occasions as agent for Virginia in London. The inheritor of more than twenty-five thousand acres of land, he had an enormous task to administer his property. He also served as colonel of the militia for his county and as a judge of the county court, and he had to fulfill other civic obligations, many of which brought no reward except prestige and hard work. When he could obtain a post that was lucrative, he seized it, as in his appointment as receiver of customs in Virginia.

Byrd became one of the busiest tobacco planters in Virginia and was active in developing his estate at Westover. He planted all sorts of fruit trees and encouraged the growing of flowers and new vegetables. All his life Byrd fancied himself as something of a scientist, and was interested in botany and medicine. He was proud of his early election as a member of the Royal Society and did his best to prove his right to belong to that body of scientists and virtuosi.

When he was a young law student at the Middle Temple in London, Byrd had made friends with writers like Wycherley and Congreve and had tried his own hand at light verse and prose satire. Busy as he was as a planter and as an official in the colonial government, he continued his interests in literature and in learning.

For many years, Byrd was known to the world of letters only because he wrote "The History of the Dividing Line betwixt Virginia and North Carolina Run in the Year of Our Lord 1728." This was an amusing narrative of his adventures as head of the Virginia Commission that collaborated with a similar group from North Carolina in determining the borders between the two colonies. The work, which circulated in manuscript in Byrd's lifetime, was not published until 1841, when Edmund Ruffin printed it and other pieces from Byrd's pen under the title of *The Westover Manuscripts.* But in 1941 a hitherto unknown diary by William Byrd was published. The next year a second volume of Byrd's diary, discovered in the University of North Carolina library, was also published. Still a third section turned up in the Virginia Historical Society and was published in 1958. If Byrd's diary did not place him at once in the class with Samuel Pepys, the document is nevertheless one of the most fascinating pieces of self-revelation surviving from the colonial period. It throws a vivid light on the daily life of a Virginia planter of the upper class, and though it is often repetitious and gives a vast amount of information seemingly irrelevant to anyone except the writer (such as what he ate every day and how often he forgot to say his prayers), it is a mine of information for the social historian.

Byrd found life with Lucy Parke tempestuous, and he confides his troubles to his diary. She was young, headstrong, violent-tempered, and a poor manager of the household. Byrd himself was not too easy to live with, for he had a vast complacence and almost invariably reports in his diary that Lucy was in the wrong. One crisis occurred on February 5, 1711

[illegible]

cloistered pedant; he led an exceedingly busy and sometimes a merry life. When the Council of State met in Williamsburg, he enjoyed convivial evenings with his friends. Frequently he played at cards and usually he lost money on his gaming. On November 20, 1711, for example, he notes: "I went to court and gave my judgment in several cases. About one o'clock I took some sage and snakeroot. Then I returned into court again and we sat till three. Then I wrote a letter to my wife and after that I went to the coffeehouse where I played at hazard and lost seven pounds and returned home very peaceable."

Byrd took his duties as administrator of his estates and as an officer of the colony very seriously, and put in long hours of hard work. He notes in his diary his personal efforts in the supervision of crops, the planting of his orchard, the sale of his tobacco, and the promotion of business enterprises like the development of lands on the Roanoke and Dan Rivers. To induce Swiss immigrants to come to Virginia, he provided the notes for a German treatise published in Switzerland in 1737 as *The New Found Eden.* As colonel of the militia he conscientiously drilled his troops and made ready to resist rumored invasions from French privateers during the War of the Spanish Succession. Particularly he notes his pleasure in the respect shown him as commanding officer.

In 1716 Byrd returned to England as agent for the colony of Virginia and took along his wife Lucy, whose beauty and style made a favorable impression on London society. Tragically, she took smallpox and died. Within a year Byrd was diligently looking for an heiress to become the second Mrs. Byrd. A certain

Mary Smith, daughter of a wealthy commissioner of the excise, excited his interest and he wooed her violently. But when, at the request of his prospective father-in-law, Byrd produced a balance sheet showing his income, Smith coldly replied that he would as soon have a son-in-law on the moon as one in Virginia with no larger cash income than Byrd's. Forthwith, Mary married a baronet; Byrd wrote her a spiteful letter expressing his disdain, and continued his quest for a rich wife. In the meantime, he solaced himself with countless love affairs and wrote down the details in his diary. For example, the diary for October 4, 1718, records a visit to the house of one Mrs. A-l-n. The object of his affection was out, but Byrd improved his time by courting her maid. When the lady of the house returned, he completed the evening with an intimate rendezvous with her and added complacently in his journal that he "went home and ate a plum cake." Not until 1724, on another trip to England, did Byrd manage to snare an heiress, this time one Maria Taylor of Kensington, with whom he lived for many years quite happily.

Although Byrd was constantly writing verse, translating bits from the classics, and scribbling short prose pieces, he published only one work in his lifetime, and that anonymously. Called *A Discourse Concerning the Plague with Some Preservatives Against It, By a Lover of Mankind,* it was printed in London in 1721. If Byrd was inspired merely by a love of mankind, the treatise suggests a certain amount of self-interest, for it advocates the wide use of tobacco as a preservative against the plague and other ills afflicting the human race. Tobacco prices had taken a drop and Byrd undoubtedly hoped that a plague-frightened England would rush to buy the Virginia commodity.

In the magnificent house that he erected at Westover, a house that is still a monument to the good taste exhibited in colonial architecture of the eighteenth century, Byrd brought together one of the finest libraries in colonial America. He took great pride in his books and his house became a center of literary culture in Virginia. He was not always typical of the ruling planter-class of colonial Virginia, but in many respects he exemplifies a type of society that made a profound impression on British America before the Revolution. He brought to a distant frontier of the British Empire the urbanity of London with its virtues as well as some of its vices. Byrd represented one element in the civilizing influence that emanated from England in the eighteenth century.

Peter Harrison

[illegible] by comparison to their European contemporaries, it remains true that when they turned to the construction of houses, the fabrication of furniture, and other practical crafts, the colonists produced some of the loveliest achievements of their times. As Samuel Eliot Morison has said, "the generation which planned the New England villages, divided the fields, and built the first houses, seemed incapable of making anything ugly."

Colonial furniture, silverware, and ironwork are justly famous, but nowhere was this practical artistry more effectively demonstrated than in architecture. Colonial building was not outstandingly originial. New Amsterdam was a miniature Leiden, the old State House in Boston as "Georgian" as any contemporary British structure. Indeed, most builders seem to have relied heavily on English architectural manuals, which were evidently imported into America in large numbers. But the best of these amateur architects made skillful use of local materials and produced works of real merit. In this chapter Carl Bridenbaugh, Professor of History at the University of California, tells the story of Peter Harrison, the outstanding American architect of the eighteenth century. In addition to a full-length biography of Harrison, Bridenbaugh has written the definitive accounts of colonial urban life, Cities in the Wilderness *and* Cities in Revolt, *and a number of other important works dealing with early American history.*

". . . greatest of the colonial architects"

CARL BRIDENBAUGH

THE growing interest we are now displaying in our past has resulted in a series of restorations that are visited every year by thousands of citizens. There is an increasing public interest in architecture, especially in what are popularly known as "Georgian" or "colonial" buildings; and it is only natural that we should want to know about the men who designed and erected the structures which we now preserve so lovingly. Peter Harrison claims our attention because he was the greatest of the colonial architects.

Time, neglect, and the weather have taken a heavy toll of eighteenth century buildings, but almost miraculously every public building that Peter Harrison is known to have designed is still standing and in excellent condition. At Newport in Rhode Island the visitor will find three public edifices planned by Harrison. On Bellevue Avenue, in the middle of a large shaded lot, stands his first effort, the Redwood Library, a small Greek temple which has served as Newport's cultural center since 1749. Not far distant, on Touro Street, is another kind of temple: The Synagogue of Congregation Jeshuat Israel, dedicated in 1763 and now the oldest Hebrew temple in this country. Its exquisite interior has few, if any, rivals for beauty and finish among American religious edifices. The Newport Market House, located at the foot of the Parade, was the last and most elaborate of Harrison's architectural undertakings, having been opened in 1772. It is now the office of the Chamber of Commerce and its preservation is assured.

Peter Harrison's work for other communities was confined principally to church architecture. On Tremont Street in the heart of downtown Boston, King's Chapel stands resolutely at the foot of many tall buildings—peaceful refuge amidst the clangor and clatter of the modern city. Opened for services in 1754, this first cut-stone structure to be erected in America is still one of the country's most interesting and handsome churches, though the beautiful spire drawn for it has never been added. Across the Charles River in Cambridge, near Harvard Square, is Christ Church, a frame building of fine proportions planned by the architect to suit the needs of a country village. Recently-adduced evidence indicates that the Rev. East Apthorp, rector of Christ Church, called upon Peter Harrison to plan his residence. "The Bishop's Palace," as those Yankees who feared Episcopacy labelled it, is today the Master's Lodgings of Adams House in Harvard University. Almost a thousand miles away in South

first place, in England itself, prior to 1750, architecture was not considered a profession for which one prepared. Structures were erected by "master builders" or "surveyors," usually recruited from the ranks of the carpenters or masons, who followed plans supplied by the gentlemen who employed them. It was then the height of fashion for a wealthy aristocrat, possessed of ample leisure, to study the dozen or so available books of designs of Roman and modern classical buildings published in England, and to create out of various elements a successful solution of his particular architectural problem. Thus design was a gentleman's avocation: architects were amateurs, not professionals. Peter Harrison never charged any fee for his work; in so doing he remained always a "gifted amateur" architect.

Born into a middle-class family of Quakers at York in 1716, Peter Harrison grew to manhood in the England in which the Earl of Burlington and his associates were throwing up handsome edifices imitated from Andrea Palladio's superb neoclassical prototypes at Vicenza in Northern Italy. Although reared in modest circumstances, Harrison enjoyed an unusual opportunity to learn the ways of the wealthy and the elegant by long visits with some connections of his parents in the gentry of Yorkshire and Nottinghamshire. During these visits he acquired his taste for architecture. But he had to make his own way in the world, and his practical Quaker parents saw to it that he learned a trade. He mastered a number of crafts and became an expert wood carver and ship builder before he went to sea to learn the art of ship handling and navigation under the tutelage of his older brother Joseph. Somewhere, sometime, he also developed a talent for drafting and map making, as well as for surveying and military engineering. Each of these skills contributed directly to that recognized mastery of architecture that has led some historians to assert that he must have served an apprenticeship in England under a professional architect. But his training, such as it was, was accidental or incidental to his interest in architecture.

Realizing that for him England offered few if any avenues to fortune and social position, he sailed for America in the year 1739 as a cabin boy in the ship *Sheffield* commanded by his brother. Its destination was Newport on Rhode Island, a fortuitous landing for this nearly penniless immigrant. Making the bustling seaport his home, Peter Harrison rose to the top of colonial society within seven years by a brilliant marriage to Elizabeth Pelham, which brought him both wealth and a country estate. He further assured his place among the gentry of New England by joining the Church of England, by then the most fashionable of religious bodies. Through a successful partnership with his brother in a mercantile house, Peter Harrison not merely added to his wealth but was enabled to make several trips back to England in the 1740s, where he purchased most of the best known books on architecture and military fortifications then available. These and other works formed the finest architectural library assembled by any American before Thomas Jefferson.

By 1748 Harrison was ready to devote his leisure time to the combining of practical skills learned in his early years with the knowledge gained from the books in his library whenever the occasions called. The first request to design a building came from the Company of the Redwood Library in 1748. The success he achieved in this first Palladian structure won plaudits and impelled his fellow Anglicans at Boston to ask him to prepare the drawings for the new King's Chapel. Shortly thereafter, in all probability, it was he who planned St. Michael's Church which Samuel Cardy, the carpenter, built for the Episcopalians of Charleston, South Carolina.

Peter Harrison's reputation as "a masterly architect" was now secure, but the French and Indian War deflected his interests to more pressing matters of public concern. He participated with his brother in the erection of the third lighthouse in the colonies at Beavertail on Conanicut Island in Newport harbor. When it burned down in 1753, he designed a new one with an improved lanthorn and a dwellinghouse for the keeper. In 1745 he had planned a fort for Goat Island to defend Newport, and a decade later he superintended the construction of a new fort, whose intricate design he worked out from his books. When he dispatched the plans of Fort George to London for approval, he included a handsome map of the town and harbor of Newport.

With the return of peace after 1759, Peter Harrison withdrew

pass many a pleasant hour with his friends, the Episcopal gentry who were the King's most ardent supporters in New England.

This idyllic life ended in 1766 when Harrison accepted an appointment as Collector of the Port at New Haven in Connecticut, a reward for his service and loyalty procured through the good offices of Lord Rockingham. While not itself a lucrative position, this customs post promised greater economic security; and, moreover, the elevation to the ranks of officialdom signified his arrival at the very apex of colonial society. Shortly thereafter fellow colonials honored him with election to the newly-founded American Philosophical Society at Philadelphia.

By performing a host of public services without any request for compensation, he amply repaid the society that had helped him to his exalted position. His career is a colonial chapter in the celebrated American success story. But it has a very tragic end. After Peter Harrison moved to New Haven, his tide of good fortune began to ebb. His health, never robust, broke; and the death of his son Thomas, whose artistic gifts had promised so much, was a very heavy blow. As a faithful royal official, the Collector clashed with smuggling merchants, and suffered indignities accorded all prominent members of the Tory group, whom Whig patriots despised. Harrison lived in constant fear of a physical beating such as his brother received while performing his official duties at Boston in 1768. In fact his world suddenly began to tumble down around him. He did not live to suffer at the hands of the mob, for he died only eleven days after the Battle of Lexington. But several months after his burial, a New Haven mob led by "King" Isaac Sears from New York ransacked his house, destroying or carrying off all his books and priceless drawings. Today his buildings are his only monument.

Henry Bouquet

The average citizen of any land tends to see his country's history too much from his own viewpoint, and we Americans, full of pride in our unquestionably great national accomplishments, have been no exception to this rule. This has been true despite the efforts of some of our foremost historians to place our history in its true perspective.

Nowhere does this prejudice seem more deeply rooted than in the common interpretation of the French and Indian War. As Kemp Malone points out in the following chapter, "We owe it to the redcoats that the French lost their American empire," but in the popular image of that war the British army is pictured as a blundering, stiff-necked force marching blindly in columns of fours through the tangled wilderness into a long series of bloody ambushes. The eventual victory, according to the traditional view, was won by brave, devoted, and canny colonists, who beat the French and Indians at their own game. General Braddock's overwhelming defeat at Fort Duquesne and Washington's devotion to duty and shrewd understanding of the nature of forest warfare have been taken as typical, which neither was. Colonial soldiers, by and large, were undependable and ill-led. James Wolfe, the brilliant captor of Quebec, thinking of Boston militiamen of his acquaintance, said: "It seldom happens that a New England man prefers service to a lazy life." Wolfe insisted on fighting the crucial battle for control of North America with an army made up almost entirely of British regulars. "Most [American] officers, except the higher ones," another British general reported, "are an extremely bad collection of broken innkeepers, horse jockeys and Indian traders."

British soldiers, it is true, did not take naturally to forest warfare, but they and their generals learned from experience. Even the unfortunate Braddock was the victim more of bad luck than of stupidity, and before the conflict was over officers like Wolfe, John Forbes, and Jeffrey Amherst had won a series of spectacular victories. Henry Bouquet is less well known than any of these, but as Professor Malone makes clear, he was a brilliant com-

mander whose career offers an excellent example of the true worth of the British military in the French and Indian War.

Kemp Malone is Professor Emeritus of English at Johns Hopkins University, and past President of the Linguistic Society of America and several other scholarly organizations. He is the

THE Irish dramatist Richard Sheridan, in *The School for Scandal,* gives a list of noted wayfarers: Mr. and Mrs. Honeymoon, Miss Tattle, Lord Buffalo, Sir H. Bouquet, and Mr. Tom Saunter. The honeymooners are on their travels as a kind of fling before settling down to married life. Miss Tattle goes from place to place in order to spread gossip. Tom Saunter does his aimless wandering for no particular reason; he is simply a born vagrant. These characters are all mere inventions of the playwright, of course. I know nothing about Lord Buffalo, but my guess is that "Buffalo" was the nickname of some nobleman, a nickname well known to Sheridan's audience but a mystery to us.

Sir H. Bouquet remains. He at least was not invented by the playwright. He was a man of flesh and blood, a professional soldier who fought on many fields of battle in Europe and America, a man who had wandered so widely over the face of the earth that he was eminently in place in Sheridan's list. Sheridan, when he called him "Sir," was giving him a knighthood that he never got, but he fully deserved the honor. Unhappily we hear nothing more about him in the play—there he is only a name on a list. But in the British Museum the Bouquet papers run to no less than 30 manuscript volumes devoted to his American career alone. He played so important a part in our colonial history that every American ought to know his name and have some idea of what he did.

Henry Bouquet was born in the year 1719 in a Swiss village not far from Geneva. As his name indicates, he came from the French part of Switzerland and French was his mother tongue.

But he was no stay-at-home. When only seventeen years of age he went to Holland to join the Dutch army as a soldier of fortune, and it took him only two years to win a lieutenancy. In those days, national armies as we know them did not exist. The army of the Netherlands in particular was made up of professional soldiers drawn from many countries. Switzerland had long been an important source of supply for such soldiers, and Henry Bouquet was not doing anything out of the way or unpatriotic in entering the service of a foreign state. His European career as a soldier lasted for twenty years, during which he mastered the military profession in all its branches, theoretical and practical, and rose to a lieutenant-colonelcy. His soldierly parts made him so well known in professional circles that the British craved his services and finally persuaded him to come to America as commander of a battalion in the so-called Royal Americans, a regiment organized for duty in the colonies. Here he spent the rest of his days, rising to the rank of brigadier general before his death of a fever in 1765, when he was in his middle forties.

Bouquet was the greatest leader in the Indian wars of the 18th century that the British army in America ever had. One may indeed go further and say that he was the only great leader, in that kind of warfare, to be found on the British side among the professional soldiers of the day. The colonists, or the frontiersmen at least, could often beat the Indian raiders at their own game, but they were not soldiers; they resented military discipline and intensely disliked long campaigns far from home. When their own firesides were threatened they took up arms at once, but from the moment the immediate danger was past their one thought was to get back to their families and farms. Their periods of enlistment were short, and many cut them shorter by simply deserting. The French and Indian War was won by the regular British army, and it was the regulars again who put down the conspiracy of Pontiac in the spring and summer of 1763. The colonial militia helped, of course, but they did not bear the main burden of the long, hard campaigns. We owe it to the redcoats that the French lost their American empire, and that the Indian lands west of the Alleghenies were opened up to our pioneer forefathers for settlement.

These redcoats paid a heavy price for their final victory. At first they fought as they had learned to fight on the battlefields of Europe, advancing in close order, unwilling to take cover, picked off at leisure by invisible foes. Both officers and men adapted themselves slowly and reluctantly to the tactics required in fighting Indians. Bouquet was the outstanding exception. He was a man of flexible mind, able to adjust himself readily to new situations and changed conditions. In particular, he soon mastered the principles of forest warfare. His scouts, thrown out on every side, kept him in touch with the movements of the enemy,

his career came to an end not only the battalion he had personally trained but whole regiments knew how to fight the Indians.

Bouquet's leadership, though important, was not decisive in the French and Indian War proper. He served as second in command to Brigadier General Forbes in the march to Fort Duquesne, soon to become Fort Pitt, and but for him this expedition might well have failed. The war was won, however, by General Wolfe when he defeated Montcalm at Quebec. The conspiracy of Pontiac in 1763 brought to Bouquet general recognition as the greatest Indian fighter of them all. In this conspiracy the Indians made their supreme effort to stem the tide of European conquest. Pontiac, an Ottowa chief, gathered in the common cause nearly all the Indian tribes of the frontier, from the Great Lakes to the Gulf of Mexico. He started his strike for freedom in the late spring of 1763. The uprising was tremendously successful at first. In less than a month's time Pontiac made himself master of the wilderness west of the area of white settlement. Most of the fortified posts that the British had built or taken from the French in that vast region fell into his hands and those that held out were besieged or threatened. In this emergency the British called Bouquet back to active duty.

The colony of Maryland had made Bouquet a citizen and he had settled there, but now he left his farm and took command of the meager forces put at his disposal for the relief of Fort Pitt —now Pittsburgh. With characteristic speed and efficiency he got his troops ready for the campaign, made the needful arrangements for supplies, and set out. On the afternoon of August 5, 1763, as he was making his way westward, the Indians attacked him in force. They took him by surprise in spite of all his precautions: his scouts had failed him, outwitted by the enemy. But he rose to the occasion and made good his retreat to a hill, where he took his stand. Here he held out the rest of the day, repulsing all assaults, though heavily outnumbered and hard pressed on every side.

The next morning the battle began anew. It is known to history as the Battle of Bushy Run. At the psychological moment Bouquet made a tactical move that would not have been possible but for his understanding of Indian ways of fighting and his complete control of his troops, who were splendidly disciplined and had every confidence in their commander. He ordered a part of his little force to fall back. The Indians took this move to be the beginning of a rout, and they rushed forward in a wild charge, leaving their cover and exposing themselves to a counterattack which ended in their utter overthrow. Bouquet's victory led to the relief of Fort Pitt and the reconquest of the whole upper valley of the Ohio River. In 1764 Bouquet was transferred to the south, where he headed an expedition against the Indians that was equally successful and even more important in its effects.

The Battle of Bushy Run and the southern campaign made clear to all the greatness of Henry Bouquet as a military leader. He won the thanks of King George himself and the gratitude of the southern colonies, whose legislatures passed resolutions of praise and appreciation. But his greatest service to our country remains to be mentioned.

He pacified and opened to settlement the frontier from Lake Erie to the Gulf, and thereby set going that swift expansion westward which was not to end until our nation stretched from the Atlantic to the shores and islands of the Pacific. This expansion gave us a way of life all our own, and made us at last the dynamo of western civilization, the great upholder of democratic ideals, the chief stronghold of the free world. Henry Bouquet stands in the front rank of the men who made it possible for these United States to grow from thirteen to fifty and from insignificance to world leadership. To this Swiss soldier of fortune and his fellows we owe much. It behooves us ever to be mindful of the great work they did for us in those momentous days when we were becoming a nation.

John Dickinson, Patrick Henry,

were also lawyers like John Adams, printers like Franklin, poets like young Joel Barlow, doctors like Benjamin Rush, and every other sort. So, too, the Revolutionary Fathers ran the gamut where personality was concerned. Angry agitators like Sam Adams stood side by side, so to speak, with quiet but determined patriots like James Madison. Romantic rebels like Alexander Hamilton worked shoulder to shoulder with staid burghers like John Jay. Men like Jefferson wielded their pens for the cause while others—Nathanael Greene for example—turned their talents toward military affairs.

Many of the leading patriots were descended from the earliest settlers; by tradition and in training they were completely American. Others, such as General Charles Lee and Hamilton, were recent arrivals who adopted the cause almost as soon as they set foot on American soil. Some were rich, some poor, some old, others young. Northerners and Southerners, frontiersmen and those from the settled areas close to the Atlantic—every section provided its share of revolutionaries.

Among so many diverse groups there were many feelings and opinions. Indeed, the wonder is that the movement for independence did not explode into a hundred separate fragments.

Franklin provided one explanation of why it did not when he pointed out to his fellows that if they did not "hang together" they would certainly "hang separately." But while this was good advice and logical, revolutions are not often conducted logically. And Franklin's advice was offered after the die had been cast. What held a majority of the revolutionary generation together through the trials and torments of the war years were two atti-

tudes, relatively new but of growing importance: that America was a special place, different fundamentally from the Old World. And that there was basic injustice in England's efforts to subordinate the interests of her colonies to her own. While most settlers continued to think of themselves as Englishmen right up to the end, and while a great deal of their indignation against the mother country was based on Great Britain's denying them their rights as *Englishmen*, nearly everyone in the colonies recognized the uniqueness of America and the unfairness of England. About these matters radical and conservative, rich and poor, the impetuous and the deliberate, the learned and the ignorant, indeed, even the brave and the cowardly could not really disagree.

The four following essays illustrate both the diversity of the revolutionary leaders and their basic similarity. Henry was the hot-headed patriot orator ready to toy with the idea of rebellion ten years before the fighting began. Dickinson was the cautious, conservative lawyer who had grave doubts about the wisdom of independence even in 1776. Paine was a bold newcomer who, with one inspired pamphlet, helped thousands of Americans to see their destiny clear. Madison, modest and well-mannered, was a careful student of government convinced of the need for independence; his main contribution came later when he served as chief architect of the Constitution. Paine was an American nationalist from the start, whereas Henry saw himself, even after the long war had been won, primarily as a Virginian. Madison was able to be both a Virginian and an American, while Dickinson had to fight a battle within his own mind and heart to convince himself that he was no longer an Englishman. But all four were aware of America's distinctive place in the world, and all agreed that England's colonial policies were morally wrong.

Bernard Bailyn, author of a number of books and articles on seventeenth and eighteenth century America, is Associate Professor of History at Harvard University. Thomas J. Wertenbaker, Emeritus Professor of History at Princeton University and former President of the American Historical Association, has written a long series of important volumes on many aspects of colonial history. Alfred Owen Aldrich is Professor of English at the University of Maryland. His *Man of Reason* (1959) is the most recent biography of Thomas Paine. George Dangerfield has written many books, including *The Strange Death of Liberal England* and *The Era of Good Feelings* (which was awarded both the Pulitzer and Bancroft prizes).

". . . voice of the colonists' conscience"

BERNARD BAILYN

biographies of the great and powerful? They tell us much, but they hide much too by keeping our attention focussed on a few personalities. And the ordinary man, powerful in the mass, stands too far from the sources of historical decisions. But between the great and the obscure are the middling men of history, involved in large affairs but not dominating them, expressing common feelings but not shaping them. Their lives tell much of the meaning of great events.

One such man was John Dickinson of Pennsylvania, a reluctant participant in the American Revolution who vaulted into early fame as the voice of the colonists' conscience but who fell into disrepute by holding back when independence was declared. He was a lesser light among the luminaries of the Revolutionary era; but an understanding of his career brings us close to an answer to Adams' question: "What do we mean by the American Revolution?"

Fortune favored John Dickinson from his early years. Born in 1732 the son of a Delaware lawyer, judge, and gentleman farmer, he was educated by tutors and studied law in the colonies and in England. Settled as a lawyer in Philadelphia, he was quickly and solidly successful. In 1765, when the first evidences of serious trouble between England and her colonies appeared, the thirty-three-year-old Philadelphia lawyer was well-established and had entered politics in the Pennsylvania Assembly.

Politically, he was already what he would remain throughout his life, an enlightened conservative. His conservatism, created in part by the circumstances of birth and education, had been confirmed by his early success in the established order of society and by his temperament, which was fastidious, scholarly, and mildly aloof. But Dickinson's conservatism was not of an obvious sort. At its heart lay a passionate conviction which gave it depth and complexity; in the light of it he appeared now well ahead, now far behind the line of liberal advance. It was his conviction that England's brilliant and tolerant enlightenment, indeed, the progress of civilization, rested and must rest on the rule of law. What distinguished England and her colonies was in the last analysis the British legal system and particularly the common law, which, embodying the inherited wisdom of the nation, expressed reasonable and universal principles of justice. It was law uniformly enforced that alone set limits to man's inhumanity to man. Nowhere in Britain and her colonies, as Dickinson saw it, were individuals endowed with unlimited or arbitrary authority. Even the king and his ministers must rule by the law. All stood before it, none above it.

This belief in the wisdom of English law and in the unwritten constitution that gave it power was the ruling conviction of John Dickinson's life. It was to defend it in the colonies that he entered the stage of history.

He first found his voice in behalf of a most unpopular cause. A large and vocal group in Pennsylvania, of which Benjamin Franklin was a leader, was working to eliminate the privileges of the Penn family, derived from the charter for colonization that had been granted to William Penn by Charles II. Why, they asked, should the lands reserved by the Penns go untaxed while all others were burdened more heavily year by year? Because, Dickinson answered, the legal charter that guaranteed these tax privileges to the Penn family also guaranteed to the people of Pennsylvania important civil rights. Nowhere, he pointed out, was religious freedom so broad as in the Quaker colony, and these rights of conscience, fuller even than those of England, were given the force of law by Penn's charter. Should these legal guarantees be sacrificed for a few hundred pounds a year? Be patient, he advised. "Why should we have any aversion to deliberation and delay," he asked in the Assembly, "when no injury can attend them?"

For this outspoken attack on a popular cause he was condemned as an arch-reactionary, a hireling of the proprietors. Within a single year, however, when he used these same principles in defense of colonial rights, he found himself a popular leader. The Stamp Act of 1765, placing duties on printed matter and on legal documents, was the first direct tax ever levied by England's Parliament on the American colonists. It shocked Dickinson. Here was a profound violation of the principles of English law carried out by England herself. To Dickinson, as to William Pitt, who argued the colonists' cause in Parliament, it

comply with the Act would be "to rivet perpetual chains" on themselves, to enter voluntarily upon slavery. Do not allow the law to take effect, Dickinson said. Fight it now. "Power," he warned in a memorable phrase, "is of a tenacious nature: what it seizes it will retain."

To some in England such views, presented formally in the Stamp Act Congress' "Declaration of Rights," which Dickinson drafted, amounted to rebellion. But this Dickinson denied. The colonists owed "all due" subordination to Parliament, but surely compliance with laws that violated the constitution was not justly due.

The repeal of the Stamp Act in 1766 justified Dickinson's faith in England and fortified his confidence in the power of reasonable argument and peaceable resistance. When in 1767 the Townshend Acts were passed, placing duties on importations into America, Dickinson threw himself into the resulting controversy, defending his now familiar views brilliantly and with great effect. From his pen came the most powerful constitutional arguments against the duties, arguments which became steps in the progress of revolution. The form they took was a series of essays in the "Pennsylvania Chronicle" entitled "Letters from a Farmer in Pennsylvania to the inhabitants of the British Colonies." These "Farmer's Letters," which in pamphlet form were widely circulated and had great influence as the most forceful expression of colonial opinion, raised Dickinson to the pinnacle of fame. The calm and elegant lawyer overnight became the hero of the radicals. Yet at bottom he was saying little more than what he had said four years earlier in defense of the unpopular proprietary charter: man in his nature has certain rights; laws exist to protect these rights; such laws and the principles behind them must stand inviolable.

Again Dickinson's position was vindicated. The Townshend duties were withdrawn. But in the four years that followed, a series of events—the burning of the *Gaspee*, the Tea Act, the Coercive Acts of 1774—brought the situation to a crisis. The Pennsylvania Farmer was deeply involved. He was a member of the Continental Congress and drew up some of its most important papers, including the "Declaration of the Causes and Necessities of Taking up Arms."

But fate in its turnings was beginning to face away from him. The course of events was surpassing the point of reasonable argument. There was violence in the air; mob agitators appeared to be grasping for power; and England, the home of liberty under the law, was increasingly deaf to all appeals. Logic seemed to be leading toward the dark frontier of political action where law no longer operated. At the brink of revolution Dickinson hesitated. Hanging back as others moved ahead towards independence, he asked himself: is it reasonable, is it necessary to destroy all law and government in order to defend liberty? He hesitated to say that it was. Economic sanctions and petitions to the Crown for justice he favored; he would accept if necessary a resort to arms; but to cast the colonies adrift, to declare them independent states, to rip the fabric of an empire's constitution—was this reasonable? Was it necessary? And what would follow independence, he asked in a speech before Congress. With sovereign authority removed, would not the irresponsible elements of society "prostrate all barriers and involve the state in ruin?"

The task, he insisted, was to convince England that her government was in the hands of those he called "profligate men," "villains and idiots," who were plunging a brave and generous nation into "unmerited and inglorious distress." He pleaded in Congress for caution and prudence. But he could not control events. He succeeded only in obtaining temporary delays and the scorn of the radicals. When, on July 2, 1776, the irrevocable moment came and Congress voted on the resolution declaring the colonies free and independent states, John Dickinson was purposely absent. His abstention, based on conviction, reflected his devotion to law and his respect for authority.

Though he had not favored the Declaration, once it was passed he did what he could, as a soldier and for a short period as a member of Congress, to support the Revolution. But his talents were better employed in the reconstruction of the state governments that followed the war. In the 1780's, as president of the Council first of Delaware and then of Pennsylvania, he worked

story than this. His cautions and hesitations were characteristic of the American people. Few of the colonists were anxious for independence. A large number remained loyal to England. The great majority, devoted to the principles that Dickinson proclaimed, hesitated to throw off allegiance to England, and after that was done proceeded to recreate under local conditions the institutions and laws, in origin British, that they considered to be the bulwarks of liberty.

"What do we mean by the American Revolution?" We mean that moment in history when a people overthrew constituted authority to defend the principle that law, written or unwritten, must guide the workings of the state and limit the uses of power. The colonists entered into rebellion reluctantly. They were essentially conservative. Though they rejected imperial sovereignty they conserved in all ways possible the fundamental beliefs that, as none knew better than John Dickinson, lay at the heart of English law.

". . . a fire alarm in the night"

THOMAS J. WERTENBAKER

TARQUIN and Caesar had each his Brutus, Charles I his Cromwell, and George III . . ." These words of Patrick Henry rang out in the Hall of Burgesses in the Capitol at Williamsburg in protest against the Stamp Act. As the orator paused, cries of "treason! treason!" came from all parts of the room. Henry denied that he was disloyal, but he made no apology for what he had said. And his words resounded through the colonies like a fire alarm in the night to awaken the people to the danger that threatened.

Patrick Henry was born at Studley, Virginia, about sixteen miles north of Richmond. His education was meager. At an early age he and a brother opened a country store, and when this failed he became a farmer. Later he studied law—the only available textbook was *Coke-on-Littleton* and this he mastered from the first page to the last. He managed to secure his license to practice from the Board of Examiners, but he did so poorly that George Wythe, a great Virginia lawyer, later a signer of the Declaration of Independence, refused to sign it.

Patrick Henry first came into prominence in the famous Parsons' Cause, a lawsuit which foretold the coming of the American Revolution. The issue was of great significance, for it involved the right of the King to veto acts of the Assembly. In 1758 the Assembly had passed a law to permit all obligations to be paid in money for a year rather than in tobacco, the usual currency. Since this prevented the tripling of the salaries of the ministers, they complained to the British government, and the King vetoed the act. As a result hundreds of men in Virginia were threatened with ruin.

The matter came to a head in 1763, when the Reverend James Maury brought suit in the Hanover County court for his salary in tobacco. Patrick Henry was attorney for the defendants. When he rose to speak he seemed hesitant and awkward. But gradually he grew in confidence. His eyes kindled, his gestures were bold, his voice became commanding. The listeners hung on his every word. The clergy, he said, by appealing to the King to annul a law enacted by the Assembly were attempting to rivet the chains of slavery upon the people. The law of 1758 was good and just, and a King who disallowed good laws was no longer the father of his people but a tyrant who forfeited all right to their obedience. When he had concluded, the jury, in less than five minutes, returned a verdict of one penny damages. Spectators lifted Henry on their shoulders and bore him from the room.

The decision of the Hanover County jury in the Parsons' Cause was a forerunner of the Declaration of Independence. If the Virginia courts insisted on enforcing laws which the King had vetoed, the Assembly was, to all intents and purposes, supreme in the colony. Virginia was ripe for revolution.

Ten years earlier, in protesting against Governor Dinwiddie's charge of a fee of a pistole for the use of the seal in granting patents for land, the House of Burgesses had made a declaration of historic significance. "The rights of the subjects are so secured by law that they cannot be deprived of the least part of their

body in which they were not represented, was to turn the clock back a century and a half. Not only in Virginia, but in all the colonies, men said: "This means slavery."

But there was little thought of resistance until Patrick Henry made his fiery address in the House of Burgesses. Before rising to speak he wrote down on a flyleaf of his *Coke-on-Littleton* several resolutions. There was deep silence in the room as he began to read. The subjects of the King in Virginia were entitled by their charters to all the privileges possessed by the English people. The exclusive right of taxation belonged to them. The usurpation of this right by any body other than the Assembly tended to the overthrow of both American and British liberty.

A bitter debate followed. Some of the ablest men among the Burgesses urged more conciliatory resolutions. But Henry's eloquence carried all before it. Although the most extreme of his resolutions was later rescinded, it, with the others, became known throughout all the colonies and inspired the people to resistance. Perhaps Henry himself, as he left Williamsburg wearing a pair of leather breeches and leading his bony nag by the bridle, did not realize that he had set the American colonies on the road to revolution and independence.

Henry served in the Continental Congress in 1774, and the next year was a member of the Virginia Convention which met in St. John's Church, in Richmond. Here he made one of his greatest speeches. "Gentlemen may cry 'peace, peace', but there is no peace," he said. "The war is actually begun . . . Is Life so dear, or peace so sweet, as to be purchased at the expense of chains and slavery? Forbid it Almighty God! I know not what course others may take, but as for me, give me liberty or give me death."

After the Declaration of Independence and the adoption of a constitution by Virginia, Henry was elected governor. It was appropriate that under his administration Virginia should make one of its greatest contributions to the nation, the conquest of the Northwest. In November 1777, George Rogers Clark, garbed like a frontiersman, appeared in Williamsburg to propose an expedition to drive the British out of the region beyond the mountains. When the matter came before Governor Henry he persuaded the Council to advance £1,200 to finance the expedition, and appointed Clark the leader. So, a few weeks later, Clark mounted his horse, told Henry goodbye, and set out to begin the expedition which was to add an empire to the United States.

Henry opposed the ratification of the United States Constitution by Virginia. At the convention which met in Richmond he declared that the Constitution would create a consolidated government, not a federation.

This was obvious from the wording of the preamble: "We the people of the United States . . . do ordain and establish this Constitution," he said. Madison, who was the chief advocate of ratification, explained that the Constitution was to be ratified by the States, but in each State the people, not the legislatures, were to decide. "The people—but not the people as composing one great body, but the people as composing thirteen sovereignties." Henry was far from being satisfied. He pictured the slavery that would follow ratification; the tyrant on his throne, the mercenary troops, the cries of the oppressed people. The President would send his tax-collectors to take their property, he would be a Caesar, a Cromwell. Henry's pleadings were in vain. Nine States had already ratified, and Virginia had to decide whether she should join the new Union or become an independent nation. The final vote was 89 for ratification and 79 against.

When Thomas Jefferson organized the Democratic-Republican Party, Henry's friends and followers thought that he would throw in his lot with it. Instead he became a Federalist. In 1795 President Washington offered to make him Secretary of State, and when he declined because of ill health Washington urged him to become Chief Justice. But he declined this also. Yet in January 1799 he became a candidate on the Federalist ticket for the House of Delegates. Though elected, he did not live to take his seat.

Patrick Henry always showed great interest in education. He was an early trustee of Hampden-Sydney College. He was one of the greatest orators America has produced, perhaps superior even to Clay or Calhoun or Webster. George Mason said of him: "He is by far the most powerful speaker I ever heard. Every word he utters not only engages, but commands, the attention; and your passions are no longer your own." It was the dedicating of this talent to the cause of freedom which has won him so

THE son of a humble Quaker stay-maker, Thomas Paine was born in England in the year 1737. After spending several years at sea and then trying a number of occupations on land, he traveled to London where he found employment, and supplemented his meager education by attending science lectures.

While inconspicuously employed as a schoolmaster in London, Thomas Paine first met Benjamin Franklin, who advised him to try his fortune in the New World. Almost as soon as he landed, in 1774, Paine saw the country set on fire—the battles of Lexington and Concord were fought and the Continental Congress came into being. He immediately began scientific experiments to produce gunpowder, and started a literary campaign to blast the British out of America. Before his pamphlet *Common Sense* had been sent throughout the colonies, no one dared to breathe of independence in public; afterwards no one dared to dispute it. The work produced "the greatest sale that any performance ever had since the use of letters," according to Paine's grandiloquent but not quite accurate statement. In it Paine advocated the convoking of a constitutional convention, and set out the policy of independence from European involvements which, for nearly two centuries, became traditional in American foreign policy.

Paine fought in the Pennsylvania militia with the rank of brigade major and later accompanied Washington on the famous retreat from the Hudson to the Delaware. Then, to bolster the army's shrinking morale, Paine wrote his *American Crisis,* beginning with the now famous expression: "These are the times that try men's souls." He denounced the "summer soldier and the sunshine patriot," but praised the manly and martial spirit of those who would persist until the glorious triumph he predicted was won. Washington ordered the *Crisis* read in camp to every corporal's guard, and the flagging spirits of soldiers and officers were greatly revived. "Hope succeded to despair, cheerfulness to gloom, and firmness to irresolution." Throughout the war, whenever there was need for inspiring troops, molding public opinion, or ridiculing British blunders, Paine took up his pen. When Congress lacked the funds to continue the war, Paine embarked with John Laurens for the French court and proudly returned with silver requiring sixteen ox teams to transport. He served entirely without compensation, and it was not until the end of the war that Washington and Robert Morris arranged a yearly salary for him to continue his writing in the public interest.

When peace came, Paine turned to scientific research and invented an iron bridge of a single span, which foreshadowed modern methods of assembly. Unable to find sufficient American capital for construction, he took his model to France and England, and a bridge on his plan was eventually constructed over the Wear River, near Sunderland in the county of Durham, England. In 1791 his interests were sidetracked from bridge-building by the publication of Edmund Burke's *Reflections on the French Revolution,* a bitter attack on the principles of popular government. Paine, who had formerly been in close association with Burke and considered him a political ally, answered this anti-democratic manifesto with *The Rights of Man,* a powerful philosophical vindication of representative government. Repudiating Burke's designation of the common man as the "swinish multitude," Paine defended the dignity of the individual and his natural and inalienable right to live in freedom and political equality with his neighbor. In contrast to Burke as the spokesman of privilege and British colonialism, he described himself as "a man who considers the world as his home, and the good of it in all places as his object."

These were the times when France as well as England suffered under the tyranny of despotic kings and unfeeling aristocrats. As soon as *The Rights of Man* was published, Paine left for Paris. In company with a young colonel of the French Army, he covered the walls of that city with an incendiary manifesto urging the citizens to proclaim a republic. In so doing, Paine put himself in the vanguard of a movement that was to change the face of Europe. He was literally the first to call for the creation of a republic in France, as he had previously been first so to do in America.

Paine returned to England to face government prosecution of *The Rights of Man* in a series of legal actions against the principal agents in its publication and sale. The circulation of *The*

quently the French people in four different electoral districts elected him to the National Convention, where he took his seat in September 1792. Although he could speak no French, he was almost immediately appointed to a committee to frame a new constitution. The most important debate of the Assembly concerned the destiny of the deposed king, Louis XVI, and by means of an interpreter Paine delivered two significant opinions. One was received with general acclaim, the other with abuse and derision. In the first speech Paine argued that the deposed monarch should be tried for treasonable actions against the state; in the other he pleaded that Louis' life be spared and that he be banished to America.

From this moment Paine, along with the moderate constitutional members of the Assembly, became suspected by the majority group, the ruthless Jacobins. When the Assembly grew alarmed at the dictatorial tendencies of Jean Paul Marat, one of the Jacobins, Paine gave evidence against him. Unfortunately for Paine, Marat was triumphantly acquitted; thereafter the Jacobins had a double reason to silence Paine. The notorious Robespierre forced the Convention to condemn him as a counter-revolutionary, and in December 1793 he was imprisoned, which at that period was a virtual commitment to the guillotine. A delegation of English and American liberals appealed vainly at the Convention for Paine's release, but the American minister, Gouverneur Morris, seemed indifferent to his plight.

When James Monroe arrived in France during the summer of 1793 as the new minister, he immediately claimed Paine as an American citizen; since the Reign of Terror was then at an end, French officials released him and restored his seat in the Assembly. Suffering from fever contracted in prison, Paine lived with Monroe as an invited guest during a period of eighteen months, and he repaid Monroe's kindness by introducing him to such prominent international personalities as the Irish republican Hamilton Rowan and the South American adventurer General Francisco Miranda.

While in Monroe's house, Paine wrote and caused to be published a famous examination of Washington's administration; and he subsequently composed several influential tracts on French constitutional affairs and international law. The cause of the French people, he believed, was the cause of all mankind. Later, on retiring from active political life, Paine served as unofficial liaison agent between the French and American governments, advising both Talleyrand and Napoleon on western affairs. In 1802 he returned to America at the invitation of his friend, President Thomas Jefferson.

Paine, a staunch supporter of reason and moral integrity, said in *The Rights of Man:* "Every religion is good that teaches man to be good; and I know of none that instructs him to be bad." In France he saw that the old order had fostered religious superstition to perpetuate its abuses, and that the atheism of the Revolution was incapable of satisfying man's spiritual urges. To combat both extremes he wrote his own theological treatise, *The Age of Reason,* the world's most influential deistical book. His creed was positive and humanitarian. "I believe," he said, "in one God, and no more; and I hope for happiness beyond this life. I believe in the equality of man; and I believe that religious duties consist in doing justice, loving mercy, and endeavoring to make our fellow creatures happy."

Since Paine had refused to endorse the creed of any church, the orthodox attacked him as an atheist and minion of the devil, and since his political and religious beliefs were identical with Jefferson's, the Federalists attacked him in order to disparage Jefferson. A sacrifice to political propaganda, Paine became in America the symbol of French atheism, as in England he had been the symbol of bloody revolution. Although he continued to write newspaper articles supporting the Jeffersonian administration, his influence waned. In June 1809 he died, and was buried with little public attention. But now that the clouds of prejudice and political partisanship have been lifted, grateful

Americans recognize the achievements of Thomas Paine, the patriot who could say to all mankind: "My country is the world, and my religion is to do good."

hear him read his Inaugural Address, which he did in a weak, trembling voice, saw a short man with the deeply lined face of an invalid and the indrawn expression of a scholar and a recluse. He was dressed, as was his invariable habit, all in black, with black knee breeches, black silk stockings, black buckled shoes. His hair was powdered and tied at the back. Old-fashioned, meagre, meticulous, prim, he must have seemed a very chilling, a very unimpressive successor to Thomas Jefferson.

It is this unflattering image of James Madison that, in spite of the best efforts of apologists and biographers, still coldly persists in American mythology. Even his semi-official title, "Father of the Constitution," has served to increase rather than diminish his remoteness; for the nineteenth-century notion that the Founding Fathers were almost abstract figures, especially endowed with wisdom and virtue, has not altogether vanished. Madison had all the attributes of a great public servant—loyalty, disinterestedness, incorruptibility, intelligence—but none of the outward characteristics.

The private Madison, however, was very different from the public one. "A gentleman of great modesty," said William Pierce of Georgia, "with a remarkably sweet temper. He is easy and unreserved among his acquaintances, and has a most agreeable style of conversation." Augustus Foster, the British Minister whom Madison sent packing in 1812, described him as "a social, jovial, and good-humored companion, full of anecdote, sometimes rather of a loose description, but oftener of a political and historical interest." His hospitality was famous. He was happily married to the most generous and warm-hearted of women, who once, in the days of their courtship, called him her "great little Madison." These three words about sum up the truth.

If you go to his letters and writings you will find them, at their best (as, for example, in his contributions to the *Federalist Papers*), temperate, lucid, and logical, but never warm and rarely inspiring. Yet a curious freshness—"freshness" seems to be the only word—diffuses itself through them. He feels that the American republic and the American people are giving to words like "liberty" and "freedom" a practical meaning they have never before possessed in the long history of Christendom. It is only in the light of this belief—touching, heroic, even innocent—that his character can be understood; and it was this belief that illuminated his lifelong intimacy with Thomas Jefferson.

This intimacy might be explained in some respects though not in all as the attraction of opposites. Jefferson was sanguine and experimental; Madison relied on logic and common sense. Jefferson held as a cardinal belief that the will of the majority must and should prevail; Madison accepted the principle of majority rule, but had a profound suspicion of local majorities. On the question of centralized government, which Jefferson abhorred, their views were very different. What held them together was, first, social compatability; second, a disposition to compromise and an acceptance of change; and, third, an inflexible devotion to civil liberties. It was Madison who, as a member of the Virginia House of Delegates in 1784, secured the enactment of Jefferson's Bill for the Establishment of Religious Freedom, one of the three acts by which Jefferson wished most to be remembered. In 1798, in the presidency of John Adams, Congress passed the Alien and Sedition Acts which threatened, among other things, the freedom of the press. Madison replied with the Virginia Resolutions, and Jefferson with the more fiery Kentucky Resolutions. As political doctrine these Resolutions were unworkable, but as affirmations of American freedom they were both timely and great.

Madison was born in 1751 into the slave-holding aristocracy of Virginia. Like Jefferson and many other Virginians, he detested the institution of slavery; it is one of the paradoxes of early American history that the men most concerned with the preservation of freedom were men who were forced to countenance the denial of it in their own communities and on their own estates. He was educated at the College of New Jersey, now Princeton University, after which he drifted into the political side of the

Revolution. His demure and retiring personality did not conceal from those who sat with him in the Virginia Convention, in the Virginia Council of State, or in the Continental Congress his supremely lucid and logical mind, his capacity for business, and

ward to make him very suspect to the more rigid Jeffersonians. Neither the complexities of the Convention's debates nor the nature of its many compromises can be set forth here. It must be enough to say that Madison himself showed a leaning toward a strong central government, and a certain tenderness for property rights that, in combination, might not seem very democratic.

It is well to remember, however, that he was an eighteenth century gentleman who still believed that the small independent property-owners, who were then the chief democratic force in America, might locally behave like a starving and desperate London mob. Shays' Rebellion of 1786, an uprising of sorely oppressed Massachusetts debtors, provoked from Jefferson the cheerful remark that "a little rebellion now and then is a good thing." But it filled Madison with horror. He could not see that its purpose was not to destroy but to protect property.

When the text of the Constitution reached Jefferson in Paris, where he was American Minister, he could not conceal his alarm. He saw that it was over-conservative, even while he admired some of its structural features. His chief objection, however, was that it contained no Bill of Rights. But as a Representative from Virginia in the First Congress, Madison proposed the first ten amendments which gave Jefferson what he wanted.

It was as a Representative in Congress that Madison did some of his most courageous work when under Jefferson's inspiration he became a leader of the Republican (or Democratic-Republican) Party. We do not know the exact date of the formation of this party. Perhaps it was in 1791. At any rate, by that year Madison perceived that a strong central government, which allied itself with bankers and stock-jobbers, sought to perpetuate a political elite, and also professed an admiration for the monarchical element in the British constitution, might be very able but would certainly prove destructive. His opposition to Alexander Hamilton and the Federalists became rigorous and extreme. As a spokesman for the agrarian and debtor elements in the nation he demanded a narrow, literal, and inhibiting interpretation of the Constitution and seemed, in the intensity of his arguments, to be denying what he had once asserted in the *Federalist.*

This was not really so. He was always a nationalist, a believer in national supremacy in the federal republic. But he assumed that the object of this national supremacy was to maintain a balance between competing interests. What he fought in Hamilton was economic nationalism, that is to say national supremacy dedicated to the satisfaction of one economic appetite at the expense of all the others. His nationalism was never again to be so strong as in the days when he helped to write the Constitution and afterwards defended it in the *Federalist.* But it remained. It made him unpopular with the more strict agrarians of his own party—unpopular when he was Jefferson's Secretary of State and even more unpopular when he became President. And, in fact, almost his last acts as President were the rechartering of a National Bank and the signing of a mildly protective tariff bill. These acts were necessary and therefore statesmanlike, but they seemed to align him with bankers and manufacturers.

His career as Secretary of State and as President is too involved in the effort to keep out of the Napoleonic Wars to be reducible to a few words. One can say that the principle of peaceful coercion by which Jefferson and he hoped to make England and France respect America's neutrality was an honorable principle, and their concept of Neutral Rights a noble concept. In the end, perhaps because he was too weak a President, perhaps because circumstances were too strong for him or for any man, Madison was sucked into the War of 1812. He managed it badly for he had no talent for warlike leadership or wartime administration, and he endured the supreme humiliation of being chased out of his burning capital by the British in 1814. Never was his reputation so low. The sudden arrival of peace in 1815, however, more than restored it. For the rest of his life, which he spent in somewhat embarrassed financial circumstances on his Virginia estate of Montpelier, he was, if not exactly a popular, at any rate a deeply respected figure. His wonderful friendship with Jefferson flourished until Jefferson's death in 1826. He himself died ten years later.

Aside from his constitutional labors, his great legacy to us—his great common cause with Jefferson—was his dedication to civil liberties. He had only a qualified trust in the people, but he

Michael-Guillaume de Crèvecoeur

If no one can speak a language quite like a native, it is equally true that no one can understand a country quite so well as a foreigner. This has been the American experience, at any rate. Men like Denis W. Brogan and André Siegfried in our own day, James Bryce in the 1880s, and Alexis de Tocqueville half a century before Bryce, have been able to catch the distinctive qualities of life in the United States and describe them with a clarity and persuasiveness that no native observer has ever matched.

Of course, mere foreign birth, even when combined with high intelligence and great literary ability, will not alone make a man into a Bryce or Tocqueville. To write an incisive account the foreigner must also have a thorough knowledge of the land based at least in part upon on-the-spot analysis. And in addition he must possess a basic sympathy for the people he describes. The lack of this last quality, for instance, is what makes Charles Dickens' American Notes *only a caricature of the United States in the 1840s, albeit a valuable and interesting one.*

Michael-Guillaume de Crèvecoeur, as Whitfield J. Bell, Jr., makes clear in the following chapter, loved America and knew it well. He was a shrewd and dedicated observer, and his background in France, England, and Canada enabled him to study America "in perspective," as Henry Steele Commager has put it. The third of his Letters from an American Farmer *was the first really insightful commentary on the force of the environment in changing the European settler into an American.*

It is a curious fact that whereas the writings of most first-rate foreign observers have attracted instant and widespread attention in this country, no matter how critical their tone, Crèvecoeur's friendly, entertaining, and illuminating Letters *attracted little notice here until recent times. There was no American edition until 1793 (by that date there had been four editions in the British Isles as well as French and German translations) and thereafter the* Letters *were neglected until the twentieth century.*

Professor Bell, of Yale University, is associate editor of The Papers of Benjamin Franklin, *the first two volumes of which have recently been published.*

". . . *sense of wonder and exultation*"

WHITFIELD J. BELL, JR.

menagerie that was the home of improbable creatures like the possum, the buffalo, and the porcupine. But to every thoughtful man, whether he contemplated the New World from a distance or shared at first hand its fresh, turbulent life, America was a social process achieving something unlike anything the world had seen before.

Such a thoughtful man was Michael-Guillaume de Crèvecoeur. Born in Brittany in old France in 1735, educated in England, he came to Canada when he was 19 or 20. There he joined the French army under Montcalm; but, after the expulsion of the French from Canada, instead of returning to France he came into the English colonies, explored the Great Lakes and the Ohio Valley, and travelled in New York and Pennsylvania. In 1764 he was naturalized. Five years later he bought a farm, called "Pine Hill," in Orange County, New York, and married an American girl from nearby Yonkers.

The next few years were the happiest of his life. He was a good farmer: he worked hard; he was eager to try new crops and new methods; and he prospered. More than this, Crèvecoeur was an observant man and a philosopher. He studied his neighbors closely, noting and pondering the meaning of all that he saw happening around him, so different from what he had known in France. Soon he began to write down his observations and reflections. Some of the essays he collected together; he called his book *Letters from an American Farmer,* and it was published in London in 1782.

Written in honest, artless prose, the American Farmer's *Letters* had all the simplicity, originality and compassion of a great book. Its pages still glow with the sense of wonder and exultation that immigrants from Europe felt as they confronted the American continent and their own futures. And in these essays that Crèvecoeur wrote 175 years ago there are insights that help to explain the America of today.

Like so many other Europeans he was fascinated by the American wilderness, its teeming life and wild extremes, by the sudden death that lurked and by the beautiful, delicate creatures that lived there. In one chapter of the *Letters* Crèvecoeur described the poisonous rattlesnake and copperhead and the harmless blacksnake, which hypnotized the birds and squirrels it fed on: "When they have fixed their eyes on an animal, they become immovable; only turning their head sometimes to the right and sometimes to the left, but still with their sight invariably directed to the object. The distracted victim, instead of flying its enemy, seems to be arrested by some invincible power; it screams; now approaches, and then recedes; and after skipping about with unaccountable agitation, finally rushes into the jaws of the snake, and is swallowed. . . ." Much pleasanter woodland companions were the humming-birds, which he used to watch as they fed on wild flowers, their wings beating so unbelievably fast that he could not see them. "On this little bird" he wrote, "nature has profusely lavished her most splendid colors; the most perfect azure, the most beautiful gold, the most dazzling red, are forever in contrast, and help to embellish the plumes of his majestic head."

Far more than snakes and birds, of course, did the inhabitants of America excite Crèvecoeur's interest. Though a new American himself, he nevertheless observed his neighbors with penetrating detachment. He devoted several chapters of his book to the Nantucket Islanders, those whalers, herdsmen, and merchants who had made a neat, prosperous city with 500 houses and 200 sail in in the harbor out of a miserable sandbank. They were, Crèvecoeur reported, a simple, sober people, above all industrious. They spun great quantities of wool and flax, for example; and any woman whose family was not clad in good, neat, and sufficient homespun would be reckoned an idler and be disgraced. Because their husbands were at sea so often and so long, Nantucket wives played an unusually important part in the family business. In Crèvecoeur's day the richest man on the island was John Coffin; and it was common knowledge that he owed his success to his wife Keziah, who may have taken the teachings of *Poor Richard* the closer to heart as she was a cousin of Benjamin Franklin. When John Coffin first went to sea, Keziah traded in pins and needles and kept a village school. Soon she stocked more costly goods, which she sold with such judgment that she developed a prosperous store. She formed trading connections on the mainland and with London merchants, and became, in short, the arm, voice, and brain of her husband's business.

the island lived in cheerful enjoyment of "the full rewards of their industry," happily unoppressed by any civil servitude. "I saw neither governors, nor any pageantry of state, neither ostentatious magistrates, nor any individuals cloathed with useless dignity; no artificial phantoms subsist here, either civil or religious; no gibbets . . . no soldiers."

But to Crèvecoeur, as to all attentive observers, the most significant aspect of America by far was the process that transformed European peasants into American freemen. More eloquent than anything he wrote on snakes or the customs of the Nantucket Islanders are Crèvecoeur's accounts of the American frontier-farmers. His information came from his own life in Pennsylvania and New York, his deep feeling from his knowledge of the German, Scots, and Scotch-Irish farmers he knew there.

Repeatedly and in great detail in his *Letters* he analyzed the painful lessons in the hard school where the new immigrant learned how to live in America, how to use the axe and plough, how to work the land, to fish and hunt. He related in graphic terms the new settlers' struggles against the weather, Indians, and cheating land agents; and in glowing words he described how the newcomers bought a farm, got a freehold, acquired a reputation, and established a family. This farm, Crèvecoeur pointed out, speaking from his own experience for thousands like him, was the foundation of "our rank, our freedom, our power as citizens, our importance as inhabitants of such a district." Thus the new settler became truly independent, living off what he grew or killed by his own efforts; and, living thus, he became different from what he had ever been. He became, in short, a new man, an American.

Not only was the American a man with a new idea; he was also, Crèvecoeur saw, a new physical creation, the amalgam of many nationalities. "What then is the American?" he asked; and answered his own question. "He is either an European, or the descendant of an European, hence that strange mixture of blood, which you will find in no other country. I could point out to you a family whose grandfather was an Englishman, whose wife was Dutch, whose son married a French woman, and whose present four sons have now four wives of different nations. . . Here individuals of all nations are melted into a new race of men, whose labors and posterity will one day cause great changes in the world."

The wilderness that Crèvecoeur described in 1782 has vanished forever; nor are we of the twentieth century that nation of free-holders, each living at peace on his own homestead, which our ancestors seemed to him on the verge of becoming. Yet much of what Crèvecoeur said of his America is also true of ours. A new man *has* been created— a new mixture of the nations, with new principles and a new goal. This goal, even more than the mingling of the nations, is what made the American a new man. As Crève-coeur sensed, the essence of the American's—and of America's—strength is not fact, but dream; not the solid realities of fertile farms and thriving trading towns, however inseparable they may seem from the actual America; but the noble dream, not yet realized but not forgotten, that all men should be free and walk in simple dignity. "Here," exclaimed the American Farmer ex-ultantly, but humbly too, "here man is free as he ought to be."

Paul Revere

Actually he was an outstanding craftsman in several different media. Probably he was the greatest of American silversmiths. In addition he was a powerful political cartoonist and an effective organizer of men in the patriot cause. He designed the first Continental money and the official seal of the Commonwealth of Massachusetts, which is still in use. In later years he developed a new method of rolling sheet copper, cast bells, and cannon of brass, and supplied various metal parts for the U. S. S. Constitution *and for one of Robert Fulton's early steamboats.*

Revere was also in many ways an "ideal" ordinary American. He was the son of an immigrant (who changed the name from De Revoire to Revere to make it easier for Americans to pronounce). He learned his trade in his father's shop, and when his country needed him he served like a good American jack-of-all-trades as messenger, propagandist, artist, and soldier. Throughout his life he played an active role in civic affairs and died, respected and prosperous, at the ripe age of eighty-three.

O. M. Dickerson, Professor Emeritus of History and Political Science, Colorado State College of Education, is the author of The Navigation Acts as a Cause of the Revolution *and other books on the colonial period.*

"... *the fatal day had come*"

O. M. DICKERSON

PAUL REVERE was much more than the midnight rider of Longfellow's famous poem. He was one of the key men in organizing the successful engagement that opened the American Revolution.

By occupation Revere was a silversmith. In any collection of eighteenth century silver, pieces made by him stand out as superior to others. Even the most casual visitor to such a collection notices that Revere pieces have an artistic something that others do not have. He was also an artist with pencil and brush. The most famous picture of the "Boston Massacre" is said to be his. Everything related to his trade he did with scrupulous care. His mechanical and organizing genius laid the foundation for later successful business enterprises, such as Revere Copper, that still makes the name Revere outstanding.

The mastery of his trade alone would have made him famous. His skill in organizing lines of communication made him one of the great Revolutionary leaders.

In Boston there were two Masonic lodges. One was St. Johns, to which the Tories belonged. It founded no other lodges. The other was St. Andrews—the lodge of the patriots. St. Andrews had a charter from the Grand Lodge in Scotland which gave it authority to organize other lodges anywhere in America. This lodge became highly missionary in the years just before the Revolution and founded many new lodges, especially in the northern colonies. Paul Revere was Grand Secretary of these lodges and is referred to in the newspapers of the day as "Grand Secretary of all Masonic lodges in America."

With the Stamp Act controversy came the wholesale organization of lodges of Sons of Liberty—a secret organization strongly masonic in form. Revere was a top man in this organization and probably instrumental in its rapid growth.

Thus Revere acquired a personal acquaintance with patriots outside Boston probably greater than any other man in the colony. This experience made him a key man in all patriot plans. Others made the speeches, drafted the resolutions and protests; Revere helped pass them on to patriots elsewhere.

Whenever confidential messages needed to be carried from

Boston to leaders in other colonies, Revere handled the details. He was the personal messenger of the merchants in Boston to those in Philadelphia during the non-importation movement against the Townshend Acts. When the First Continental Congress met in Philadelphia in 1774 Revere set up a regular messenger service

of Parliament to tax the colonies and denounced as unconstitutional measures that had just been taken against Massachusetts.

Events in 1774 made it clear that Americans must submit to military force or resist. They chose to resist. Successful resistance required armed forces subject to the call of the patriot leaders. The result was the organization of companies of Minute Men sworn to obey only the orders of their own officers, who in turn were sworn to respond immediately when called upon by the head of the Provisional Government. Warren, as head of the Massachusetts Provisional Government, had the authority to summon the entire military force of the province to resist attempted aggression from the British army under Gage. These companies were organized into regular military units with dependable officers. Thus the patriot leaders, on paper, had an armed force to oppose the British army in Boston. But it was scattered in every hamlet of Massachusetts. To be effective they had to be able to assemble it quickly. There was no telegraph, telephone, or radio, so a system of rapid personal communication was needed. The job fell to Revere.

He attacked the problem with all his skill in handling details. Lines of communication were arranged to pass calls from trusted persons in one hamlet to those in another. Those receiving the call in turn notified the local Minute Men of the impending danger. These in turn sent riders to alarm the Minute Men in other villages in the county. In case General Gage closed all roads out of Boston, signals were agreed on and responsible leaders informed of their meaning. Thus the leaders in Boston could summon help in any emergency.

It was a good plan on paper. But would it work? It was tested.

In the winter of 1774-1775 a false alarm was started. Within hours thousands of armed Minute Men were on the roads leading to Boston and had to be turned back. Revere's plan worked. The patriot leaders in Boston now knew they could call up massive resistance if the British attacked.

Such was the situation in Boston on April 18, 1775. General Gage had orders to seize any military stores of the colonists and to arrest John Hancock and Samuel Adams and send them to England to be tried for treason. He had postponed action, for he was loath to start hostilities. But time was forcing his hand.

Hancock and Adams were known to be staying at the inn at Lexington preparatory to leaving for Philadelphia to attend the Second Continental Congress, which was to meet on May 10. In another day they might be beyond his reach.

Gage decided to send out a fast moving secret expedition, ferry it across the Charles river, where a direct road led to Lexington only ten or twelve miles away. Such a force could leave Boston after dark, reach Lexington, and capture Hancock and Adams while they slept, then move on to Concord, only six miles farther, destroy the colonial supplies, and return to Boston by the close of the next day. It looked like a good plan, but it failed to reckon with Revere and his methods for spreading information.

The unusual movement of troops attracted attention in Boston. Dr. Joseph Warren, head of the Massachusetts Committee of Safety, was notified. He verified the rumors and sent for Revere, who was already fully informed of what was going on. Obviously the fatal day had come.

The emergency required that three things be done at once—summon aid from the Massachusetts Minute Men; warn the patriots in Concord to remove the military supplies so as to prevent their capture or destruction; warn Hancock and Adams of their danger and make sure they started safely on their way to Philadelphia.

Roads out of Boston were closed and guarded by British troops. Messengers could not get out. Revere decided to use the agreed upon signal—two lanterns in the belfry of Old North Church. A trusted friend was detailed to put them in position with the coming of darkness. These were seen and reported to leaders; soon the network of communication arranged by Revere was in operation. Massive resistance was on its way to Boston.

William Dawes was assigned the task of pushing through to Concord to warn the patriots to save what supplies they could.

Revere personally assumed the most important job of all—that of making sure that Hancock and Adams escaped British capture and were started safely on their way to Philadelphia. The fate of the American cause hinged on them and their success in securing aid from the other colonies.

home of the pastor of the Lexington church. They had no suspicion of their possible danger. Revere awakened the captain of the Lexington company of Minute Men and told him of the advancing British force and its probable mission. The captain started at once to assemble his men—some soon to die in their own dooryards.

Revere then sought out Hancock and Adams and warned them of the rapidly approaching danger. After considerable difficulty he persuaded them that it was their duty to leave at once. Revere provided them with transportation and laid out a route that would be clear of the advancing British troops. He then returned to the inn, secured their personal belongings, including valuable papers that would be needed at Philadelphia, and forwarded them to their owners by trusted messengers. Thus Revere insured that Hancock and Adams safely escaped the British net and were on their way to Philadelphia to help create a new nation.

Daylight saw the firing on the Lexington green. The afternoon saw the British expedition fighting its way back to Boston. The communication system long planned by Revere had worked. General Gage was learning the meaning of American massive resistance.

Revere's work was done. No other American had rendered a greater service than he to the cause of ultimate independence. The fate of a nation was indeed riding that night, not only in Revere's saddle but in those of the hundreds of others that helped carry the alarm planned by him to every village and farm in Massachusetts. Americans can never forget what he and his helpers did that day and night.

John Paul Jones

The American naval tradition has always been a proud one, and Edward Ellsberg has contributed his full share toward creating that tradition and preserving it in books. In this chapter he takes us back to its beginnings.

The exploits of John Paul Jones in the Revolution—here recorded—as well as the triumphs of men like Captain Isaac Hull of Old Ironsides *and Captain Oliver Hazard Perry ("We have met the enemy and they are ours") during the War of 1812, and the brilliant heroics of Captain Stephen Decatur against the Barbary Pirates, have obscured the fact that on the whole the American Navy was inadequate to the task of defending our shores throughout the early years of the nation's history. The British fleet was in control of the coast during most of the Revolution, and it burned Washington and blockaded our seaports during the War of 1812. In our legitimate pride over Andrew Jackson's victory at New Orleans in 1815, we must remember that General Pakenham's army was brought to New Orleans by a British fleet that operated boldly and unopposed all up and down the coast.*

Because the Navy was so small and suffered so many defeats, it was especially important that a few brilliant commanders like Jones were able to win in single encounters with British warships. Their triumphs, often against larger and more powerful vessels, inspired their fellows in the dark early years and laid the basis for the high morale that has characterized the service in its years of power and triumph.

Rear Admiral Edward Ellsberg, as a midshipman at Annapolis in 1913, marched in the final funeral procession of John Paul Jones. Graduated in 1914 as honor man of his class at the Naval Academy, Ellsberg received the Navy's Distinguished Service Medal for his submarine salvage exploits in the 1920s. During World War II he directed salvage operations in the Red Sea, in the North African invasion, and in the Normandy invasion, for which services he was decorated both by England and by the United States.

". . . just what this country needed"

EDWARD ELLSBERG

No one ever spoke in tones of moderation respecting John Paul Jones.

John Paul was briefly (and unhappily) a midshipman in the Royal Navy, then in swift succession ex-merchantman, ex-slaver, aye, even ex-pirate! Finally, at 26, again a merchant shipmaster in the West Indies, likely to be charged with murder for the death of a mutinous seaman, he abandoned his ship and posthaste fled the Caribbean. When next he appeared, John Paul, Scotch master mariner, was no more. Beneath the pseudonym of Jones a friendless shipmaster was striving to lose himself in colonial America. Yet now at the Naval Academy in Annapolis lies Jones, sepulchred in marble. Strange metamorphosis—from fugitive British seaman to American naval saint! Yet Fate managed it more, perhaps, because America desperately needed him then than because he ever needed America.

At a critical moment in the turmoil leading to our birth as a nation, Fate tossed the fugitive John Paul Jones ashore into our southern colonies. There in that bubbling cauldron of revolt it made him friend and companion to some of the best stokers of the fires of rebellion against tyranny this world has ever looked upon—Patrick Henry, Thomas Jefferson, and (most important to Jones' future) the North Carolina Quaker, Joseph Hewes.

Under the canny stoking of Jones' newly found friends, the bubbling pot of colonial revolt soon boiled over into open war. Embattled farmers (some of them, at any rate) seized their flintlock rifles and went gunning for redcoats. But America then was wholly agricultural. Patrick Henry and Thomas Jefferson could by their flaming words inspire farmers to revolt. It took, however, something wholly beyond the power of words to provide the gunpowder needed to make their flintlocks effective. Only via sea could agricultural America get the badly needed munitions of war.

For successful revolt America imperatively needed a navy. Congress set about providing one. To Joseph Hewes, workhorse of the congressional committee appointed to provide that navy, went as his share of the patronage the privilege of naming one man to be a Lieutenant in the new service. Hewes named his seagoing Scotch friend, young John Paul Jones. And so to John Paul Jones came opportunity. Aged now 28, intoxicated by the glowing phrases of his friends, Jones became First Lieutenant on the flagship of the new fleet, the *Alfred.* He fitted her out, drilled her crew at the great guns, and with his own hands proudly hoisted to the *Alfred's* masthead the first flag ever to fly above an American man-o'-war.

The infant fleet went to sea. To Ezek Hopkins, the bungling Commodore of our new fleet, and to his equally inept captains, their first enemy encounter, with a solitary British frigate, *H.M.S. Glasgow,* brought only disgrace and courts-martial. But to young Lieutenant Paul Jones, his skillful handling in that action of the flagship's guns brought promotion to Captain and elevation to the quarterdeck of the sloop *Providence*—a quarterdeck left suddenly vacant by a court-martial outraged by the lack of eagerness of its late captain to come within gunshot of the *Glasgow.* A tiny spit-kid, the *Providence* was insignificant as a warship by any standard, even in her own day. But she was a man-o'-war. With her quarterdeck beneath him, his to command, the flaming muzzles of young John Paul Jones' long guns, speaking the only language tyrants ever have or ever will understand, put the solid substance of shrieking cannonballs behind the scintillating phrases of Jefferson's Declaration of Independence, to make of it something more than just a brilliant exercise in rhetoric.

Young Captain John Paul Jones—handsome, small in stature, soft of voice, soon more at home than any courtier in the boudoirs of the grand dames of European courts—looked little like a seadog, but he turned out to be just what this country needed. Embodied in this one person was the sailor to whom the sea was second nature from early childhood, the valiant knight in whose breast beat a heart of matchless courage, the ardent student of naval tactics and of naval history—a naval genius. Alone among all the commanders of our Continental Navy he was never captured, never defeated. Whenever he managed to get beneath him a floating tub of any nature in which to get to sea, a stream of invaluable prizes taken by his guns started to flow into American ports.

From seizing British shipping on our coasts, Paul Jones soon moved across the Atlantic to become the terror of Britain's own

[illegible]

the menacing *Drake* bear-ing down on him, Jones at pistol point had first to quell his mutinous crew, intent, not on fighting the *Drake,* only on murder-ing their captain and fleeing to safety. And then he performed the miracle of leading the recently cowed mutineers into a broadside to broadside gunnery action in which the *Ranger* savagely cut the *Drake* to pieces and finished by towing her into a French port, his prize!

Outraged Britain shrieked for vengeance on Paul Jones, but shortly, at his hands, worse came to her. Soon off her shores a heterogeneous collection of tubs masquerading as warships ap-peared. Leading them was John Paul Jones, his flagship a dilapi-dated French ex-East Indiaman renamed the *Bon Homme Richard,* her decayed sides pierced now for a battery of badly worn out guns. Contemptuous of the entire Royal Navy seeking him, Paul Jones circumnavigated Great Britain, paralyzing all shipping, till, homeward bound with his holds jammed with prisoners from his prizes, he arrived off Flamborough Head on the North Sea coast. And there, between his improvised flagship and a newly-built two-decker, *H.M.S. Serapis,* captained by Richard Pearson, under the weird light of a September moon was fought a vicious action unique in the annals of war at sea.

For three harrowing hours in the moonlight, Paul Jones in his decrepit ex-merchantman slugged it out with the best two-decker the Royal Navy had. At his first broadside, his heaviest guns ex-ploded. By the end of the first hour of close range cannonading with what artillery he had left, the swift-sailing *Serapis* had dis-mounted and silenced the remaining guns in Jones's ancient ark. The beaten *Bon Homme Richard* was lost now unless Jones somehow could grapple his nimbler antagonist and continue the fight hand to hand alongside her—a hopeless maneuver to a sadly crippled sailing ship. Still, by dazzling seamanship, Jones managed just that! Lashed finally broadside to broadside to the *Serapis,* with yards overhead interlocking, the unequal combat recommenced—American pikes, rifle bullets, and hand grenades opposed now to British cannonballs.

Swiftly Pearson's guns cut the rotten hull of the *Bon Homme Richard* almost in two horizontally. The shattered flagship began to flood. Below, a misguided master-at-arms released from her holds some hundreds of fear-crazed British prisoners, lest they drown. Instantly these swarmed on deck, easily capable of taking the *Bon Homme Richard.* Paul Jones, sensing immediate disaster, turned it into salvation by singing out to them: "The *Serapis* is sinking alongside us! If you want to save your lives, man the *Richard's* pumps! It's your last hope!" The panic-stricken prisoners did, the sinking *Bon Homme Richard* was temporarily kept afloat, the battle raged on.

Next, seemingly to insure defeat, came treachery. The *Alliance,* one of Jones's consorts, captained by a half-mad Frenchman, Pierre Landais, sailed up in the moonlight to pour her broadsides as she passed, not into the enemy, but into the already shattered *Richard!* Finally, to complete the nightmare of disaster, came fire. There was no option. To fight that blaze, such of Jones' powder-stained and bleeding seamen as could still stagger about amongst the mangled bodies of their shipmates had to cease even their rifle fire on the *Serapis.* The *Bon Homme Richard* lay at last a silent flaming wreck, from which amidst the crackling of burning rigging a terrorized shriek drifted across the bulwarks to the *Serapis*: "Quarters! For God's sake, quarters! Our ship is sinking!"

Captain Pearson, gazing across at the obviously beaten wreck alongside him, was nevertheless loath to call a halt to gunplay till he was sure. "Have you surrendered?" he demanded.

From the silent deck of the sinking *Bon Homme Richard,* loud and clear, in a voice fit to raise the dead lying all about him, echoing above the roar of English guns, came Paul Jones' answer, his passport to the company of immortals: "Surrender? *Never! I have just begun to fight!*"

An idle boast? Pearson soon learned not. For almost immediately a boarding party, mustered by Jones from amongst the bleeding remnants of his crew, swarmed from the disintegrating

Bon Homme Richard over the bulwarks of the *Serapis* with pike and cutlass to sweep all before them.

The *Bon Homme Richard* swiftly sank. But on his enemy's vessel, the captured *Serapis,* John Paul Jones sailed back in triumph

But not wholly. For soon the eye of Catherine of Russia, seeking a sailor who could defeat the Turks in the Black Sea, lighted on Jones in Paris. With America's permission, John Paul Jones became a Russian admiral. In his natural element, with the deck of a warship once again beneath his feet and the enemy before his eyes, he made short shrift of Catherine's foes. But back at Catherine's court, Russian chicanery soon made short shrift of him. A gross blunder on Jones' part put him in great disfavor. It seems he failed to laud with sufficient fulsomeness to Catherine her paramour, the powerful Prince Potemkin, as the very Prince of Admirals who singlehandedly had encompassed the defeat of the Turks. Swiftly a despicable intrigue, as typical of Russian methods then as now, was sprung to disgrace him as a man. Extricated with difficulty from a Russian dungeon by the British Ambassador, who could not bear to see a one-time Britisher, even one of Britain's enemies, so scandalously maltreated by the Russian court, Jones returned to Paris. And there, in 1792, hardly turned forty-five, John Paul Jones died, a broken man.

But in 1905, reverently carried aboard one American man-o'-war, escorted across the Atlantic by a combined squadron of French and American warships, the body of John Paul Jones made its final voyage back to our shores. And in 1913 America enshrined his body in deathless marble beneath the Chapel at Annapolis as a symbol of what training, blended with supreme courage, can produce to defend her in emergency. There the spirit of John Paul Jones will, the Naval Academy hopes, prove inspiration to all his successors at sea.

George Rogers Clark

Most American frontiersmen possessed all the qualities that go to make up good soldiers. They were physically tough and used to life outdoors. Most were expert riflemen, and they knew the woods thoroughly. Courageous, quick-thinking, patriotic, they should have left an unparalleled record against the Indians, the French, the Spaniards, and the British, all of whom plagued them from time to time during the years they were pushing over the Appalachians and swarming into the Mississippi Valley.

But they did not always perform as one might have expected, and the reason is easy to find. Americans generally have been independent and resistant to taking orders, and Westerners more so even than the average. Fierce and determined in defending their homes, they were often indifferent soldiers when called upon to defend the homes of others. They resented being ordered about and having to accommodate themselves to the interests of a large group. When affairs did not develop as he wished, the average Western militiaman tended to decide for himself how to deal with the situation, and as often as not he decided to abandon his military obligation and go back to his farm. Desertions, even mutinies, were perennial problems for those who commanded Western armies. Little wonder that British generals during the French and Indian War were so contemptuous of provincial troops.

However, under a powerful and respected leader, Western soldiers could perform great deeds. Andrew Jackson proved this conclusively in his campaigns against the Creek Indians and in the Battle of New Orleans. So, in an earlier period, did George Rogers Clark. Walter Havighurst describes thoroughly Clark's qualities of leadership in this account of his career. Havighurst is Professor of English at Miami University. He has written some fifteen volumes of fiction and regional history dealing with the Middlewest, including The Upper Mississippi, The Long Ships Passing, Land of Promise, *and* Wilderness for Sale.

"... a man in buckskin"

WALTER HAVIGHURST

But no other period was so changing as the Revolutionary years, when thirteen seaboard colonies became a nation extending to the Mississippi. One man's shadow falls across the whole interior country, the great valley of the Ohio. He saw it first as a youth, steering down the wilderness river. He claimed wild land and surveyed the sites of future cities. As a political delegate he voiced its hopes and fears in the Virginia Assembly. As a commander he defended it from Indian attack and captured British posts north of the Ohio. In a few momentous years he won the Old Northwest for the new nation.

In the spring of 1772 George Rogers Clark, nineteen years old, did not plow his father's corn field. Tall and strong, with a man's stride and a boy's wonder, he tramped off toward the western mountains. He would come back, on many errands, in the years ahead. But from that April day in 1772 he was a western man.

Braddock's Road began at Will's Creek, which was a frontier name for Cumberland, Maryland. The creek itself joined the Potomac and turned eastward, but the frontier post was faced to the West and the wilderness. There in 1750 the Ohio Company of Virginia had built a trading house, a depot of goods for the Indian commerce. They also built Fort Mount Pleasant, which later became the base of Braddock's expedition and was renamed Fort Cumberland.

On the bright May day when Clark arrived at Cumberland the old trading house was empty and the log stockade was falling down. But he paced its walls and peered through cobwebbed loopholes. Mute and ruined, it yet told him something: the West was a disputed country, to be entered with caution, to be won with courage, to be held with boldness. It was not a land to be accepted, it was a country to be won.

In a trading canoe he went west from Pittsburgh. Forty miles below the tiny settlement of Wheeling he marked his claim. He cleared ground and planted corn. But he was not cut out for a farmer. Soon he was a captain in the frontier militia, fighting Chief Cornstalk's Shawnee warriors. Then came news of the Boston Tea Party and the meeting of the First Continental Congress. Clark and his western comrades sided with American liberty. A new struggle with the British was beginning.

From Detroit the British sent war parties of Indians against the Kentucky settlements. Through the long year 1777 the settlers lived in terror. They called it the "Year of the Bloody Sevens." Young George Rogers Clark was made commander of Kentucky's defense. He sent two spies across the Ohio, on the pretense of buying beaver skins. They brought back information about the British troops at Kaskaskia and Vincennes. In that dark year Clark planned a march into enemy country. The only defense was to attack the British seats of power.

The next spring he gathered his troops on the Ohio near the future site of Louisville. He had a tiny army, 170 men, in a vast and hostile land. Knowing that the British watched the Mississippi shores, he marched his men across the empty Illinois prairie. On the evening of the Fourth of July, two years after the Declaration of Independence, they crept upon the town of Kaskaskia. In darkness they slipped through the river gate. They swarmed over the startled British soldiers and captured the governor in his bed. Kaskaskia was taken without a gunshot.

When news of Clark's invasion reached Detroit, General Hamilton marched seven hundred British troops and Indians down the Wabash to Vincennes. With such a force he could drive the Americans out of the country. But winter rains had flooded the prairie, and Hamilton waited for good weather. At Kaskaskia Clark had few men. But he was a bold leader, and now an audacious plan gave him confidence. No one would suppose that a weak force would cross a flooded country to attack a stronghold. It was a hazardous plan, against enormous odds, but it was the only way to victory. Clark ordered his men to muster. He wrote to Governor Patrick Henry in Virginia: "Great things have been effected by a few men well conducted. Perhaps we may be fortunate."

On a gray February day, in a thin, cold rain, his troops filed out of Kaskaskia. Ahead of them lay two hundred miles of sodden prairie. At the end waited a strong army in a massive fort. Day after day they sloshed on. Clark kept them jesting, singing, whooping. He fanned their humor and courage. They were young

chorus, the men joined in. They were a wretched, exhausted army, shoulder-deep and singing.

On the night of February 23rd, after an eighteen-day march from Kaskaskia they entered Vincennes and crept toward the fort. The invasion had been silent but the battle was noisy. Cannon roared from the British stockade and rifles spat back in the darkness. Clark kept his men shifting, whooping, shouting. Confused and bewildered, the British surrendered. On the morning of February 25, 1779, the scarlet ranks marched out and the mud-stained men moved in. Thirteen times the cannon thundered, for the thirteen stars in the new flag over old Vincennes.

This was Clark's great hour. He was just twenty-six. The rest of his life was downhill—quarreling with jealous generals and politicians, watching speculators wrangle over the country he had won. The achievement left to him was anticlimax, after the Illinois campaign. He led an expedition against the Ohio Indians, he directed the building of a fort at the Falls of the Ohio, and there he laid out the future city of Louisville. To the new settlement came the Clark family from Virginia. George Rogers Clark had claimed a section of land for his father, and on a spring day in 1785 he led them to a handsome site overlooking the cabins of Louisville and the island-strewn river. "Mulberry Hill" his mother called the new home.

For nearly twenty years Clark lived in his father's household at Mulberry Hill while the country that he had known as wilderness became a settled region. A brooding man, he shared his memories and feelings with his youngest brother, William, who was a lanky fifteen-year-old when the family came to Kentucky.

In 1803-6 William Clark with Meriwether Lewis would explore the vast "Louisiana" territory and find the way to Oregon.

In 1803 military bounty lands were tardily allotted to the veterans of Clark's campaign in Illinois. The lands were located north of the Ohio, across from Louisville. On a hill above the river Clark built a cottage of his own, and there he sat in his worn chair while the sun set over the western hills. Sometimes an old soldier came to see him. Occasionally a moody chief sat with him, smoking in Indian silence and staring across to the busy streets of Louisville where people had forgot the fear of scalping knives.

One winter day Clark slumped in his chair, his big head nodding and his right leg jerking out. He tried to move his hand, his knee, his foot. He was paralyzed. The rest of his life was spent in a wheel chair. Another stroke left him voiceless. Still he hung on, his eyes staring out of memory and silence. But at last the stubborn heart faltered. He died on a winter day in 1818—the year when Illinois became a state, and when the National Road ran over the mountains to Wheeling where a red-haired youth had once built a lean-to camp on the empty shore.

Now in the old town of Vincennes, on a graceful curve of the Wabash, there stands a dome of marble. Around its walls is pictured the conquest of the West, and in the center of the room stands a bronze figure of George Rogers Clark. Clark was a man in buckskin. Bronze and marble would have puzzled him. On the site of his memorial his hungry men poured rifle fire into the loopholes of an enemy fort. On the trampled ground he met the British general and demanded his surrender. The marble dome can be seen three miles down the river, though no one comes up the Wabash any more. In the leafless winter it rises white as frost across the lowlands, where no gaunt regiment wades through the bottoms now.

Joel Barlow

led to the Jay Treaty of 1795 and Jefferson those with Napoleon that resulted in the purchase of the vast Louisiana Territory in 1803. Indeed, it was perhaps even more important in the early days when America was weak than at present when she is strong, that the country play an active role in international affairs. Then, as now, survival depended upon our understanding the world situation and adjusting intelligently to it.

The difficulties faced by American diplomats in the early period were very great. The nation was young and without significant military power. It was also cordially despised in the royal courts of Europe because it was a republic and born of revolution. The French Revolution changed this condition somewhat, but the wars of the Revolution, which broke out in 1793, posed new problems. The United States as a neutral trading nation found her shipping attacked and her seamen mistreated by the navies of both sides. For years the chief efforts of our leading statesmen were directed toward questions involving trade and the rights of neutrals on the seas.

Some of these problems are considered in this chapter dealing with the poet Joel Barlow and his diplomatic adventures at the court of Napoleon. It is the work of Irving Brant, author of the latest and most detailed biography of James Madison, and an expert on the diplomacy of the period.

". . . hatred of despotism"

IRVING BRANT

IN FEBRUARY 1811, President James Madison nominated the Connecticut poet, Joel Barlow, to be American Minister to France. The United States at that time was drawing close to war with England, and many people thought there was equal cause to go to war with France. For eighteen years, except for one short interval of peace, England and France had been pouring out their blood in the wars that followed the French Revolution and the rise of Napoleon. Our country was neutral, but it did not enjoy the blessings of neutrality—the British Government had issued Orders in Council forbidding trade with France or her allies, and Napoleon had issued decrees prohibiting trade with England. Both restrictive decrees violated international law. The United States was caught between the two warring nations when both sides seized and confiscated American ships.

But there was a belief, also, that England was trying to prevent the development of American commerce. British warships took American seamen from their ships and compelled them to fight in the European war. This caused sharper resentment against England than against France, although most Americans were bitter against both. That was the attitude of Presidents Jefferson and Madison and of their political adherents, the Democrats (then called Republicans). On the other hand, the out-of-power Federalists either supported England outright or stiffened her anti-American policies by claiming that Jefferson and Madison were vassals of Napoleon Bonaparte.

Early in 1810 Congress passed a law providing that if one of the belligerents should revoke its edicts against American commerce, the President would cut off trade with the country that failed to revoke. Napoleon directed his Foreign Minister to notify the United States that the French decrees were revoked—it being understood by France that the United States should then make its flag respected by Great Britain. President Madison proclaimed non-intercourse with England when Napoleon's action became known to him. But many uncertainties remained—Napoleon was regarded as tricky; American trade with France was hampered by other French restrictions; and the American minister, General John Armstrong, was returning to private life.

So President Madison sent the name of fifty-seven-year-old Joel Barlow to the Senate. Barlow, born at Redding, Connecticut in 1754, had been known at Yale University as one of the "Con-

Barlow brought his fortune back to America and built a fine home, Kalorama, in Washington, D.C. He became the confidential friend of Presidents Jefferson and Madison and was the author of a long poem, *The Columbiad*, extolling the future greatness of democratic America. His chronicle of future triumphs in welfare and scientific progress included the conquest of disease and the building of a canal across the isthmus of Panama.

Barlow wanted to be Madison's Secretary of State, but disappointment did not reduce his loyalty. His appointment as minister was pounced on in the Senate by a faction personally hostile to the President. The appointee was derided as a poet and visionary, and it was brought out that he had been made an honorary citizen of France during the French Revolution. But to the astonishment of the Senate itself, some of the most conservative New England Federalists came to his support and he was overwhelmingly confirmed.

Federalist newspapers still opposed the appointment. One journal expressed surprise that Madison did not save trouble by letting a French diplomat represent him in France. The editor thought that the United States would lose nothing by so doing, "for if Joel be not a complete Frenchman in his habits, principles and attachments, report does him singular injustice." The report did do him singular injustice. Going back as American minister, Barlow carried strong instructions. Repeal of the decrees, it was supposed, had put an end to interference by France with American commerce on the ocean, but severe restraints were still imposed in French seaports. Barlow was to seek the repeal of these trade-killing restrictions, and he was to demand indemnities for American ships and cargoes already confiscated by France.

The French Foreign Office did not seem to think it was dealing with a visionary poet or vassal of the Emperor. Barlow arrived in Paris just as Napoleon and his foreign minister, the Duke of Bassano, were leaving for Holland, and for two months he held diplomatic conversations with a subordinate who reported the progress of events to Bassano. "My first talks with Mr. Barlow," wrote Jean Baptiste Petry, "yielded me nothing. I thought that with a man so cold, who seemed to me to wish to know the ground on which he stood, I should place long intervals between my visits in order to show him that, like him . . . I was not governed by desire and curiosity to learn his secrets."

Barlow had some serious faults as a negotiator: he put too much faith in assurances of good intentions, and he was so self-confident and so anxious for big results that he went beyond his instructions. He had no authority to negotiate a treaty, yet in his first formal note to Bassano, after the imperial party had returned to Paris, he proposed that they draft a treaty of commerce. He was overjoyed when the Emperor told him in a loud voice at a crowded court reception that the answer would be favorable.

The slow sailing ships took nearly two months to carry this news to Washington. President Madison then wrote a gentle but critical letter to his minister. The Emperor's public attitude, he said, was pleasing, but against it he placed half a dozen indications, set out in Barlow's own report, that the French were merely playing for time. "The prospect suggests distrust rather than expectation," he wrote. Furthermore, there was no need of a treaty, which would have to be submitted to the Senate for ratification. The only need was for France to revoke her unjust laws against American trade.

As it took several months to get this word back to France, Barlow kept working for his treaty, and the French kept on stalling. Madison thought Barlow was being duped by clever negotiators, but the truth was that Bassano was vainly appealing to the Emperor for authority to bring the treaty to completion. In the meanwhile, Napoleon's ruthless militarism turned Barlow more strongly than ever against him. There was probably nobody in America, he wrote to Madison in the spring of 1812, who felt such a horror as he did of a war between the United States and England. The reason, he said, could be seen in England's difficult position in the struggle with Bonaparte, and in the character of the master of Europe.

But that conflict, centering then in Spain, was about to be enlarged. Russia joined the coalition against France, and both Napoleon and his Foreign Minister left the army of invasion that was to capture Moscow. Once more Barlow negotiated with a diplomat assigned by his superior, and constant reports were

[illegible] declared war on England. You can read in many histories that after news of the declaration of war reached France, the impractical Joel Barlow made a foolish attempt to visit Napoleon on the Russian war front, hoping to promote Franco-American cooperation in the war. He went there all right, but the circumstances were quite different. In September 1812, Barlow, in obedience to instructions, showed the French Foreign office a private letter, dated August 11, which he had just received from President Madison. The President said that England was reported to be repealing her orders in Council. If that should be followed by peace, the President wrote, "the full tide of indignation with which the public mind here is boiling will be directed against France." He declared that unless France made reparation of past wrongs, war would be called for by the nation almost with one voice and measures of hostility could be expected at the coming session of Congress.

As soon as that threat reached the Duke of Bassano, who was then in Vilna, Barlow was asked to come at once to the imperial headquarters to complete the treaty. Petry also was summoned. At the beginning of winter, Barlow set off with his nephew, Tom, to drive nearly two thousand miles into the frozen wastes of eastern Europe. Bassano had told him that Napoleon was on his way back from Moscow and would spend the winter at Vilna. Treaty prospects looked good. But a few days after Barlow's arrival a half-frozen messenger brought news of disaster. The French armies were beaten and demoralized; the Emperor was in headlong flight for Paris.

Barlow started to return by way of Vienna, accompanied by his nephew and Petry, but he fell gravely ill on the road. At the little Polish village of Zarnowiec, on December 22, he could go no farther. In that village, wrote Petry, Barlow had the care and attention of an excellent family (that of Idzi Bajorkiewicz) with whom they lodged, and two physicians were summoned. But he died of pneumonia on December 26.

Shortly before Barlow sailed for France as American minister, he had expressed doubt that he would ever see his native country again. The prophecy could have been broadened, for the mortal remains of this Connecticut poet who died in his country's service still lie beneath a marble slab in that little village near Krakow. On the fatal mission Barlow wrote his finest poem, "Advice to a Raven in Russia." While waiting for the Emperor to return from Moscow, and not knowing of the French disaster on the Beresina River, he poured out his hatred of despotism and senseless wars in lines beginning "Black fool, why winter here?" The frozen skies of Russia should warn the raven back to southern climes:

> You fear perhaps your food may fail you there—
> Your human carnage, that delicious fare,
> That lured you hither, following still your friend
> The great Napoleon to the world's bleak end.
> * * * * * * * * * * * * * * *
> You fear he left behind no wars, to feed
> His feather'd cannibals and nurse the breed.
> Fear not, my screamer, call your greedy train,
> Sweep over Europe, hurry back to Spain,
> You'll find his legions there; the valiant crew
> Please best their master when they toil for you.

That mood was forced on Joel Barlow by the times he lived in, not by his nature. Life was to him a bright and joyous adventure. He lived it with zest, in his family relationships, in his poetry, in his political idealism, in his devotion to his country—the devotion that led him across the frozen wastes from which he did not return.

Thomas Cooper

lands. As a consequence many of them migrated to the United States, where economic opportunity and political liberty seemed alike assured.

Of course from the time of the Pilgrims to that of the young Swiss aristocrat, Albert Gallatin, who arrived in 1780, America had been a haven for Europe's disaffected rebels, but the influx was greatly speeded up after 1789. The arrival of large numbers of aggressive and forthright immigrants, such as Thomas Cooper, the subject of this chapter, and his friend Joseph Priestley, coincided with the growing radicalism of the French Revolution and produced among some American conservatives an irrational fear of revolution and subversion.

The result was a reaction against radicals and foreigners and the passage in 1798 of the Alien and Sedition Acts. Some of the victims of these harsh laws scarcely deserve sympathy. Pamphleteers like James Thompson Callender, a Scot who had been expelled from England, and John Daly Burk, an Irish-born playwright, probably deserved to be punished for their libelous attacks on the conservatives, although it seems clear that they were denied fair trials. But the suppression of honest radicals like Cooper marks a dark page in the history of the United States.

Fortunately, the hysteria soon passed. Nothing shows up the foolishness of these laws better than an examination of the later careers of some of the "dangerous" foreign radicals of that day. One thinks of "Citizen" Genet, who became a respectable New York farmer, the du Ponts, who became rich manufacturers of munitions, and Cooper himself, who, while always a firebrand, ended his days defending slavery and John C. Calhoun's version of states' rights.

Dumas Malone, Professor Emeritus of History at Columbia University and former editor-in-chief of the Dictionary of American Biography, *is the author of a biography of Cooper and has also published, among other works, two volumes of a definitive life of Thomas Jefferson.*

"*. . . foe of governmental centralization*"

DUMAS MALONE

TOWARD the end of his life more than a century ago, one of Thomas Cooper's admirers said that he was famous on two continents. Even at that time this was an exaggerated statement. But if his American contemporaries were alive now, many of them would probably be surprised to discover how little he has been remembered. To those acquainted with this versatile and pugnacious man, who spread learning and started rows wherever he went, he must have seemed unforgettable.

Even his physical appearance was astonishing. He is said to have been less than five feet tall, with a massive head and a tapering figure, so that he looked like a wedge with a head on it. In his day he was noted—among other things—as a scientist, economist, jurist, and educator, while he was notorious as an agitator. He never held elective office, but he was one of the most conspicuous victims of the Sedition Law in the presidency of John Adams, and he proclaimed extreme state-rights doctrines in South Carolina well ahead of John C. Calhoun. His stormy and colorful career cannot be summed up neatly in a sentence, but he is chiefly significant in history as a foe of governmental centralization and as a champion of the freedom of the human mind.

Thomas Cooper was born in England in 1759, came to Pennsylvania thirty-five years later, removed to South Carolina when he was past sixty, and died there at the ripe age of eighty. His life fell into three main parts.

In England, he went to Oxford, dabbled in medicine, became a barrister and member of a firm of calico printers in Manchester, where he applied his growing knowledge of chemistry to his business. At the same time he poured his superabundant energies into reform activities, advocating the abolition of the slave trade, the removal of all religious disabilities, and parliamentary reform. His own efforts seemed futile, but all of these causes were ultimately successful. He bore the fraternal greetings of the Manchester Constitutional Society to the Jacobins in France in 1792, being denounced in Parliament by Edmund Burke for this action

conservative reaction against the revolutionary developments in France had set in. The church and personal property of his friend Dr. Joseph Priestley, the Unitarian clergyman and distinguished chemist, had been destroyed by rioters, and the spirit of repression was growing in the government. Therefore Cooper and Priestley went to America, hoping to find a haven of freedom such as the Old World did not offer.

Cooper made a prospecting trip to America before he settled permanently, and published a book containing his observations. He found no fault with the government, describing it as "the government *of* the people, and *for* the people," anticipating the greater part of Lincoln's famous saying. He planned a settlement project in Northumberland County, Pennsylvania, which did not work out, but he and the Priestleys established a home in the village of Northumberland. During the next few years he supported himself chiefly by practicing law, while sometimes serving informally as a physician, without pay, and availing himself of the opportunity for scientific experiment provided by Priestley's library and apparatus. He attracted little public attention at first, although Priestley was soon the object of scurrilous attacks by Federalist editors as a "firebrand philosopher." Thus both men were virtually forced into the opposition camp and became identified with the Jeffersonians. With the passage of the notorious Alien and Sedition Acts in the presidency of John Adams, this alignment became inevitable. Though Cooper was naturalized, Priestley was not, and many believed that the Alien Act, authorizing the President to expel from the country any alien judged by him to be "dangerous to the peace and safety of the United States," was directed against Priestley. Actually, he was not ordered out. Cooper was more affected by the Sedition Act, which forbade "false, slanderous, and malicious" criticism of the government, and was designed in fact to silence those opposed to the party in power.

This was just the thing that Cooper had left England to avoid, and he would have been false to his own deepest convictions if he had not objected to such a partisan attack on freedom of opinion. He did so forcefully when serving for a time as editor of a local newspaper. His newspaper essays were published separately, and his criticisms of the government led to his trial for sedition in the election year of 1800. For saying no worse things about Adams than were said thousands of times in later presidential campaigns, he was tried before Justice Samuel Chase, who charged him with a brazen attempt "to poison the minds of the people." He was sentenced to six months' imprisonment and a fine of $400. Upon emerging from jail he sought an indictment of the arch-Federalist Alexander Hamilton, whose attacks on Adams were far more violent and extreme than his. Nothing came of this maneuver, but the Federalists lost the election and, long years after Cooper's death, his heirs recovered his fine with interest. The Sedition Act was completely repudiated and Cooper fully vindicated.

His writings and political martyrdom attracted the attention of Jefferson, but Cooper received no political reward commensurate with his own merits as he perceived them. Actually this champion of freedom of political opinion was temperamentally unsuited to public office. He was too opinionated, too belligerent, too impatient. As a state judge in Pennsylvania he reacted strongly against the attacks on the judiciary by extreme democrats. His desire to maintain decorum was commendable, but there was some ground for the charges of arbitrary conduct which led to his removal by the governor, after seven years of service.

These circumstances caused Cooper to turn to science and to enter the field of education. He became professor of chemistry at Carlisle College—now Dickinson College—and after a time held a similar post at the University of Pennsylvania. When he was about sixty he received the honorary degree of M. D. from the Regents of the State of New York, and thereafter was known as "Dr. Cooper."

Jefferson, with whom he was carrying on a fascinating correspondence, wanted him as the first professor at the University of Virginia, but because of delay in opening the University and the powerful opposition of religious leaders, nothing came of the matter. Instead Cooper in 1820 became a professor in South Carolina College—now the University of South Carolina—and was soon elected president of that institution. Thus opened the last and most interesting phase of his life; in South Carolina, if

All this was consistent with his own past, but he reversed himself on slavery and became a defender of the institution.

Valuing Union too little because he loved political liberty too well, he accelerated the movement which finally led South Carolina to secession. While John C. Calhoun was Vice-President and keeping quiet, Cooper stated publicly that it was time for South Carolina to "calculate the value of the Union," and he urged nullification of the objectionable tariff laws while Calhoun was still counseling moderation. Daniel Webster condemned him in the Senate as Edmund Burke had done in Parliament, but the extreme state-rights group in his own locality hailed him as a prophet and supported him in his personal controversies as president of the College.

These controversies were chiefly with religious groups, especially the Presbyterians, who regarded him as a materialist and unbeliever and sought to oust him from his high educational position. In the pamphlet warfare which ensued, very extreme things were said on both sides. Cooper's religious views were not unlike those of Jefferson, but his manners were far worse. Unlike Jefferson, who made no public attack on any man's faith, he made fun of orthodox theology, and he injured the cause of religious freedom by his own vehemence and intolerance. He finally resigned, leaving the College in a parlous state. Admirers of his political views found work for him to do; and in his late seventies this incredible man edited the statutes of South Carolina in five volumes, which remain as a monument to his legal learning.

The inscription on his tombstone in Columbia, South Carolina, says that the stone was erected by *a portion* of his fellow citizens. Opinions about him were generally divided, and he can hardly be termed a practical success. But a major reason for his many failures was that he was so often ahead of his own age; and, if he did not always act wisely, modern scientific progress would have been impossible without the freedom of the mind which he championed throughout life. He was a minor prophet and generally a true one. This impassioned man of learning often over-reached himself, but he was never dull.

opening up new vistas, whether he wished to or not, and the frontiers were not limited to the country's geographical boundaries. Everything was so new, so different from Europe, that men of vision found frontiers of knowledge to explore long after the first wave of settlement had passed over any particular region.

One area of tremendous potentiality that attracted many Americans was nature study. The great and trackless continent contained countless species of plants and animals previously unknown. Everyone seized quickly upon those new varieties that could be put to practical use. Potatoes, Indian corn, the turkey, and tobacco, for example, were soon familiar to the whole western world. But eventually certain men began to collect, classify, and describe the flourishing flora and fauna of America simply as an end in itself. Few of these men were specialists. Jefferson, for instance, made the study of nature but one of his myriad activities. Yet so great were the opportunities that even amateurs could add importantly to human knowledge, and many, like Jefferson, did so.

Some of the most fruitful intellectual contacts between the Old World and the New developed from the exchange of information and specimens between American and European naturalists. The first important American botanist, John Bartram of Pennsylvania, was famous in European scientific circles long before the Revolution. Jefferson's friendly argument with the French naturalist Buffon about the effect of American conditions on the size of animals (which Jefferson finally won by importing into France at great expense the hide and skeleton of a huge moose) is another instance of this.

During the early national period, the boundaries between

natural history and various other disciplines were vague. Doctors, being students of the highest of all forms of life, were particularly important among naturalists in the United States. Richard Harlan, whose Fauna Americana *(1825) was the first systematic study of American mammals, was a physician and surgeon, and nearly half of those who subscribed to his book were doctors. When natural science was taught at all in the period around 1800 it was taught in medical schools, and the best source for studying the work of early nineteenth-century American naturalists is the old* Medical Repository.

Similarly, in the days before the camera, there was a close relationship between nature study and art. Charles Willson Peale, for example, one of the finest portrait painters of his generation, dug up and assembled the bones of two mastodons, and painted a large canvas, "Exhuming the Mastodon," to celebrate his accomplishment. Peale also established a natural history museum in Philadelphia and staffed it with a number of professional naturalists. Other artists, such as George Catlin and Karl Bodmer, made careful pictorial studies of the American Indian and his surroundings.

The two following essays deal with artists who were important ornithologists. Audubon, of course, is famous, but Alexander Wilson, who was almost his equal both as scientist and painter, is scarcely known at all to the general public.

Robert Cantwell, an editor of Sports Illustrated *and a lifelong student of birds, has written, in addition to two novels, a biography of Nathaniel Hawthorne. Donald Culross Peattie numbers among his many books* Singing in the Wilderness, Flowering Earth, *and* Audubon's America.

". . . transformed a science into an art"

ROBERT CANTWELL

LONG before Audubon, the United States possessed one of the greatest of ornithologists in the person of Alexander Wilson, a Scottish-born poet, weaver, and school-teacher who set out at the age of forty to picture all the birds of America. He has always been an obscure or even a mysterious character. Tall and awkward, with long bony features and a strong Scottish burr to his speech, Wilson is as little known as any figure who has made a comparable contribution to literature and to science. It is true that he appears in standard reference works as "the father of

His father, marrying again, returned to smuggling, and the boy was apprenticed to a weaver, his formal education ending at that time. For about ten years Wilson was a journeyman weaver and a peddler of cloth throughout Scotland, meanwhile publishing two volumes of poetry that has won him a secure place among Scottish poets of the rank just below Robert Burns. His most popular poem, *Watty and Meg,* a study of a lower-class husband-and-wife quarrel and reconciliation, and a masterpiece, was published anonymously and was generally attributed to Burns.

Wilson was beginning to make a name for himself, and had been offered the assistant editorship of *The Bee,* one of the best Scottish literary magazines, when he was jailed in the suppression of Scottish radicals during the French Revolution. Wilson had published a series of poems attacking mill-owners in Paisley. One of these poems was called *The Shark.* All weaving was piece work, and Wilson's poem charged that William Sharp, the owner of the Long Mills, had subtly lengthened the measuring devices by which the weavers were paid. The alteration was so slight as to be scarcely noticeable, but it made a great difference when multiplied over thousands of yards from hundreds of looms. Wilson expected to face political martyrdom, but to his horror he was arrested as a common criminal, charged with blackmail. The uproar was great; he was roughly handled, and perhaps injured, released on bail, returned to jail, released and jailed again repeatedly; and at last fined and sentenced to burn his poems with his own hands in the public square of Paisley.

He fled Scotland for America in 1794. For a time he worked as a weaver and peddler around Philadelphia, eventually establishing himself as a teacher in country schools at Bustletown,

Milestown, and Gray's Ferry. Much of the mystery in his life stems from his deliberate concealment of his past in this period, for he avoided contact with other political refugees from Scotland and lived with the greatest respectability in an effort to overcome the suspicion he felt was directed toward him. Ten years after his release from a Scottish prison, he still found his American friends growing cold because of whispers concerning him that had reached them. And so he came to believe that no human companionship would ever be possible for him. He wrote a little poetry—"There was no better poet in America during the years in which he lived and died here," in the words of the literary historian Van Wyck Brooks—but his best poetry was in the Scottish dialect, and his separation from the old country cut him off from his inspiration.

In his loneliness he began to study wild life, and especially the colors, songs, habits, migrations, and the marvelous interwoven economy of the world of American birds. Thus he became the father of American ornithology in the isolation that his reputation, or more precisely his lack of reputation, forced upon him.

There had been earlier students of American birds: Mark Catesby, who pictured many in his magnificent *Natural History of the Carolinas* nearly a century before; John Bartram, who sent specimens of American birds to English naturalists; even Thomas Jefferson, an amateur ornithologist of no mean ability. But as the great English naturalist Sir William Jardin put it, Alexander Wilson was "the first who truly studied the birds of North America in their natural abodes and from real observation, and his work will remain an ever-to-be-admired testimony of enthusiasm and perseverance. . . . If some plates and illustrations may vie with it in finer workmanship or pictorial splendor, few, indeed, can rival it in fidelity and truth of delineation."

Wilson taught himself to draw, and began picturing birds from life before he knew the names of those he painted. With borrowed tools he also taught himself engraving, prepared to produce the plates for his book single-handedly if necessary. In 1806 he became assistant editor of *Ree's New Encyclopedia,* a superior reference work of the time published by Samuel Bradford in Philadelphia, with the understanding that Bradford would publish his *American Ornithology* if Wilson could secure 200 subscribers. The nine volumes of work—Wilson died before completing the tenth—appeared between 1808 and 1813, with incalculable effect on American culture.

They were dazzling to Wilson's contemporaries: hundreds of radiant bird paintings, vivid and exuberant, coupled with some of the most concise, informed, exact and entertaining nature writing ever put into print. Here were the bluejays with their odd nods and gesticulations; the humming birds, more numerous

of books ended with sandpipers, fish hawks, ducks, geese, herons, flamingos, and the other water birds—not quite all that were then known, for Wilson had twenty-four still to paint when he died. Working thirty years before Audubon, he covered the ground so thoroughly that in the century after his death only twenty American birds were discovered that he had not known about.

While the books were being published, Wilson explored the American wilderness from Canada to the Gulf of Mexico. "Few Americans have seen more of their country than I have," he said, "and none love it more." He collected rare specimens for the later volumes, and sold subscriptions to the set. In all he sold 500 sets at $120 each, a great investment for books at that time. His subscribers included Jefferson and most of his cabinet, public figures like Robert Fulton, Benjamin Latrobe, Elias Hasket Derby, Nicholas Biddle, Benjamin West, De Witt Clinton, Rufus King, the presidents of colleges, generals of the army, and many plantation owners, most of his books being sold in the South. As his pictures appeared he had a brief, belated success. His poems, including his long narrative, *The Foresters,* were published in *The Port Folio,* the outstanding literary magazine of the country. Each volume of the *Ornithology* was greeted with fresh praise. His personal life was brightened by professional recognition, and by engagement to a Philadelphia heiress, Sarah Miller. But during the War of 1812 the old suspicions of him revived, and his colorists all left him, forcing him to color all the plates by his own hand. Overwork weakened him, and he died after a brief illness in 1813.

So little was known about him that his closest friend and literary executor could not learn the date of his birth. Another friend of many years, Dr. Charles Caldwell, who was present at his deathbed and wrote his obituary, admitted he knew nothing about Wilson's life. The obscurity continued after Wilson's death, for his books were locked in private collections and the general public had no notion of them, color printing being unable to reproduce the quality of the hand-painted plates. A contributing factor in his obscurity was the conflict many years after his death between his literary executor, George Ord, and Audubon, in which Ord accused Audubon of stealing some of Wilson's work, a conflict that involved technicalities wearisome to the general public, and that dragged on for so long that popular interest became exhausted. The loss was unfortunate, for no American writer except Emily Dickinson wrote of birds with the wit of Alexander Wilson. His great work, so rare, strange, and hauntingly beautiful, transformed a science into an art.

His life-long struggle with the state made him a peculiarly modern figure. His escape from a political impasse was into nature, not by evading the political scene, as Thoreau tried to do by living on nature's bounty outside society, but by infusing into political and cultural life a sense of the natural wonders that restored perspective to political disputes. "Amusement blended with instruction," he wrote, "and a wish to draw the attention of my fellow-citizens, occasionally, from the discordant jarrings of politics to a contemplation of the grandeur, harmony and wonderful variety of Nature exhibited in this beautiful portion of the animal kingdom, have been my principal, and, I might say, almost my only motives."

What drew Wilson to the study of birds was their wildness, something apart from what man could control and direct, the eternal opposite of the artificial and the contrived. Other ornithologists, and especially Audubon, created more spectacular plates, but Wilson surpassed all others in capturing the wildness of wild life, the mysterious quality of being different from tame. His birds were really wild, and their wildness came from something in his own view of nature. To Wilson, birds were a part of the original wilderness life of America carried over into the world of the white man. They stood for a natural order of life, a native terrestrial pattern, to which their flight, colors, habits, melodies, migrations provided a clue. He felt that a fragment of the prehistoric American wilderness existed, diffused around towns and farms, singing in fields and orchards, and casting a radiance in its intangible and constantly shifting pattern of vivid and vibrant life. The unspoiled past of nature could still be studied in the New World, and it remained a living influence in this new nation that began its Declaration of Independence with an invocation to nature's God.

born the one who was to capture the birds of that lost wilderness forever in his paintings—John James Audubon. He was born far away, on a tropical plantation in that part of Santo Domingo which now we call Haiti. His father was an officer of the French navy, his mother a lady of that island who died soon after this brief love with the gallant lieutenant. But in France, tender arms awaited the little boy. There Madame Audubon, his father's childless wife, gladly consented to his adoption. So in the country near Nantes he grew up, a loved, light-hearted youngster, good-looking, ardent, sensitive, and with a will of his own.

That will was from the beginning bent toward what was to prove his destiny. He had lessons in English, fencing, dancing, and music, but his one passion was to draw birds. "None but aerial companions suited my fancy," he later quaintly wrote. His father, firm though fond, put him in a naval training school. The boy broke out of that iron cage. Lieutenant Audubon then sent him to Paris as a pupil in the studio of the painter Jacques Louis David. But drawing from plaster casts was dull work to this born genius of the free and winged. So in 1803 it was arranged that he should sail for America, to look after some interests his father had near Philadelphia.

There, as the young master of a country house, he spent carefree days in the woods with his fine fowling piece, dressed like a dandy in polished pumps and ruffled shirt. So he fell in with a fellow hunter living nearby, an Englishman named William Bakewell, who genially invited him to call. When the young man presented himself, only his neighbor's daughter was at home. Lucy Bakewell was fifteen years old, the love of Audubon's life at sight, and the one right woman in the world for him.

Back to France went John James, to ask his father's consent to the marriage and to seek his practical help. The lieutenant advanced his son funds from his future inheritance, and made a plan for him. This was for a business partnership with a young merchant named Ferdinand Rozier, to open a store on the frontier in Kentucky. So presently, in New York, the two young men bought a stock of goods and turned west to seek their fortunes. In Louisville, then a village of a thousand souls, they set up their enterprise. The year was 1807, and already the frontier was darkening with the financial depression brought on by Jefferson's Embargo Act. But John James Audubon, young and in love and daring always, came back to Pennsylvania one June day to claim his bride and take her into his singing wilderness.

Always bad at figures, with no head at all for business, Audubon found the store one more of life's tight cages. He escaped it as often as he could. After a long day in the forest he would return happily, bringing game for the table and subjects for his swift brush and pencil. His partner grumbled; Lucy sighed and smiled. So badly did the little business go that the owners decided to move it on to Henderson, in hope of better trade. Audubon labored long and hard—but not at storekeeping. Instead, the pile of his drawings grew. Each was the fruit of days of woods-wandering and keen observation. Each met with Lucy's loving praise. But wistfully she made the comment: "I have a rival in every bird."

Rozier had less patience. Goading Audubon to a new venture, he set out with him to the old French settlement of Ste. Genevieve on the Mississippi, seeking trade. But their boat became ice-bound, and Audubon was free meanwhile to follow the wild swan and make fellows of the Osages. Soon after the ice broke up, so did the unequal partnership. Back to Henderson went John James, to Lucy and the little boys John and Victor.

Now for nearly a decade of the prime of his young manhood John James Audubon struggled to find his fate. Here in the log-cabin town of Henderson, with the primeval American wilderness at his door, he lived as deeply as any man can. Here he knew bliss and sorrow, failure and unrecognized success. Of Lucy's four children, two died. But this was a marriage that could lift the lovers from the depths of grief to the heights of communion. Always she upheld him in his passion for the birds and that glorious record of them which now numbered hundreds of drawings. Always she stood bravely beside him through one business failure after another: a store, a mill, a commission business. He was sued, reviled, attacked, taken to jail for debt. When in a last desperation he declared bankruptcy, the sheriff came and took all that the little family possessed—Lucy's china and silver, the furniture, the house itself. All but those drawings; those, of

[illegible]

his way. In those days before the camera, people would pay for a quick portrait. Thus he made his way to Cincinnati, where he found a job as a taxidermist in a museum. Lucy joined him with the boys. Now, out of the conjoined powers of science and art, was born the great concept of Audubon's immortal work. He determined to paint all the birds of America, life-size, in attitudes of life and in full color. On this peerless adventure, with the blessing of Lucy, he set forth in October of 1820 into the young American wilderness.

It was by flatboat that he drifted down the Ohio and then down the Mississippi to New Orleans, happy in the wings that haunted those shores. In Louisiana his French grace found favor; he kept himself as tutor and portraitist, and soon sent for his family again. Lucy got a place as governess; for the next twelve years she was to carry on her slim shoulders the burden of bread-winning. Audubon himself was dedicated to his chosen task. He collected and painted from dawn to dark. Under his hands grew the brilliant, lively record of our unsurpassed American avifauna, as it was in the beginning.

More, he set out now to find a publisher for his prodigious work. In Philadelphia, then our cultural center, he was advised to go abroad. Scraping together all the money he could, with Lucy's savings readily added, Audubon in 1826 sailed for Europe to show his drawings. In Liverpool, Edinburgh, London, and Paris their wild free beauty took the public by storm. The giant publication called *The Birds of America* was launched. Subscribers flocked to Audubon; he, who had failed so many times in business, succeeded with this boldest of all his ventures.

The famous "elephant folio"—really a double elephant, or a

page thirty by forty inches—is the one that all Audubon collectors seek. Audubon chose this gigantic format because he wished to represent all the birds of America life-size, and this took considerable ingenuity; to get a flamingo even on a page 30 by 40 inches meant that the bird had to be arched over into something like a croquet hoop.

The illustrations of the elephant folio were engraved on copperplate, the first few by Lizar's of Edinburgh and all the rest by Havell and Sons of London. To their exquisite workmanship from Audubon's originals (which were done in an odd mixture of crayon and water-color) Audubon owed a great deal. But it is also owing to them that too many Audubon birds look as if cut out of metal, for Havell and Sons were not ornithologists, or anything but engravers. They were not even artists enough to handle background, middle ground, and foreground successfully. Yet there is the compensating glory that every engraving has been hand-colored, so that when a man says he has an original Audubon, he means one of the plates from the elephant folio. The additional landscape and flowers seen in most Audubon pictures are almost always the work of some collaborator. For instance, the first hundred or so plates are filled with the flowers painted by the boy of thirteen whom Audubon took down the Mississippi on a raft. The flowers and scenes of the birds of the Gulf States were largely done by Miss Maria Bachman, and for the birds of the Far North the accessory materials were drawn by Isaac Sprague, so that almost every Audubon painting is a collaboration by three people at least. But the presiding genius—the man who makes the birds come alive instead of looking like stuffed specimens in a museum—is Audubon himself.

America loves success, and when her French-born son returned with it, he found more waiting for him. He had funds now, for travel and work and to take Lucy with him when he went back to England in a year. Then Florida, with its unsurpassed bird life, called him; in Charleston he met John Bachman, fine old zoologist, whose two daughters were presently to marry Audubon's sons. From the Texas coast and Key West to Labrador Audubon roved, working to complete his mighty task. Then he began another, in collaboration with Bachman, on the quadrupeds of North America. Lucky it was that he had sons to carry this on, for old age overtook him too swiftly. The illustrations for this work were begun by Audubon Senior, and are his last fine work; they had to be completed by Audubon's two sons after his death. Hand-colored copperplate engravings were too costly. As a result they are printed in colored inks, and for some reason too often over-colored. The plates are less good than the text, on the whole, but every Audubon collector owns a few be-

De Witt Clinton

Now that man can span the continent almost as fast as the sun, it is hard to keep in mind that for centuries the search for rapid and efficient transportation was one of the most important in American history. In order to preserve economic and political unity an effective system of transportation had to be developed, and this was difficult because the country was large and sparsely settled. Wagons and stagecoaches might serve to move men and goods from London to Liverpool, but they were hopelessly inadequate for moving them from New York to Chicago or St. Louis.

As a result the United States pioneered in the development of new methods of transportation. The Mississippi River steamboat, for example, is an illustration of a highly specialized vehicle brought to a peak of efficiency by American ingenuity. The railroad, although first developed in Europe, proved so useful to Americans that by 1840 this country had 3,300 miles of track to Europe's 1,800.

In the years before the Civil War the canal was even more important than the railroad in providing cheap transportation, especially for the movement of bulky farm products. More than 3,000 miles of canals were built between 1824 and 1840. The 364-mile Erie was by far the most significant, for it made possible a direct East-West water connection between the Mississippi Valley and the Atlantic seaboard. Designed by ingenious amateur builders like Benjamin Wright and Jonas Geddes, the Erie brought untold wealth to New York State, eased the lot of westward moving pioneers, tied East and West together, and thus changed the course of American history.

In this chapter Nathan Miller, of the History Department of Rutgers University, discusses De Witt Clinton, a truly unforgettable American whose vision and administrative skill made the "Big Ditch" possible. Dr. Miller's The Enterprise of a Free People *won the Ansley Prize of Columbia University and the Albert J. Beveridge Award of the American Historical Association.*

"... through the Appalachian barrier"

NATHAN MILLER

York City, as Governor of New York State, as Senator both in the State Senate and in the Senate of the United States, and as a candidate for the presidency, he had frequently been party to shrewd political deals. Nor was the path of expediency unknown to Clinton.

But who remembers Clinton the politician? Who recalls that as a candidate for the presidency in 1812 he was presented to his Federalist supporters as one who would bring the war with Great Britain to a swift end, and at the same time to his Republican supporters as the man who would infuse greater vigor into the war effort than President Madison had done? Who wonders at the way this man succeeded in confounding the leadership of both the Republican and Federalist parties in New York State for a period of twenty-five years, muddying the political waters to a point where the group that emerged was recognized as being neither Federalist nor Republican, but Clintonian? Clinton was essentially a creature of "the miserable squabbles" of politics, but it is not for this that he is remembered. Rather, his fame rests on the fact that he did stick closely to the cause of internal improvements, and particularly to the cause of the Erie Canal.

Military and naval operations on and around the Great Lakes during the War of 1812 emphasized the need to improve arteries of transportation between the eastern seaboard and the trans-Appalachian West. Migration and settlement beyond the mountains, once the war was over, added even more compelling reasons for providing improved transportation connections between East and West. By this time farmers in the western country, restricted as they were to two unsatisfactory arteries of transportation for shipment of their produce to market, were clamoring loudly for improved shipping facilities for their surplus products. The Mississippi River and its northernmost tributaries, which provided one route, involved a long voyage to New Orleans; Lake Ontario and the St. Lawrence River to Montreal provided the other. Both were long, dangerous, and expensive. Moreover, many Americans feared that their continued use would lead to national disintegration, with East and West separating along the line described by the Appalachian Mountains. To reduce costs of transportation and to preserve national unity, a direct connection between the Atlantic seaboard and the growing western country was required. Clinton shared these conclusions with many of his contemporaries, and like them believed that the best route through the Appalachian barrier lay in New York State. To link the Atlantic Ocean with the Great Lakes via the Mohawk Valley and the Hudson River had occurred to a few men as early as 1724, but it was destined to remain an unrealized objective until a small band of "visionary enthusiasts," as they were afterwards mockingly called, met at the City Hotel in New York in December 1815 to plan the great enterprise that became the Erie Canal.

Only the briefest mention of the meeting appeared in the newspapers of New York City at the time, and perhaps that was all it deserved. The meeting is noteworthy only because it was there that Clinton was assigned the task of composing a Memorial to the Legislature recommending the construction of the Erie Canal by the state.

The Memorial incorporated Clinton's extensive knowledge of the financial, technical, and administrative problems that canal construction posed both in America and abroad. Based on his own immediate experience as a Canal Commissioner in New York, it represented a combination of study and experience that marked it as especially authoritative. Clinton's reasoning led irresistibly to a single conclusion: the canal promised a dazzling future to New York State. It "would convey more riches on its waters than any other canal in the world," and would "render New York the great depot and warehouse" of the entire continent. By carrying the products of the West to eastern markets and by making the new regions more accessible to settlers, the canal would accelerate the growth of the western territories into prosperous states. The canal would serve the national interest by establishing stronger bonds between East and West, thereby counteracting whatever tendencies towards regional separation the facts of geography seemed to encourage.

Had the Memorial been Clinton's only contribution to the canal project, it would have been sufficient to connect him with

Thousands of citizens endorsed copies of the document that were forwarded to the Legislature.

Sectional jealousies threatened to defeat the project in the state legislature; and its enormous cost made it appear truly visionary. "Only a madman, fool or knave," declared Peter R. Livingston, would advocate such a costly experiment. Taxation, he predicted, would soar. "Call the canal what you please," said Livingston, call it "a ditch—you will find it a ditch that will bury you all. It will make a pauper of the State." But neither legislative delays nor the refusal of the national government to grant aid nor the expressions of doubt or incredulity on the part of men of importance in public life could stop the movement for "Clinton's ditch." Sectional opposition to the canal in the eastern and southern parts of the state diminished as a result of compromises which were carefully worked out and in which Clinton, no doubt, had a hand. By 1817 excavation was begun, and thereafter work went rapidly forward under the guidance and supervision of amateur American engineers. By 1824, long after Clinton's first term as Governor had expired, the canal was well on its way to completion and its success was certain.

The completion of the canal boded ill for Clinton's opponents, since it threatened to revive the political fortunes of the man whose name was most intimately asociated with the project. Clinton's political power had declined notably even before he left office in 1822; in fact, fear of defeat had accounted for his refusal to stand for reelection at the conclusion of his first term. To prevent his reemergence as a powerful political figure, Clinton's opponents in the legislature removed him from the post of Canal Commissioner that he had held for more than fourteen years

—a post which he had occupied with distinction and which carried with it no remuneration. Clinton wielded the weapon of martyrdom that his opponents had thrust into his hands with consummate skill. Assuming the attitude of a humble servant of the people, Clinton watched an outraged citizenry rally to his support. In the next gubernatorial election he was re-elected Chief Executive of the State, a position that he suitably occupied during the pomp and ceremony that marked the official opening of the Erie Canal in 1825.

The immediate evidence of the canal's success—the large revenues from tolls that made possible the repayment of the canal debt in less than a decade, the drastic reduction in the costs of transportation between Buffalo and New York City, the spectacular technical achievements of the engineers who supervised construction—had vast implications for the nation. Eastern port cities and western states that were clustered around the Great Lakes regarded the Erie Canal as a guide to the solution of their own transportation problems. The country became afflicted with a raging "canal fever," and canals became part of a transportation revolution that affected large portions of the country.

What sort of man was DeWitt Clinton, this politician whose interests transcended the problems of getting and holding office? Clinton held a variety of posts other than political. He served as a Director, and later as President, of the American Academy of the Fine Arts. The importance that he placed on education was reflected in his early organizational work for the Common School Society and in his dedication to the cause of free public schooling. Clinton was a founder and president of the New York Historical Society, a vice-president of the American Bible Society, and a founder and active member of the Society of Arts and Manufactures. His scientific researches, the work of an intelligent amateur, won for him a modicum of honor and recognition from some European institutions and scientific groups, such as the Linnaean and the Horticultural Societies of London and the Wernerian Society of Edinburgh.

Clinton was a self-conscious intellectual, a dilettante without the training or ability to undertake serious work in either the arts or the sciences. But he was also a man of broad interests, with a standard of values that those who derided his intellectual pretensions overlooked. Dedicated to the objective of "exciting the prosperity" of his state and his country, Clinton esteemed material progress as a necessary basis for the fulfillment of man's intellectual and artistic capacities. He expressed this belief in his Memorial to the Legislature; here he wrote of the United States of the future, a nation engaged in "great public improvements . . . encouraging the arts and sciences . . . patronizing

Mary Moody Emerson and Elizabeth Cady Stanton

Although great progress has been made over the years in improving their opportunities, it has always been true that intelligent and ambitious American women have had to struggle against odds to fulfill themselves in our society. Indeed, in her recent volume, Century of Struggle: The Woman's Rights Movement in the United States, *Eleanor Flexner comes to the discouraging conclusion that women have still not achieved real equality with men. "While most of the legal barriers are down, others remain, some of them rooted in physiology, others rising more from prejudice than fact."*

Foreign visitors have frequently commented on the relatively high status of women in the United States, and the deference shown to women by American men. Even in colonial times, when, as Miss Flexner acidly remarks, "women had many duties, but few rights," they were generally better off than their European sisters. The shortage of women and of all labor in early America help to account for this. In any case, by the middle of the nineteenth century great steps had been taken to improve the education of women, and to grant married women the right to own property, for instance.

But in general, American women were expected to remain in the family and to excel only in the social graces. "The leading features of the female character," wrote the English observer, James Silk Buckingham, in 1841, "are domestic fidelity, social cheerfulness, unostentatious hospitality, and moral and religious benevolence." Most women accepted the prevailing pattern. "When a woman marries," Alexis de Tocqueville noted, "it's as if she entered a convent. . . . I ventured the other day to ask one of these charming recluses just how, exactly, a wife could pass her time in America. She answered me, with great sang froid: *'In admiring her husband'." Even among those who sought some self-expression, the majority were probably like the women a Boston lawyer had in mind when he told the Austrian commentator, Francis J. Grund: "No sooner do they find out that their husbands or fathers have laid up a couple of thousand dollars in the bank, than . . . they want to ride in their own carriages . . . give parties to which they invite people whom they never met before . . . rake up a relationship with some colonel in the revolutionary army, or some noble family in Europe*

agitators in behalf of all mistreated minorities. They devoted their energies to such causes as the abolitionist crusade, the labor movement, and especially to the movement for women's rights. Elizabeth Cady Stanton was one of the most important of these, as Robert E. Riegel brings out in his account of her life, but there were many others, such as Lucretia Mott, Frances Willard, Susan B. Anthony, and Carrie Chapman Catt.

Finally, there were those women who achieved self-expression indirectly by influencing the men in their lives. Of course, countless American women by their love and devotion have influenced and inspired their husbands, sons, and other relatives, but some have had a real intellectual impact as well. Of these, in no case is the evidence clearer than in that of Mary Moody Emerson, whose story is told here by Odell Shepard.

Mr. Shepard, a former professor at Trinity College, is best known for his life of Bronson Alcott, Pedlar's Progress, *which won the Pulitzer prize. Robert E. Riegel is Professor of History at Dartmouth College. Among his many books are* The Story of Western Railroads, America Moves West, *and* Young America.

". . . the prompt production of heroes"

ODELL SHEPARD

IT HAS been said that some men are born great, some achieve greatness, and others have greatness thrust upon them. An example of the third class is Ralph Waldo Emerson, often called "the wisest American." He never tried to achieve fame, wealth, or power, and had he been left to himself he would probably have smiled his way through life as an amiable mediocrity. But Fate would not have it so. The Emerson who left an indelible mark upon his country and the modern world was made out of rather unpromising materials by a woman of queer but unquestionable genius.

Emerson was still a child and had recently lost his father when his maiden aunt, Mary Moody Emerson, took charge of him and his brothers, impatiently brushing their mother aside as unfit for the holy task. Ralph was not the most brilliant of the brothers, nor was he her favorite, but with each of them she strove to fulfill her exalted ideal of what an Emerson ought to be.

Family pride was one of her motives, but motherly longings may have been stronger. A spinster by choice, she was determined that her mind should bear worthy children. For years she had sought out young people of promise and "stormed their castles," as one of them said, "by flattery, raillery, wit, and rebuke." Always she demanded perfection of them, and when it was not forthcoming she quarrelled soon or late with them all. Ordinary goodness she neither admired nor encouraged, but for sin as a means of spiritual awakening she had a deep respect. Indeed she once advised a respectable matron, the mother of several children, to commit a crime for the good of her soul.

Such instruction was too advanced for her nephews, but she gave them its equivalent in such commands as "Lift your aims!" and "Scorn trifles!" and "Always do the hardest things!" These injunctions—stinging, staccato, war-headed by verbs of action in the imperative mood, barked out as though by an exasperated drill-sergeant—were not meant for the coddling of children but the prompt production of heroes. When poverty sent the boys supperless to bed she told them about the ancient Spartans. When Ralph and Edward were ridiculed by their schoolmates for having only one overcoat between them she let them know what to think about the laughter of fools. For this woman, thirty-five years old and four feet three inches tall, life had been one long battle. She hoped that the brothers would find it so, and wished them to be armed betimes.

Mary Emerson's acquaintance with war began on April 19, 1775, when at the age of nine months she watched a skirmish at Concord's North Bridge from a window of the "Old Manse," her birthplace. "I was in arms at the Fight!" she told Lafayette half a century later, and the remark holds good for all her eighty-eight years. She never forgot, or let others do so, that her father, the minister of Concord, had greatly helped to foment that fight and had died in the war that followed. Stoutly determined that his heroic spirit should live on in her, and fully aware that the

reach. Milton's *Paradise Lost,* Young's *Night Thoughts,* a powerful poem by Robert Blair called *The Grave,* the sermons of Jonathan Edwards and Michael Wigglesworth's *Day of Doom,* led the girl's thoughts far into the valley of the shadow, but she was neither dismayed nor saddened by what she saw there. Once and for all, she fell in love with death—or rather with eternity. Whatsoever was nobly heroic and stern in the Puritan tradition she kept and put to vigorous use, while rejecting its bigotry, superstition, and fear. Though by no means saintly or pious, indeed scarcely a Christian, she became in early youth and remained all her days intensely, even passionately, religious. Out of the depths of her loneliness and destitution there came this triumphant cry: "To be alive with God is enough! It is rapture!" Again and again she declared her entire willingness to be damned forever if that would conduce to the glory of God.

The ardors and audacities of the Revolution were oddly conjoined in this woman with the fervor of early Puritanism, but the combination was highly effective. From the one she drew her delight in combat and from the other those ideals of personal independence for which she fought. The time and place of her conflict, moreover, would seem to have been providentially arranged, for she emerged from solitude when the Federalist Party —blindly conservative and pseudo-aristocratic—held Boston in a firm though chilly grip. The political principles involved did not much concern her, but she was quick to discern their benumbing effect. Where was the Spirit of Seventy-six? Could these genteel and enfeebled conformists really be descendants of the Puritan Fathers? They measured personal worth in terms of dollars.

Death to them was an unmentionable horror, because they were not really alive. What they wanted from God was not the sense of an infinite presence but health, wealth, respectability, and peace of mind. She set herself to disturb that peace as much as she was able.

For that effort she was well equipped. Tiny, lean, bright-eyed, crop-haired, often dressed in a shroud of her own manufacture, always taking with her on her travels a bed made to her measure in the shape of a coffin, continually harping upon death as an eagerly awaited bridegroom, fearing no man and contemptuous of most women, atrocious in manners, habitually violent in speech, with a wit like the sting of a wasp and wrath like the pounce of a hawk, she fluttered the dove-cotes of Boston and round about for many a year while living, as she said, "to give pain." Her purpose, to be sure, was no more cruel than that of a surgeon, but inevitably it was misunderstood. Many of her victims must have sighed for the days when scolds were sent to the ducking-stool and witches were summarily hanged.

By far the most important of Mary Emerson's victims and beneficiaries was her nephew Ralph. In him she found an inert goodness, an apathetic intelligence, and a quite incorrigible optimism that called forth her utmost powers. She was his harshest critic and chief inspirer. She guided his early reading, told him what to think of it and what its use might be. Her unquestionable affection for him, slightly mingled with pride, was chiefly expressed in fault-finding, rebuke, and occasional revilings. Her main purpose was to arouse him from his constitutional langor, to kindle the dry faggots of his thoughts until they blazed into utterance. She was often with him in person, sometimes as a quarrelsome member of his household, and when she went to live in Maine there were always her astonishing letters and diaries—villainously scrawled and often as hard to interpret as the oracles of Delphi—to be read, reread, copied into his journals, and passed about among his friends. Seldom indeed, and never for long, did he escape from her influence. It is descernible in his first book, *Nature.* In his essays on "Heroism" and "Self Reliance" he is thinking of her as a prime example. Quite possibly his favorite doctrine of Compensation was suggested by the way her mind had been set free by imprisonment and greatly enriched by poverty.

Without the severe ministrations of his Aunt Mary, we may be sure, Emerson might have succumbed to the gentilities and docilities of his time and place—might himself have been one of those "meek young men," as he calls them, "who grow up in libraries," feeding mostly on paper and ink. She herself was a voracious reader, and she taught him how to read great books while avoiding their tyranny. For the inborn chill of his blood

Boston and Harvard—both of them strongly European and Anglophile in his time—could not have provided. Thus his address on "The American Scholar," one of his boldest utterances, owes much to her. He felt, however, that she was much older than America, and that there was something primitive, all but prehistoric, about her. When he called her a prophetess, a pythoness, a weird woman, he was trying to express the feeling that there was in her wisdom and her total lack of self-restraint something supernatural. At times she seemed to be possessed by a power which he could not name and could not disobey. For that reason it was that in every main crisis of his life he sought out her counsel.

But Emerson was not a thinker primarily, although he was a great one. It is when we consider his mastery of the spoken and written word that we begin to comprehend his achievement and influence. While still a boy he had wished "to put on eloquence as a robe," and that he manifestly did in later life. Now it is precisely in his style, where we might expect him to be most original, that the influence of his aunt is most clearly discernible.

Emerson had, in fact, two sharply contrasted styles, and these he learned to use in a subtle collaboration like that of a pianist's two hands. One of them, native to his mild disposition, is suave, smooth, and serene. Its effect is that of a quietly flowing river, and in extended passages it can be a bit dull. But such long passages seldom occur. When he is writing at the top of his form they are broken abruptly by rhythms totally different, and by sounds that are harsh, brusque, peremptory. This second style is heard in the familiar words: "Trust thyself! Every heart resounds to that iron string." It comes again in the sentence: "Never strike sail to a fear!" It sounds like the snarl of a trumpet in: "What I must *do* is all that concerns me, and not what the people think!"

One of these styles is feminine, and the other is all male. What adds piquancy to the comparison is the fact that the masculine element in Emerson's writing is due to the life-long influence of his maiden aunt. That influence was brought to bear almost in his infancy, and it continued until he finally laid down his pen. While still a youth he hinted that he would like to borrow some of her "images," and was sharply rebuked; but she could not keep from him the intonations and rhythms of her speech. They are heard today whenever we read or hear the words we call his. Some of them have passed into common parlance, as, for example, "Hitch your wagon to a star."

Those words, signed by Ralph Waldo Emerson, are in the idiom of his Aunt Mary. They express the whole tenor and purpose of her life. They bring to mind a vivid picture of a tired and hungry girl standing at twilight in a New England barnyard beside a cart with up-thrust thills. The evening star is sinking. There comes to her the notion that even she, in her humble place, may set forth on a journey of infinite and eternal significance. And that she did. She converted a mild and docile man into one of the foremost citizens of the Monarch Thought's dominions. She made a good writer into a great one. Wherever his thought now goes in the world, she, his aunt in the flesh but the mother of his mind, goes also.

". . . women against men"

ROBERT E. RIEGEL

DURING July of 1848 a little band of reformers met at the hamlet of Seneca Falls, in the Finger Lake region of New York State. This small convention had a large purpose—to open a campaign for the rights of women. Impressed with the importance of the occasion, it passed a Declaration of Sentiments which paralleled the national Declaration of Independence. It began: "When, in the course of human events, it becomes necessary for one portion of the family of man to assume . . . a position different from that which they have hitherto occupied . . ." But it was the second paragraph that held the real dynamite. Its opening words were: "We hold these truths to be self-evident; that all men and women are created equal." The remainder of the document consisted of a list of grievances of women against men.

[illegible] midst of bearing her seventh child. She loved her family and was a hard-working housekeeper. Her protest against limitations affecting women represented no personal frustration.

Elizabeth had been born into a prosperous and well-known family. Her father, Judge Daniel Cady, was a lawyer and judge, and had sat in the state legislature and in Congress. While he was a trifle old-fashioned and conservative, he was also loving and generous. Elizabeth herself was sensitive and imaginative, but also plump, fun-loving, and daring. Her education, good for the day, included two years at the famous academy of Emma Willard in Troy. Possibly she was affected by the often expressed wish of her father that she had been a boy, and undoubtedly she was bitterly disappointed at not being able to go to college, but these difficulties did not prevent her from having a happy girlhood.

Important in forming Elizabeth's general interests and outlook upon life was her cousin Gerrit Smith, one of the best known reformers of the area. Periodically Elizabeth visited at the home of her cousin, where she was impressed with his high ideals for the improvement of human society, and particularly with his favorite reforms of temperance and abolition.

Elizabeth Cady's marriage was more than a trifle unusual, and this fact may have had some influence on her outlook. She fell in love with her sister's husband, and almost violated all current morality by running away with him. Bounding back from this unhappy affair, she met one Henry M. Stanton, ten years older than she, at the Smith home. Immediately they fell in love, and on May 9, 1840, they were married. As emancipated young people believing in the equality of the sexes, they dropped the word "obey" from the marriage ceremony. As earnest reformers they spent their honeymoon attending an anti-slavery convention in England. Indelibly impressed on Elizabeth's mind was the refusal of the meeting to allow women delegates to sit on the floor of the hall.

The young couple settled in Boston, where Henry practiced law and Elizabeth kept house, with spare hours devoted to the theater, concerts, and all sorts of reform lectures. When Henry's health deteriorated the couple moved, in 1847, to Seneca Falls. Elizabeth missed the activity of Boston, and now spent her extra energy in working for abolition and temperance. Like many other such women workers, she was increasingly irritated by the criticisms leveled at women who spoke in public before mixed audiences. Such criticisms, placed upon a background of protest against the position of women, inspired her to enter the struggle for greater rights for her sex, which she soon stressed as the most important of all reforms.

That Mrs. Stanton and her friends should be dissatisfied with the place of women in the United States came as a very unpleasant surprise to most Americans. Weren't American women better off than women elsewhere? Weren't they respected and honored, and practically revered? Weren't they preserved from demeaning contacts with the rough competition of the male world? Weren't they fulfilling their natural functions as wives and mothers? Weren't they obeying God's law as stated in the Bible, and realizing their own innate desires? Most Americans concluded that the protestors must be either strong-minded married women who wanted to wear the pants of the family, or disappointed spinsters who had failed to trap husbands.

The feminists reacted far differently. They pointed out that women received inferior educations, that most jobs were not open to them, that their pay was inferior, and that they were almost completely debarred from such professions as medicine and law. Married women, according to the common law, could not control their property or services, and all women were grouped with children, the mentally defective, and criminals in not being permitted to vote.

The ladies emphasized particularly the legal rights of married women and the opportunity to vote. Now and then they caused themselves unnecessary trouble. The well-known Lucy Stone horrified the conventional by retaining her maiden name after marriage. Many of the women brought ridicule upon themselves in the early '50s by wearing a more comfortable type of feminine dress, a sort of Turkish trousers affair with a short overskirt. It was named after a Seneca Falls friend of Mrs. Stanton—Mrs. Amelia Bloomer.

For over forty years Elizabeth Stanton spent all the time she

tours. Later they traveled together. Susan always called Elizabeth "Mrs. Stanton," while Elizabeth responded with "Susan."

As a team Elizabeth and Susan were very effective. Susan was tall, gaunt, and severe-looking, with a deficient sense of humor—a fine target for the cracks about soured old maids. Susan rushed around making all the arrangements, and ultimately dropped into her seat exhausted. Elizabeth on the other hand rested, bathed, and primped before her appearance. On the platform she was dressed immaculately, usually in black with a touch of white, and with every lock of the beautiful white hair of later years in proper place. She was plump and motherly in appearance, and there was a twinkle in her eye. No wonder Mrs. Stanton always held the center of the stage.

Elizabeth was clearly the most effective of the early feminists. She gave the most appealing speeches and she had the greatest executive ability. Quite naturally she was the president of the National Woman Suffrage Association of 1869 and of its successor, the National American Woman Suffrage Association of 1890.

In the late 1880s Elizabeth Stanton began to slow down. In 1892 she passed to Susan Anthony her mantle as president of the feminist organization. By this time she had become almost a legend. Both her seventieth and her eightieth birthdays were celebrated nationally. By the 1890s her strength was declining and her vision failing. In 1902 she passed away quietly in her chair.

Elizabeth Stanton was one of the truly influential and successful people of her generation. Within her lifetime, and due in some part to her efforts, women's opportunities in education, sports, and economic affairs had expanded magnificently. Almost universally greater legal rights had been provided for married women. In various states women had been given the vote, and by the time of her death the woman suffrage amendment was not far in the future. While these developments represented much more than the efforts of any single person, the greatest credit still should go to the most effective feminist of her day—Elizabeth Cady Stanton.

Martin Van Buren

Occasionally the office has overwhelmed the man. Buchanan and Harding are good illustrations of this sad possibility, and there are some who would say that Grant's performance was so poor as to deprive him of the luster won as a general during the Civil War. Fortunately, this has not often happened.

More commonly the office has projected men of previously ordinary or unsuspected ability to the heights. Here Lincoln is the outstanding example. In the trying days before his inauguration he often seemed uncertain and evasive, his public statements trite. Once in office he became decisive and direct, his public pronouncements models of lucidity and style. In 1931 and 1932, to take another example, Bernard Baruch thought Franklin D. Roosevelt too "wishy-washy" to make a good Chief Executive and Walter Lippmann dismissed him as "a pleasant man, who, without any important qualifications for the office, would very much like to be President." Both, of course, were to change their opinion of Roosevelt completely after he entered the White House. And, although not all our Presidents have been Lincolns and Roosevelts, it nevertheless seems fair to say that the tendency has been for the office to bring out the best that its holder possesses.

In the next chapter Arthur M. Schlesinger, Jr., discusses the career of a President who has been much disparaged as a cheap and crafty politician, but who responded to the office, like Lincoln and Roosevelt, by rising to meet its challenges. Martin Van Buren did begin his public career as a politician. He ended it still a master of that trade, but a statesman as well. Professor Schlesinger teaches history at Harvard University. His many books include The Age of Jackson *and the still uncompleted* Age of Roosevelt. *These works have won him the Pulitzer, Parkman, and Bancroft prizes.*

". . . a consistent faith in the people"

ARTHUR SCHLESINGER, JR.

MARTIN VAN BUREN was not the first politician to become President; for, in their ways, Jefferson, Madison, Monroe, Adams, and Jackson were all politicians. But it can be said that Van Buren was the first professional politician in the modern sense to become President. None of his predecessors fully grasped the role in politics of the political machine, of local organization, of patronage, of the party press. Van Buren fully understood all these things—and invented and improved a good many of them. He was adept in politics on almost any level.

This is, of course, the reputation he bore when he was alive, and is the image that survives in our memory. He used to be known as the "Little Magician" or the "Flying Dutchman" or the "Red Fox of Kinderhook." John Randolph of Roanoke, a contemporary politician well known for his biting tongue, once said of Van Buren that he "rowed to his object with muffled oars." Van Buren himself was proud of his capacity to walk a tightrope on pressing public issues. In his *Autobiography* he tells of a conversation between two friends who had heard him give an important speech on the tariff. "That was a very able speech," one of them said. "Yes, very able," was the answer. Then, after a pause, the first man asked, "On what side of the tariff question was it?" It is characteristic of Van Buren that he should enjoy telling this story on himself. But beneath his political dexterity there lay a consistent faith in the people and a consistent desire to serve them. That is why Andrew Jackson so liked Van Buren and made him his political heir.

For, though Van Buren came to be an urbane and worldly gentleman, well known for his polished manners and dapper dress, he was born a poor boy, the son of a farmer and tavern-keeper in the small village of Kinderhook, near Albany. After scant schooling he entered a law office at the age of 14, and for six years, between sweeping the floor, lighting fires in winter, and copying legal papers, he pored over law books and prepared for a career at the bar. He was a first-rate lawyer; John Quincy Adams, indeed, wanted to appoint him to the Supreme Court. But his first interest was in politics. He rose steadily in the Dem-

debts. He led the fight for the extension of the suffrage in the New York constitutional convention. He advocated state regulation of the New York banking system. In the United States Senate he favored policies which would open up the western lands for settlement, and he attacked what seemed to him the political role of John Marshall's Supreme Court.

He supported Andrew Jackson in the election of 1828. Jackson in response called him to Washington as Secretary of State, and in the next years Van Buren established himself in Jackson's confidence. For his second term Jackson asked Van Buren to run on the ticket with him as candidate for the Vice-Presidency. And in 1836, when Jackson retired from the Presidency, he had the great satisfaction of seeing Van Buren nominated and elected as his successor.

Van Buren's term in the Presidency lay under the shadow of a great and bitter depression, which began in 1837, the worst depression our nation had had up to that time. The business interests blamed conditions on Jackson's refusal to renew the charter of the United States Bank, and seized upon the depression as an excuse for demanding that the government restore the Bank to its former position of power. But Van Buren instead proposed that the government place its money in its own depositories. This was known as the "independent treasury" or "subtreasury" system.

When Van Buren made it clear that he was determined to carry through his plan to divorce bank and state, he was mercilessly attacked by leading bankers, businessmen, and conservative politicians. But in 1840, after three years of violent controversy, the subtreasury measure was enacted. In the meantime Van Buren performed another act of importance. He declared that no person need work more than ten hours a day on federal public works. This government recognition of labor's demand for a ten-hour day was a vast encouragement to labor in its fight for decent working conditions.

In 1840 Van Buren came up for reelection. By now his Whig opponents had decided that they could not beat the Democrats by avowing themselves as the party of the aristocracy; they thought they might win if they could conceal their aristocratic prepossessions and present themselves as the party of the common man. This is what they did in 1840. They nominated a popular military hero, William Henry Harrison, famous for his victory over the Indians at Tippecanoe; they claimed that he lived in a log cabin and drank hard cider; and they staged great torchlight processions in which they marched the streets shouting "Tippecanoe and Tyler too!"

As part of their campaign strategy they tried to identify Van Buren as the real aristocrat. He was accused of living in luxury at the White House, drinking champagne and dining off golden plates. A hostile life of Van Buren, which Davy Crockett had been persuaded to sign before he left for the Alamo, even claimed that he wore a corset. The Democrats tried desperately to rally their forces. They called Van Buren "Old Kinderhook"—from which the expression O.K., first used in this campaign, may have been derived—and they started their own torchlight processions. But between the fury of the depression and the fury of the Whig campaign, they were beaten. Van Buren had to console himself with one of his own maxims: "The sober, second thought of the people is never wrong, and always efficient."

The defeated President was retired to Kinderhook to await the people's sober second thought. New issues were now becoming important, particularly the issue of slavery. Van Buren was at heart deeply opposed to the spread of slavery. When, in 1844, he was asked whether he favored the immediate annexation of Texas as desired by pro-slavery forces, he candidly stated his opposition. This courageous declaration angered Southern Democrats and lost him the Democratic nomination in 1844.

The Mexican War in 1846 raised the question of slavery extension in acute form. People began to ask: should slavery be permitted in the territory acquired from Mexico? Many northern Democrats in Congress said no, and Van Buren vigorously backed them up. In 1848 the anti-slavery forces decided to organize a new party of their own, the Free Soil party. When the Free Soilers met in their convention, they enthusiastically nominated Martin Van Buren as their candidate for President. And the former President now emerged from retirement to lead the fight against the slave power. He lost, of course, but

secure in his Jeffersonian belief in the people, refused to give an inch. He deserves to go down in history as a man of intelligence, of resolution, and of steady democratic faith.

Washington Irving, Edgar Allan Poe, Henry David Thoreau

American cultural standards have been largely derived from Europe, and especially from England. This fact has tended to make many Americans overly reverential of European achievements in all the arts. Until recently, to cite but one case, it has been common practice for American opera singers to take Italian-sounding stage names, the thought being that audiences in this country would not have proper respect for an American singer. Of course, it is true enough that the United States has not yet produced a Shakespeare or a Cervantes, a Beethoven or a Wagner, a Leonardo or a Rembrandt. But probably there has simply not been enough time; such genius may not even arise once in a century anywhere in the world. In any case, the American tendency to disparage its own creative artists, fortunately rapidly disappearing, was never really justified by the facts.

The first field in which Americans achieved the top rank was literature. By the middle of the nineteenth century a large number of writers born and trained in the United States were producing novels, stories, poems, essays, and historical works that were comparable to most of the similar work being done in Europe. Hawthorne, Longfellow, and Emerson in Massachusetts, Irving, Cooper, Whitman, and Melville in New York, and Edgar Allan Poe were outstanding. But there were many others of note, such as Thoreau, Oliver Wendell Holmes, Richard Henry Dana, William Cullen Bryant, John Greenleaf Whittier, James Russell Lowell, James K. Paulding, William Gilmore Simms, and the historians Prescott, Motley, and Bancroft.

The mere listing of these names is impressive, and a book such as this can draw only a scattered sample for closer inspection. Washington Irving is interesting because he was one of the first American writers to attract a large audience, and because of his versatility. In addition to developing a wide range as an imaginative writer, Irving was also a serious historian and biographer. The late Claude G. Bowers, former United States Ambassador to Spain and Chile, wrote a number of popular works of history and biography, including three volumes on Thomas Jefferson and The Tragic Era, *a study of Reconstruction.*

Thoreau is representative of the artist's dedication to his work and his rejection of everything that interferes with his self-

author of a long list of distinguished volumes of literary history and criticism, discusses the great contributions made by Poe to the development of literature in America and in the world at large.

". . . a national asset"

CLAUDE G. BOWERS

A TRULY observant and constant visitor to the piers of early nineteenth-century New York might well have noticed a young man of slender build who spent most of the day gazing out to sea. His grey-blue eyes were lost in reverie as he dreamed of far places. The dreamer was Washington Irving, who lived near the river front with his father, an unimaginative, austere man. Irving's schooling was rudimentary, for, sad to relate, he was a rather lazy youth. Then, too, his father's financial status was such (he was a successful merchant) as to promise security for a long time to come. In time Irving was admitted to the bar, more as a favor to his family than as a right he had earned. "I think the young man knows a little law," one bar examiner observed dryly. "Make it stronger," said another. "I would say damn little." Washington Irving never practiced law. He did appear at Aaron Burr's trial for treason with a retainer in his pocket from the defendant, but he was a silent spectator as the really great lawyers crossed swords in verbal combat. It had been the desperate hope of the clever Burr that young Irving's pen might help to acquit him at the bar of public opinion.

In his twenty-first year Washington Irving sailed for a two-year tour of Europe. He visited old churches and art galleries, but he was mostly interested in people. He haunted the theatres, danced, and flirted whenever he found a pretty face. In the diary of his Roman sojourn he wrote that he had visited the churches, but added "to see the faces of the ladies." In Paris he played the dandy, and his diary teems with references to shirtmakers, bootmakers, and tailors. He had money, he was young and gay. The world was indeed his oyster.

Returning to New York, Irving plunged into the social whirl. The unfortunate death of a young girl he loved cast a shadow for a time over his activities. But he recovered sufficiently to woo another, who eventually refused him. Irving was destined to remain unmarried through life, but he never lost his zest for beautiful women.

The gay life he pursued began to drain his resources, and Irving was forced to take up his pen to earn money. With his brother, William, he wrote an amusing book of satirical essays patterned on Addison's *Spectator.* This work, which he called *The Salmagundi Papers,* quickly became the talk of New York. It was followed by *A History of New York,* a humorous work written under the pen name of Dietrich Knickerbocker.

In 1815 Irving returned to Europe for a stay of seventeen years. No American visitor to England, in the days following the troubled years of the War of 1812, did as much to reconcile the two English-speaking nations as did Irving. During his long stay his charming personality and manner, his learning and keen intelligence, did much to disabuse the British mind of its dim view of the Americans. In Irving the English saw an American whom they could admire and respect. Through his eyes they could see an America such as they had not conceived could exist. In them Irving saw the real English people, and he wrote of what he saw and felt with infinite charm. His understanding and affection glow in his *Sketch Book of Geoffrey Crayon, Gent.,* and in *Bracebridge Hall.* His imagination illuminated for the Americans all he saw. His readers were thrilled, as he was, with the historical scenes, the pageantry of England, the glory he saw.

Irving was welcomed into British literary circles, then at their most glorious. Sir Walter Scott rambled with him in the Scottish hills. The eccentric father of the incredible Disraeli opened to the young American the literary treasures of both his mind and his house. Tom Moore, the Irish poet, was a boon companion and regaled him with his songs. Byron hailed his friendship with delight. He was warmly welcomed to Holland House, where the [illegible]

[illegible] peared in four volumes.

Irving's research in Seville had intrigued him with the drama of Spain's history, particularly the struggle between the Moors and the Christians. His next book was the stirring history, *The Conquest of Granada.* In Seville Irving lived in an old Moorish palace. Though his apartment was pleasant, the lower floors were let out to tramps and ruffians of the town. As always, Irving's interest in people was so great that he made friends with his neighbors. From them he heard the strange tales that were to go into his next book, *The Alhambra.* The publication of this book created a lively interest in Spain among other Europeans and Americans, an interest which persists to this day. The late Duke of Alba said that Irving's fascinating book rendered a greater service to Spain than the work of any other writer who followed him.

Returning to New York after his seventeen years in Europe, Irving was hailed enthusiastically, for he had been the first American writer to gain European recognition. The doors of the socially elite were opened to him; writers paid him homage; statesmen acclaimed him as a national asset. Millionaire John Jacob Astor, then eighty, cultivated him. It was during a visit of some days to the Astor mansion that Irving urged the millionaire to devote a part of his fortune to the building of a public library in New York. The talk was to bear fruit when Astor bequeathed money for the purpose, naming Irving as an executor of the will. Thus was started the Astor Library, now The New York Public Library.

It was during the late 1840s that Irving made his tour of the

Middle and South West. The result was another book, *A Tour of the Prairies,* filled with many descriptive passages of great beauty. At the request of Astor, Irving wrote *Astoria*, the dramatic story of the fur trade in the far Northwest, where the Astor fortune had been made.

But Europe called him again. Years earlier he had served briefly as secretary of the United States Legation in London. He had found the diplomatic life pleasant. President Tyler, who delighted in his books, offered Irving the post of Minister to Spain. Irving was not particularly fond of politics. He had, in fact, refused the offer of Tammany Hall to make him Mayor of New York. He had also declined President Van Buren's invitation to enter his cabinet as Secretary of the Navy. But a diplomatic post, remote from politics as it was, seemed different.

So, for the next four years, Irving lived in Madrid. In his diaries of the time we see him going through the numerous salons of the Royal Palace to the Porcelain Room to present his credentials to the twelve-year-old Queen, Isabella. With the unscrupulous Queen Mother intriguing to control the throne of Spain, and with the great powers maneuvering to force on the girl a husband of their own choice, Irving's sympathy went out to the little child whom he characterized as "a pawn in a dirty game." He remained the girl's staunch champion throughout his four years as Ambassador. During the civil disturbances and the struggles of various factions for power in Spain, Irving maintained his traditional partiality for the liberals.

But illness began to exact its toll. Irving found himself under doctor's orders neither to read nor to write. His very soul struggled as he spent long hours thinking of his long-projected biography of George Washington. With the election of James Polk as President, Irving resigned and returned home. He bought ten acres on the banks of the Hudson at Tarrytown. There he retired in a house he named "Sunnyside." Now in his seventies, plagued by asthma, weary with the years, Irving shut himself away from the world. Doggedly he wrote on until, a few months before his death in 1859, he finished the fifth and last volume of his biography of our first President.

His course was almost run. Sitting under the trees on the broad lawns of "Sunnyside," his eyes on the Palisades across the Hudson, he passed his last days recalling happy memories. He died in his seventy-sixth year and was buried in the Sleepy Hollow Cemetery. A simple stone marks his resting place. Washington

Irving was the first American writer to gain European acclaim. He gave to the world some of the most delightful and imperishable characters in fiction: Rip Van Winkle, Dietrich Knickerbocker, the Headless Horseman of Sleepy Hollow, and many others who still charm and delight us. His histories and biogra-

". . . magnificent and haunting phrases"

HOWARD MUMFORD JONES

In his excellent book, *The Histrionic Mr. Poe,* after summarizing Poe's biography in less than four pages, Professor N.B. Fagin of the Johns Hopkins University says: "Assuredly Poe's life, thus presented in bare outline, does not add up to anything remarkable. It promises neither the romanticism of great deeds not the exoticism of great strangeness."

I not only agree with Mr. Fagin, I shall go him one better by condensing Poe's biography into a paragraph in order to get on to more important things. Edgar Allan Poe was born in Boston in 1809, of poor and mediocre actor parents who died when he was an infant. He was adopted, or thought he was, by John Allan, a Scotch merchant in Richmond, Virginia, but the adoption was repudiated later. Poe tried the University of Virginia, the Army of the United States, and West Point, and liked none of them. From 1831 to his death he kept alive in the miserable half-world of American magazines by writing poetry, fiction, and criticism, and by editorial work, always dreaming of a magazine of his own. He married Virginia Clemm when she was fourteen; she died of tuberculosis in 1847. In 1849 he was found unconscious outside a polling place in Baltimore and died in a hospital. Add that alcohol was bad for him, that he toiled terribly and never had enough money, that he was a pleasant, quiet gentleman who liked hoaxes and saw that striking a romantic attitude was one way to get on in literature, and you have his story. But you do not have the legendary Poe.

In a moment of irritation Nathaniel Hawthorne referred to his female contemporaries as a "damned mob of scribbling women." A mob of poetesses, together with Poe's unscrupulous biographer, Rufus W. Griswold, helped to create the Poe legend. As Poe translates easily into other languages—for example, French—the later French romanticists expanded this legend, so that by 1900 Poe had become his own Raven—a dark, saturnine figure coming out of midnight to sup on horrors and solve cryptograms. He became the literary equivalent of Paganini, the violinist, supposed to have sold his soul to the devil. Even now people will tell you that Poe wrote his stories under the influence of opium or alcohol. This is of course nonsense, but it has taken scholars a century to find out what Poe was really like.

Well, what was he like? In the first place, he seized upon certain elements then present in literature and did them better than any other American of his time. These elements included the literary hoax, usually an attempt to make the public believe something preposterous because it was scientific. Poe's story, *The Strange Case of M. Valdemar,* is an example. Then there was the terror story, like *The Fall of the House of Usher* and *The Pit and the Pendulum.* There was the literary travesty or burlesque; Poe wrote a good many of these, but we do not care for them today. There was also what I call prose poetry—the sort of thing you get in famous passages from De Quincey's *Confessions of an Opium Eater.* Examples from Poe are pieces like *Silence* or *The Colloquy of Monos and Una.*

A prose poem is, of course, difficult to define, and to modern ears is more often than not dismissed as a "purple passage." In such a passage the writer tends toward a rhythmical beat that grows more and more regular, as if it were verse, and also echoes or imitates such obvious examples of stately rhythm as the Bible. Poe's *The Masque of the Red Death* gets part of its hypnotic effect (or did, when readers could be thus enchanted) by the regularity of rhythm and the "elevated diction" of a paragraph like this:

> But these other apartments were densely crowded, and in them beat feverishly the heart of life. And the revel went whirlingly on, until at length there commenced the sounding of midnight upon the clock. And then the music ceased, as I have told; and

the evolutions of the waltzers were quieted; and there was an uneasy cessation of all things as before. But now there were twelve strokes to be sounded by the bell of the clock; and thus it happened, perhaps, that more of thought crept with more of time, into the meditations of the thoughtful among those who revelled. And thus too it happened

Then there was the detective story, a field in which Poe looks backward to Voltaire's *Zadig* and forward to Conan Doyle. Poe classified his detective fiction as "tales of ratiocination"—that is, his interest was in the process of reasoning from evidence by which the criminal is detected, and not in the brutality of the crime. We are not present at the time the beast kills his victims in *Murders in the Rue Morgue*, and, in fact, Poe seldom paints brutality. It is questionable whether modern writers of mystery stories have improved Poe's formula by strewing corpses all over their books or by the wrestling matches, physical assaults, and unofficial murdering of criminals that characterize the plots of a good many detective stories. Possibly detective fiction, for lack of a really fresh formula, is running out.

Finally, the era reveled in philosophic explanations of the universe; and in Poe's *Eureka* modern critics fancy they find anticipations of Einstein. Persons more skilled in metaphysics than I am, however, are not impressed by the assertion.

In the second place, Poe was a great, if narrow, poet, whose theory and practice go back to English romantics like Coleridge and forward to French poets like Baudelaire. Nobody before him in American literature was able to produce the magnificent and haunting phrases he could invent. Here is an example. The idea of a city drowned by the ocean is not uncommon, but listen to Poe's phrasing in his poem, "The City in the Sea":

> No rays from the holy heaven come down
> On the long night-time of that town;
> But light from out the lurid sea

Streams up the turrets silently—
Up domes—up spires—up kingly halls—
Up fanes—up Babylon—like walls—
Up shadowy long-forgotten bowers
Of sculptured ivy and stone flowers—
Up many and many a marvellous shrine
Whose wreathed friezes intertwine
The viol, the violet and the vine.

Why "The viol, the violet and the vine?" Why "the light from out the lurid sea?" Why is the light upside down? What are "Babylon-like walls?" No reason can be asked or given, but the effect of these vague, yet vivid, words is to create a dream-world, the world of the surrealist painter; and though Poe has only a few main themes in his poetry, that poetry is, at its best, unique and perfect.

In the third place, Poe was a great craftsman, a critic and theorist of craftsmanship. He enunciated the principles of short-story writing, and he laid down a consistent, if narrow, theory of poetry. As a reviewer he was sometimes guilty of flattery, but in the main he mercilessly exposed shoddy workmanship, and praised good writing. His was a kind of magic eye to discover flaws in what looked like acceptable literary goods. This emphasis upon craftsmanship seems to me the most characteristically American aspect of Edgar Allan Poe, who is sometimes thought to have no connection with our national life. But in his time the steamboat, the railroad, the threshing-machine, the electric telegraph, friction matches, and a hundred other inventions came into being. Each of these was the product of the same kind of ingenuity Poe brought to the craft of writing, and each demanded special technical skills for its manufacture and upkeep. So it was with Poe. He saw that writing is a craft, and he studied the principles of that craft—how to edit a magazine, how to write stories, how to make verse do what you want it to do. To this day, though there has been a falling off in his appeal (which is to say that we are no longer as awed by him as we once were), he is interesting to the moderns because he was a superb literary technician.

Nor has his influence upon American writing disappeared. It is felt in three important fields, at least. One is the field of literary criticism, perhaps of small interest to the general reader but of great interest to the specialist; and when the "New Critics" of our time expend, as they do, a great deal of effort in examining the text of a poem, they are following where Poe went before. Like them he thought the important fact is not what a poem *says,* but what a poem *is.*

Of larger interest for the general reader are two other fields in which the influence of Poe has been very great. One is the detective story.

for its effect upon a theory of vortices; *Ligeia,* which depends upon a psychological theory of the will; *The Masque of the Red Death,* which makes certain assumptions about disease and medicine, and so on. Poe's strange landscapes and stranger seas, his imaginative excursions into mesmerism and occult knowledge, his speculations about "burning" stars prepare us for the vast library of science fiction or of fantastic science which, in our time, has included such masterpieces as Ray Bradbury's *The Martian Chronicles* and *Fahrenheit 451.*

". . . practiced what he preached"

CARL BODE

WHAT would you think of some young neighbor of yours, just out of college, if he spent his mornings and afternoons walking around in the woods? Not much probably, and even less if everyone knew he was refusing not only the kind of work a college graduate was supposedly educated for, but also any odd jobs that would give him at least a few dollars.

You would no doubt be as unbelieving as Henry Thoreau's neighbors of a century and a quarter ago if somebody told you that this young fellow would go on to become one of our finest essayists, and the author of an American classic, *Walden;* that he would, in fact, become both a great writer and a highly effective propagandist and revolutionary—for he set down some of his radical ideas so ably that they reached across the oceans to Gandhi of India and the founders of the Labour Party in England.

Thoreau the propagandist and Thoreau the man of letters are not contradictory. He practiced what he preached. He could write what he did because he refused to let the world force him to waste his time making an ordinary living. He refused to conform and he paid a penalty; but he also secured advantages for himself that we who read his great works are still grateful for.

Here is how he met his problem. Even before he graduated from Harvard in 1837, at twenty, he knew what he wanted to do with his life. He wanted to be a poet—not merely a writer of rhymes but almost a seer. So he returned to the little Massachusetts town of Concord, where his family lived, and began to roam regularly through the countryside which surrounded the village. Then at night he wrote about the scenery, the plants, and the animals he had observed and—equally important—what he thought about the things he had looked at. He viewed the woods and streams as a philosopher.

His family loyally defended him, while the neighbors sniffed. But Concord's greatest man, Ralph Waldo Emerson, some fourteen years older than Henry, quickly recognized Thoreau's genius. Thoreau would always be too independent to act as anyone's disciple, even Emerson's, yet there is no doubt that his ideas resembled Emerson's and that he, like the Concord wise man, was a Transcendentalist. He believed that the reality of mind was superior to and transcended the reality of matter, and that learning through intuition was superior to learning through our five senses.

With Emerson's blessing, Thoreau soon submitted articles and poems to a new periodical that Emerson had helped to found and edit. This was the *Dial,* one of the most noted of all "little magazines." Before it ended its brief career in 1845, Henry was drafted to do some of the editing himself. Nevertheless he was forced to realize that he could not keep himself alive by either editing or writing. In the spring of 1845 he decided to build a cabin next to beautiful Walden Pond, only a mile away from Concord, to see if he could live off the land for a while. He had tried some teaching and tutoring, in spite of his scruples about employment; he had tried the New York literary market; and—least unpalatable—he had tried living off his family at home. But none of these solutions worked out, so Thoreau moved to his cabin on July 4, thereby signalizing his personal declaration of independence.

He stayed at Walden for two remarkably fruitful years. He spent a minimum of his time in making a living. He cultivated his bean patch and supplemented his needs with trips to his …

… civilization. In the second, it was a stirring indictment of the rest of us for wasting our lives making a living instead of doing what we really wanted to do. "The mass of men," said Henry Thoreau looking straight at us, "lead lives of quiet desperation." In the third place, *Walden* was a unique literary masterpiece, written in a style of deceptive ease and lucidity.

Rewarding though his stay at Walden Pond was, Thoreau did not propose to spend the rest of his life there, so he returned to Concord for the remainder of his controversial existence. He took up where he had left off in 1845, when he had refused to pay his poll tax because he did not want to support a government that condoned war and slavery. Concord's jailer had regretfully put him in prison for a night, and out of that night came one of Henry's best essays, "Civil Disobedience." This was the one that influenced Gandhi to a marked extent; as Gandhi himself declared, "It left a deep impression on me."

As the 1850s drew to a close, Thoreau became more and more involved in abolitionism. He had started with only faint sympathy for the abolitionists, and he had no hesitation in giving his reason bluntly. He said to them in effect: why are you spending your time in trying to free the slaves when you yourselves are still chained by all kinds of weaknesses and prejudices? However, as the tension between the North and the South increased, he was drawn into the struggle. When he met the dynamic and fanatical John Brown of Kansas, he felt that here was as dedicated a man as he had ever seen. When Brown was executed after the raid on Harper's Ferry, Thoreau called a meeting in Concord to eulogize him, and wrote some of his most burning lines in Brown's defense.

In the last year or two before the Civil War, Thoreau's reputation as a writer started to spread. He began to be counted among our outstanding literary men. The newly born *Atlantic Monthly* contracted for a series of essays from him, and his book *Walden* began to attract disciples here and there. But tuberculosis, the family weakness of the Thoreaus, gradually made its inroads. He was quite a while in dying, but when he did die, on May 6, 1862, it was as a philosopher should. When his aunt asked him if he had made his peace with God, Henry's reply was that he had never quarreled with Him. And it was obvious that he had not. "Never saw a man dying with so much pleasure and peace," reported the same Concord jailer who had once held Henry overnight because of the poll tax.

Old Bill Williams

purchased in 1819, and in 1845 Texas was annexed. The following year the American claim to the Oregon territory was recognized by Great Britain, and in 1848, following the Mexican War, California and the vast regions of the Southwest became part of the United States. By mid-century, except for Alaska and the soon-to-be-acquired Gadsden Purchase, the nation had achieved its present continental limits.

One of the great tasks facing the country was the development of its huge western wilderness. Among the first Americans to push out into the region were the fur traders and trappers, the Mountain Men of whom Old Bill Williams, described here by Ray Allen Billington, was one of the most colorful. As Billington points out, the West burned its brand deep on men like Old Bill. But they, in turn, left their mark upon the West, and upon American history. In their brief heyday, from about 1825 to 1845, they roamed wide and far. They were the men who discovered the best routes over the Great Divide and into the rich valleys nestled in the mountains where agriculture was possible. The trappers' tales (tall as well as true) kindled the imaginations of the stay-at-homes, encouraging them to sell out and push westward to the mountains and California. The Mountain Men also undermined the culture and power of the Indians by introducing them to liquor and the white man's diseases, and by making them dependent upon the products of the white man's civilization. In short, although their reign was brief their influence was very large.

Ray Allen Billington is Professor of History at Northwestern University and the author of many books, including The Protestant Crusade *and* The Far Western Frontier.

"... *touched by the wand of savagery*"

RAY ALLEN BILLINGTON

THE Mountain Men who roamed the beaver streams of the Far West in the early nineteenth century showed, by their reversion to the primitive, the corrosive effect of the frontier environment on American pioneers. Faced with the problem of existence in a world of ever-present danger, they altered their appearance and the pattern of their lives until they were scarcely distinguishable from their Indian foes. Their clothes, their food, their fighting skills, were those of savagery rather than civilization. But their transformation did not stop there. After a few years in that strange world the trappers were not only living as the red men lived, they were thinking as the red men thought.

This mutation was nowhere better shown than in the person of Old Bill Williams. Born in the North Carolina backwoods in 1787, and reared in a log cabin on the Missouri frontier, Bill spent his formative years learning to trap and hunt and call the wilderness his home. Unlike many of the youths bred in the backwoods, he was deeply religious even as a boy, and it was this devotion that first led him to forsake the home of his father. When only seventeen years old Williams tucked a Bible and a handful of religious tracts into his saddle bags and started west, bent on preaching to the Osage Indians whose villages lay just beyond the settlements.

However, once among the red men, this impressionable lad was soon touched by the wand of savagery. Fitting easily into the indolent pattern of Indian life, he married an Osage maiden, and rapidly shifted his interest from preaching to hunting. By the time he reached the Rocky Mountain country in 1825, Old Bill (for he was thirty-eight now and an old man by frontier standards) was dedicated to a life in the forest.

And what a life he led! A lone wolf by nature, he was passionately fond of solitude, and happy only when far from the haunts of men. Other Mountain Men saw him only now and then, when he suddenly emerged from the forest to join them about the camp fire, his pack mule laden with a king's ransom in beaver pelts, or when he drifted into Bent's Fort or Taos with such an enormous thirst that his year's profits were squandered before it was satisfied. "Old Solitaire," they called him in awed voices, as they found the ashes of his fires amidst the pine-shaded streams of the upper Missouri country or beside the sun-drenched Gila. And Old Solitaire he remained during his years in the mountains, so divorced from civilization that he preferred loneliness or the

Indian squaw, and finally his own scalp. When Williams or any other Mountain Man lost, there was never a moment of mourning. Instead they shrugged their ill fortune away with a "There goes ha'r and beaver," and started for the beaver streams again. Misers were unknown among men who risked their lives daily; security was a concept as alien to the trappers as to their red-skinned foes.

For all his wild sprees and reckless gambling, Bill Williams retained much of the mystical nature that had turned him toward a missionary career as a boy; but even this was altered by the world in which he lived. Christianity he abandoned, borrowing from the Indians their belief that dreams portrayed future happenings and that each man had his good and bad "medicine." From them, too, he adopted belief in the transmigration of souls. As he worried about his fate in after-life, he gradually convinced himself that after death he would return to one of his favored spots as a buck elk. On more than one occasion Bill told his companions exactly what he would look like, even to the details of markings on the buck's skin, and warned them that if they saw such an elk grazing on the Bayou Salado they were not to shoot. No Indian could have accepted such a concept more literally.

From the red men, too, Old Bill and all the Mountain Men borrowed the language that they used in their rare moments of conversation. He spoke in a high-pitched voice with a strong nasal twang, emphasizing each syllable carefully as did the Indians, whose dialects he spoke as well as he did his native tongue. As he talked he gestured frequently and meaningfully, for all trappers were adept in the sign language that was used in inter-tribal communication. The language that he used showed the Indian influence in its colorful imagery. To him, and to all mountaineers, a man was a "child," or a "hoss," or a "coon." A hungry person was "wolfish" and needed to fill his "meatbag" with "cowmeat" or "buffler meat"; one drank to satisfy his "dry." To scalp an Indian was to "lift his ha'r" or "tickle his fleece," while one who had been killed had been "rubbed out" or had "gone under." Winter was "robe season" or "freezin' time"; to hide was to "cache." Nor could Bill or any other trapper utter more than a few words without injecting the "ugh" and the "wah" and the "heap" that the natives used constantly.

On one occasion Old Bill told of the time he was attacked by three braves: "Thar was a piece o' brush alongside th' river about a rifle shot distant, en this child tuk for them willows. All I had war my ha'r en' my possibles en' my toothpicker here. Them Injuns jes' kep' comin', en' this old hoss only touched the ground a time or two, fer I didn't aim ter let them Injuns rub me out. Them bucks fetched me twict, onct in the shoulder and onct in the thigh, but I made them willows. Injuns air all the same some way; they don't hanker ter take no chances an' alluz aim ter jump yer without yer lookin'. Them dogs didn't foller me fur, cuz they aimed to get me by spyin'. It sure would a taken mor'n them Injuns ter get me in them willows with th' dark all settled down. I cached, I did. Them arrers hadn't o' done no great sight o' harm, 'cept in th' meat o' my leg en I butchered it out. T'other only cut my shirt a little—th' buckskin stopped her. I slipt a' past 'em en tuk to th' hills afore mornin'. Then I war safe."

Like the Indians whose phrases they copied, the Mountain Men could no more find happiness among their countrymen than a wild animal could enjoy a cage. Old Bill tried life in the settlements once or twice, but never for long. Once, after a successful hunting trip, he invested his savings in a Taos store. For a few weeks he haggled with Mexican women over the price of pins and yardgoods, before the lure of the wilderness grew too strong to resist. Then he suddenly began grabbing up bolt after bolt of cloth, carrying them into the street and yelling to attract a crowd. To the housewives who gathered he shouted: "Here—if I can't sell you goods, I'll give them to you." After he grew tired of watching them scramble for the calico he shouldered his rifle and disappeared into the forest once more.

In 1841, Bill decided to visit his family in Missouri, but he was soon convinced of his mistake. Even the drafty frontier cabin seemed close and confining to such a child of the wilderness; he found he could sleep only by taking his blankets outside, much to the amazement of his relatives, for snow covered the ground. Nor did he make himself more popular when, hankering for some Mountain Man food, he occasionally ate raw meat. Neither Bill nor his friends breathed a sigh of regret when he returned to the

the Far West where agricultural opportunity beckoned. There was even fantastic talk of a railroad to span the plains and mountains and connect California with the Mississippi valley.

Old Bill Williams went to his death in the service of a company of explorers seeking a feasible railroad route across the Rockies. Their commander, Colonel John C. Frémont, hired Bill as guide, then refused to listen to his advice on mountain passes until disaster overtook the party. Early in 1849 Old Bill was sent to lead Dr. B. J. Kern, a scientist accompanying Frémont, and a few Mexican helpers back to a cache on the upper Rio Grande where valuable goods had been stored. Unerringly the old Mountain Man led them to the spot, where the little band camped for the night while the Mexicans packed the goods on ponies. As they sat about the camp fire they had no thought of danger.

The Utes, however, were on the warpath, and had just suffered a humiliating defeat at the hands of a company of federal troops. A dozen Indians, thirsting to avenge their brothers who had died in this battle, stumbled on Old Bill's campfire. They approached with assurances of friendship, then suddenly whipped out their guns and shot Old Bill and Dr. Kern dead. The Mexicans were allowed to return to Taos with the tale; the Indians, they were told, were at war only with the white men.

Thus did Old Bill Williams die as he had lived, amidst the snow-clad mountains that were his home, and at the hands of Indians who had been his companions. Ironically enough, the band of Utes who sent a bullet between his eyes had, when he was a young man, adopted him into their tribe; life was often cruel and unpredictable in the mountains. With him passed an age as well as a man, for the Mountain Men had played their role in history. Over the trails they had blazed were to pass the trains of covered wagons that carried the true conquerors of the Far West: the small farmers who helped win California and Oregon for American civilization.

"Thus," mourned a newspaper of the day, "died Bill Williams —a fair specimen of the old Mountaineer, a set of men now nearly extinct; a set of men who possessed as warm hearts, as noble purposes, and as courageous spirits as could be found in any state of society. Rude and unpolished, but tender and true; firm in fight, but gentle as a woman to misfortune and distress—true Paladins of the mountains and the plains."

Samuel F. B. Morse and Samuel Colt

Hall McCormick, and Henry Ford, and brilliant technicians like Eli Whitney and Thomas A. Edison.

If there is anything at all in the old saw about necessity's relation to invention, the chronic labor shortage in the United States fostered the search for machines and gadgets to do work for which human hands and muscles simply could not be found. But probably the fact that America was a new and rapidly expanding country where there was no "traditional" way of doing many of the things that had to be done is even more significant for an understanding of the inventiveness of Americans. From the earliest days Americans learned to "make do" with the materials at hand, to improvise in order to deal with novel conditions, to value versatility, practicality, and imagination. If the West produced in the Mountain Men a very special type of mentality, so the whole country placed a premium on its sons and daughters developing a spirit of curiosity, a flexibility, a quick acceptance of novelty and change, and all these characteristics stimulated not only invention but also the welcoming by the public of new machines, new products, and new ways of producing goods. While there is much truth to the theory that inventors are often cheated of the rewards of their creativity, an astonishing number of our inventors have fulfilled their dreams and accumulated handsome fortunes.

The two inventors treated here, Samuel F. B. Morse and Samuel Colt, illustrate many of the generalizations applicable to American inventors and their work. Morse was only an inventor by avocation; his profession was that of artist, and he was a first-class painter, as James Thomas Flexner makes clear. But in America one did not have to be an expert to have one's work accepted—provided the work was demonstrably useful, as Morse's telegraph so clearly was. America's tremendous growth and expansion, which meant, before Morse, long delays in the transmission of messages back and forth between far-distant points, obviously stimulated men to search for means of rapid communications with special diligence. So, too, was Samuel Colt a typical Yankee tinkerer, fooling with explosives and whittling model revolvers, and at the same time a shrewd practical businessman, capitalizing on his skills, developing an efficient organization, and displaying amazing talents as a salesman.

James Thomas Flexner is the author of The Traitor and the Spy, Mohawk Baronet, *and a number of important books on the history of American art. Roger Burlingame has written biographies of such men as Henry Ford and General "Billy" Mitchell, and, among many other books about industry and invention,* Machines that Built America.

"... the gift for practical things"

JAMES THOMAS FLEXNER

Samuel Finley Breese Morse had two separate careers. For the first half of his life he was a painter, one of the leaders of that profession. For the second half he was an inventor, the inventor of the telegraph.

The New England into which Morse was born during 1791 was in rapid social flux. His native Massachusetts was still dominated by an economic and intellectual aristocracy which had survived —had, indeed, done much to direct—the American Revolution. This aristocracy was endangered by democratic forces that, having made Jefferson President in 1800, were to sweep on, bringing to America the belief that every man was as good as every other. Son of a conservative Congregational minister, Morse was by birth committed to the losing aristocratic side. He was to see his father, Jedediah Morse, the famous author of *The American Geography*, expelled from his pulpit by a congregation which no longer believed in the old Puritan doctrine that God had divided the people by predestination into the elect and the irrevocably damned.

Because of the traditional belief that any profession that involved working with your hands was unsuitable for a gentleman, Morse's father opposed his desire to be an artist. But this prejudice was weakening all over the United States; the appearance in Boston of Washington Allston, a painter of impeccable South Caro-

mantic artists. The highest form of art, Morse was told, avoided the commonplaces of modern life and sought "the ideal" through depictions of such scenes from the past as had occupied the great masters of the Renaissance. Banning from his canvases the American world that had given him birth, Morse painted "The Judgment of Jupiter" and "The Dying Hercules."

When financial necessity drove him to painting portraits, he felt that he was, as he put it: "lowering by noble art to a trade . . . degrading myself and the soul-enlarging art I possess to the narrow idea of making money." His ambition, he explained, was to "revive the splendor of the fifteenth century, to rival the genius of a Raphael, a Michelangelo, or a Titian." That the fifteenth century was long dead, and that a new way of life was being worked out in his native land, only made his labor of reconstruction seem more important. Morse did not wish to express American culture but to elevate it.

After four student years in England, he was finally forced by lack of funds to return to a United States still devoid of museums and major examples of European painting. Since the type of art he wished to practice had no relevance to what did actually exist around him—American landscape and American life—he felt he could only mark time as a painter until he could somehow manage a trip to Italy. He had written in Europe: "If I cannot live a gentleman, I will starve a gentleman." But he could not bear to starve. He made his living from what he considered ungentlemanly work: painting portraits.

Paradoxically, this unwilling expedient produced his best pictures. Morse was not endowed with the ability to be a truly imaginative artist. Although he felt superior to the majority of his fellow-countrymen, he shared with them the gift for practical things which had been nurtured on this continent by generations of coping with the wilderness. A portrait is a practical thing, a reflection of reality. Morse painted excellent portraits, although he continued to feel that he was degrading himself.

In discouragement he turned to worldly matters, and made a very practical contribution: he spearheaded the organization of the National Academy of Design, which gave younger artists a chance to study, older artists to exhibit their work. But in his inaugural address as president of the new body, he expressed his own frustrations. The United States, he stated, was "a cold and sterile desert" where great art could neither be created nor appreciated.

His high office resulted in his receiving many commissions. Morse was soon able to afford the trip to Italy which he believed would raise him to rivalry with Raphael and Titian. But the opportunity he had dreamed of during his fourteen unhappy years as an American portraitist only threw him into despair. He found that the way of painting which had been natural for fifteenth century Italians was impossible for him. Unable, because of his long-nurtured prejudices, to accept the conclusion that all art, be it realistic or imaginative, must spring from the society in which it is created, he turned angrily on the profession which he believed had betrayed his ideals. "Painting," he wrote a few years later, "has been a smiling mistress to many, but she has been a cruel jilt to me. I did not abandon her; she abandoned me . . . I could wish that every picture I ever painted was destroyed."

Long after Morse had reached this conclusion, his fellow artists continued to elect him to the presidency of the National Academy, for the same desire for an artistic "ideal" irrelevant to American life afflicted the most ambitious of his contemporaries. Painter after painter ended his career in sterility. It was only when the younger generation applied techniques learned at home or abroad to scenes and emotions that appealed naturally to them that a true American art began to flourish. As members of the Hudson River School, these new painters gleefully depicted American landscapes and life.

Morse too found achievement and greater prosperity, but only at the price of abandoning art for business. His ideals, as he believed, shattered, he forgot his ancestral prejudices and allowed the practical side that was dominant in his nature to take over. On the ship home from the European trip that had destroyed him as a painter, he conceived the idea of the telegraph. The theoretical researches that made the invention possible had been carried out by other men with more soaring imaginations; Morse's concern was with using known properties of electricity to transmit information. This was a problem that could not have been solved in the fifteenth century of Raphael or Titian; that could not, in-

sender's key. At the receiver's end, the impulse activated electromagnets that, by pulling on a sound-making device, gave the quick or slow pattern of clicks that the operators translated back into letters and words. This was the heart of Morse's invention, although he had to solve many other scientific problems, the most vital of which was how to keep his current from fading out as it passed through many miles of wire.

With a rush, Morse had moved from the past to the present. He still talked condescendingly of his fellow Americans—that habit was too deeply seated to be abandoned—but now he worked side by side with them on a project that was a natural outgrowth of their common culture. He no longer reacted against business considerations; he was determined to secure a patent and make a fortune. This brought him into daily contact with facets of contemporary life he had once denounced or ignored. He grappled with politicians for special privileges and lured capital from money-men; he cooperated with friendly scientists and fought those who claimed he had stolen their discoveries. Organization of his environment was, indeed, as important to his eventual triumph as the wires he strung around his studio where unfinished pictures gathered dust.

Enthusiastically applying those talents which, even when applied half-heartedly, had made him an effective portraitist, on May 24, 1844, Morse sent from Washington to Baltimore his famous message: "What hath God wrought!" The telegraph was now a reality. By giving in to his own nature and making effective use of the nature of his times, Morse earned wealth and fame. Yet he carried to the end of his life a psychological wound because he had failed in his ambition to be a fifteenth-century artist.

"... *five times without reloading*"

ROGER BURLINGAME

MOST Americans know that Samuel Colt invented the revolver. What is less understood is the part Colt played, along with Eli Whitney and Henry Ford, in making mass production a reality. On the long road between the muskets of Eli Whitney in 1800 with their interchangeable parts and the first automobile assembly lines in Detroit, more than a century later, Samuel Colt stands midway. His fabulous factory at Hartford, Connecticut, in the 1850s is a real landmark in the progress of American industry. He did not invent all the elaborate pistol-making machines in that factory, but he had genius enough to pick the one man in the country who could invent them. And he master-minded the whole process. Incidentally, in addition to his mechanical talents he was a super salesman. That is a rare combination. His story is strange, full of dramatic ups and downs, but, in the end, it is above all a story of success.

At fifteen Sam was regarded as the bad boy of his neighborhood. The son of a Massachusetts dyer, he had picked up a rudimentary knowledge of chemistry from his father's shop. Nowadays there is a close connection between dyestuffs and explosives, but in the 1820s synthetic chemistry was far in the future. It was pure coincidence that Sam's mind was forever playing with explosive chemicals while he worked with the simple, natural colors his father used.

Whenever there was a startling noise near the town of Ware, Massachusetts, the people would say: "There's Sam." On the Fourth of July, 1829, something happened that finished his career in Ware, but at the same time brought about a meeting that affected the whole of his later life. He had advertised that, to celebrate Independence Day, he would blow a raft sky-high on Ware Pond. A big crowd, dressed in their best holiday clothes, came to watch. The explosion went off on schedule, but the raft had drifted from the designated spot and a shower of mud from the bottom of the pond fell on the gala throng. Two men seized Sam and would have ducked him in the pond but for the intervention of a powerful stranger. Taking Sam aside he asked how he had exploded the mine. "I know you had an electric battery," he said, "but how did you produce a spark under water to detonate the explosive?" Sam replied that, grateful as he was to his rescuer, he must keep his secret. "I aim to be an inventor," he said, "and inventors mustn't talk." "You are quite right," said the man. "I too, am an inventor. My name is Elisha Root. I hope we meet again."

[illegible]

it was the beginning, and for the next few years the boy could think of nothing else.

His father was impressed and lent him money. By the spring of 1832 a gunsmith had made a good working model incorporating the improvements Sam had designed. It had a rotating, cylindrical, chambered breech automatically revolved and locked and unlocked by cocking the hammer. Nothing like it had even been seen before. In those muzzle-loading days a firearm that would shoot five times without reloading was a weapon of inestimable value.

But the money had given out. The next ten years were disheartening for Sam. In 1832 he tried to forget the revolver, and started out on a trip determined to make money any way he could. At that time nitrous oxide, or laughing gas, had just been discovered. So Colt organized a lecture tour, advertising himself as a scientist. He delighted audiences through New England and New York by intoxicating people with the gas. On this tour he displayed the showmanship that was to make him such a high-powered salesman in later life.

By 1836 he had got English and American patents and interested some backers. A company was formed and produced in five years some five thousand revolvers. Through the mismanagement of Colt's backers, the company failed in 1842 and Sam was nearly ruined.

In the meantime the revolvers had got out to where they were most needed. In Florida and in Texas they revolutionized Indian warfare. The Indians who had won fight after fight with their accurate arrows against men who had to load rifles through the muzzle were completely demoralized by Colt's five- and six-shooters.

In 1845 an army officer named Sam Walker looked up Colt. He said there was likely to be war with Mexico and the government needed a thousand of the now-famous revolvers immediately. He offered $28,000. Colt knew where they could be made. But he did not have a single pistol to give the manufacturer as a model. Every gun shop in the East was sold out. In his poverty he had sold all his own pistols. So, as he had done at sixteen, he whittled a revolver out of wood and took it to the Whitney arms factory near New Haven. There Eli Whitney, Jr., son of the great inventor, was making fire-arms on the interchangeable parts system designed by his father. Colt made a contract with Whitney for the thousand pistols to be made in jig time. But one clause in that contract showed Colt's smartness in business. Colt knew all about revolvers but nothing about large-scale gun manufacture. So his contract stated that all the special machines Whitney would have to make for the job should become Colt's property after the revolvers were made.

With these machines Colt started his own revolver factory. He had the machines but he did not have what we call the know-how of quantity production. So he looked around for a manager. He found him in an axe factory in Collinsville, Connecticut, where this giant of a man had proved himself an inventive genius in axe-making machinery. Colt thought there was something familiar about him. His name was Elisha Root. Since the day he had rescued the fifteen-year-old boy at Ware Pond, he and Sam had never seen each other.

Together Colt and Root established in Hartford the largest fire-arms factory in history up to that date. With it came the nearest approach to mass production the world had ever seen. There were hundreds of machines for rifling, boring, drilling, and milling and arrangements for assembling that were models for later automotive shops.

Colt also established a similar factory in London, but English workmen could never adjust themselves to the American system —the Eli Whitney system of interchangeable parts manufacture. Meanwhile, however, the revolver had become famous all over the world. Colt himself played a large part in getting it known. He displayed it at the London World's Fair in 1851. He used all sorts of high-pressure salesmanship, often to the annoyance of conservative Englishmen, but they had to buy. The revolver was used extensively in campaigns in South Africa and India. It was sold in every country in Europe and in Turkey. In America it became a veritable symbol of the Wild West. It played an important part in winning the Mexican war and it was of great value in the Civil War for mounted troops.

Colt died in 1862, a milli[illegible]

Horace Mann and Francis Lieber

Americans have always been confirmed believers in the importance of education, and leaders in the development of public schools. In our own day, for example, arguments about the quality of our school programs should not be allowed to obscure the basic fact that a larger percentage of young people are being educated than in any other country in the world. Everyone realizes that a democratic system of government presupposes an educated electorate, for only the educated can be counted upon to make informed and sensible decisions on public questions.

But the history of American education has not been free from controversy. Today's axiom was yesterday's wild theory, and agreement about principles does not settle details. Should education be free for everyone, and, if so, how far should the state take the citizen along the road to learning? Does every citizen have a "right" to a college degree, or even a high school diploma, or should he have merely the privilege of competing against stiff standards and proceed at public expense only as far as his intelligence will carry him? This latter was Jefferson's view; in his day it was the radical position, but now we consider it very conservative. In any event the question remains controversial, and it is but one of many agitating the educational world.

There have always been powerful anti-intellectual influences at work in American education. The crudeness of frontier life put a premium on action rather than thought, and depreciated the importance of intellectual accomplishments. The democratic tradition led to the glorification of the ordinary man over the genius and the self-trained man over the possessor of diplomas and degrees. Our great folk heroes have been men like Jackson and Lincoln, who had little formal schooling, and like Edison and Ford, who made important contributions to science and technology without the benefit of college training. It was absurdly easy in early America to qualify as a lawyer or physician. How many cases were unfairly decided, how many lives lost because of the low standards in the professions can no longer be deter-

mined. But Americans of those times did not appear to care; it seemed more significant that Chief Justice John Marshall, to cite a single illustration, had risen to eminence despite having attended law school for only six weeks.

The two figures from the world of education in our gallery of

... formed in the politics of liberty." He would not have disagreed with Mann's basic postulates. Mann and Lieber also had in common another trait frequently found among educators. They were both reformers. The same urge that makes a teacher try to improve the knowledge and power of the individual student often expresses itself in an urge to improve society by ridding it of evils.

Philip Davidson, President of the University of Louisville, is the author of Propaganda and the American Revolution. *Frank Freidel, Professor of History at Harvard, has written many books, including a life of Francis Lieber and* The Splendid Little War. *His major undertaking is a six-volume life of Franklin D. Roosevelt, of which three volumes have so far appeared.*

". . . free, universal, and democratic"

PHILIP DAVIDSON

Horace Mann, more than any other one person, has made the American Dream a reality in education, for he made the common school universal, free, and democratic. As secretary of the Massachusetts Board of Education from 1837 to 1848 he made those twelve short years the most creative period in the educational history of this country. He came to his office in what a New Englander would call mud time. He made it seed time in education, and we today are in the harvest time of his ideas and philosophy. Out of his fertile mind, out of his devotion to children and the community, out of his tremendous energy, came a philosophy of education and a system of common schools that took deep root and spread widely throughout this land. His ideas influenced the policies and practices of many a foreign country. He is truly the father of the common school, "the greatest discovery," he once said, "ever made by man."

This man of genius was born in 1796 in the little Massachusetts village of Franklin. He was graduated from Brown University in 1819 and two years later entered the famous Litchfield, Connecticut, law school. In 1827 he was elected to the Massachusetts House of Representatives, rising to be president of the Senate in 1836. His first wife, Charlotte Messer, a frail, lovely girl, lived only two years after their marriage, and her death was a crushing blow. "My life," he wrote, "went out of itself." Eleven years later he married Mary Peabody, who was a continuing inspiration to him. She was much interested in education and in the reform movements of the time, and took an active part in his work. Her biography of him is the most revealing we have.

In 1837 he found his true career and happiness in the secretaryship of the newly created Massachusetts Board of Education. "Henceforth, so long as I hold this office," he wrote in his journal the day he accepted the position, "I devote myself to the supremest welfare of mankind on earth." Horace Mann's incomparable achievements in the twelve years that followed were made in the face of great obstacles. The Board which he served had no authority to compel, only to persuade. There were separate, autonomous school districts instead of a common system. There was apathy and indifference instead of interest and enthusiasm, active opposition instead of lively cooperation.

For twelve years he worked incessantly. In the midst of one controversy he wrote his physician: "Can you do anything for a brain that has not slept for three weeks?" The basic philosophy which guided him was simple: in a republic, ignorance is a crime. He believed in the absolute right of every individual who comes into this world to an education suited to his abilities and interests. But this education must not be given him just for his selfish purposes. "It is a monumental question," he wrote in his ninth report, "whether the children in our schools are educated in reference to themselves and their private interests only, or with regard to the great social duties and prerogatives that await them in after life." The answer, he made clear, was that education should have primarily a social purpose.

Education therefore must be free, universal, and democratic. It must promote no political or sectarian cause, but only the cause of mankind.

Throughout his life his favorite theme was the progress of mankind, for he believed in the capacity of the individual for

school construction, with the substance and content of the educational curriculum, and with the moral and spiritual values which should pervade all education. These ideas are best set forth in his annual reports to the Board. Still good reading today, they reveal the range and depth of his ideas and interests. In one he advocated the word method of reading instead of the letter or phonic method. It is being said today that Johnny can't read because he is taught by the word method; Mann said over a hundred years ago that Johnny couldn't read because he was being taught by the phonic method. In another report he attacked the concept of completely autonomous school districts, advocating the plan that is at once the paradox and the glory of the American school system—local control under a unified state system. Another stressed the importance of practical education; in another he asserted that children learn best through affection, not fear, and he urged less whipping and more understanding. The seventh report, written after a thorough study in England and Europe of their school systems, created one of the most famous educational rows in American history. His two-hundred-page report praises the German schools, their teachers, and their methods, and compares the Massachusetts schools to them most unfavorably. Outraged by his charges, thirty-one school masters wrote a stinging reply. In their attack they were joined by numerous church groups, who charged that Mann was promoting public schools at the expense of church or parochial schools. They further accused him of being anti-religious and of denying the place of religion in education. Their charge was not true. He did oppose sectarian education at public expense, but he believed in voluntary religious education and in the use of the

Bible in the schools. He won his fight, although the basic problem he faced, that of the relation between public and church or parochial schools, is still unresolved.

Mann's final report was a summary of his work and a re-statement of his faith. He had resigned in 1848 to take John Quincy Adams' place in Congress because of overwork (he was never strong) and because the controversies he had aroused threatened to divide the Massachusetts Board of Education. In this final report he reasserts the importance of the schools in upbuilding the financial, intellectual, moral, and religious condition of the state. He urges again the need for religious instruction and the use of the Bible. It is a triumphant and fitting conclusion to a series of reports unequalled by any other educator in our history.

But it was not solely in the realm of ideas and philosophy that Mann achieved success. There were solid benefits to show for his twelve years' work. Teachers' salaries had risen by over fifty percent and three normal schools had been established. Over two million dollars had been spent in new school construction, the appropriations for schools had more than doubled, and whereas in 1837 private school expenditures were seventy-five percent of the total spent for schools in Massachusetts, when Mann left office they were only thirty-six percent. The value of the Board had been demonstrated and a centralized system was well under way.

In Congress he spoke boldly against slavery and served his people well for four years. His real interest was in education, however, and in 1852 when he was offered the presidency of the newly-formed Antioch College in Ohio, he accepted. Seven years of disappointment, failure, exhausting effort, and final triumph followed. The College, founded by the Christian Church, was coeducational and was the second in the United States to admit Negroes. When Mann and his wife arrived, nothing was in readiness, he said later, "but our hearts. If Adam and Eve had been brought into this world as prematurely as we were brought out to the premises of Antioch College, they must have been created about Wednesday night!" But in the next few years Mann persisted through financial failure and religious dissension to put the pioneering little college on its feet. Its quality and freshness of view still testify today to the vigor and the enthusiasm he infused into its earliest beginnings. He died in its service, and on his monument there are inscribed the closing words of his valedictory address to the graduating class of 1859:

"I beseech you to treasure up in your hearts these my parting words: Be ashamed to die until you have won some victory for humanity."

It is nearly a century ago now that he died, and he still stands as one of the most conspicuous figures in educational history of

that we today have erected the largest and most democratic system of education of any country in the world.

". . . to America . . . European ideas"

FRANK FREIDEL

FEW native-born Americans have made more significant or lasting contributions to this nation's culture than did the German-born Francis Lieber, who for many years was a professor at the University of South Carolina and later at Columbia University. Lieber came to the United States in 1827, when he was twenty-nine years old. He brought a full cargo of old-world culture to transplant in the new, and a burning patriotism and nationalism which earlier he had directed toward Germany. He also brought a romantic and adventurous past. One of Francis Lieber's earliest memories was of sobbing at a window as he watched Napoleon's troops parade triumphantly into Berlin in 1806. He wished he were old enough to fight for the liberation of his country, a wish that came true when, aged 17, he volunteered for service against Napoleon. He witnessed the Battle of Waterloo unscathed, but was wounded a day or so later at Namur. After the Napoleonic wars he was one of those excited, nationalistic youths in Germany who engaged in gymnastic exercises with *Turnvater* Friedrich Jahn, and agitated for German constitutionalism and unification.

At the same time he became strongly interested in the worth of the individual, and in his rights and duties towards the community—an intermixture of individualism and nationalism.

Lieber was not ready to carry his discontent with the reactionary government to the point of violence, but one of his acquaintances, Karl Sand, assassinated a reactionary playwright in 1819. In the aftermath Lieber was arrested and imprisoned because he had been visited by Sand not long before the crime, but he was later released for lack of evidence. He then went from university to university, harried by the Prussian police who refused to let him enter any of them. Finally the liberal faculty at Jena admitted him, and in order to give him protection from the police bestowed a doctor's degree on him only four months after his matriculation.

In 1821 Lieber made his way with a group of romantic adventurers to Greece to participate in the Greek war for independence. He found the Greeks a half-wild, lawless people rather than the noble Hellenes he had envisaged. Thoroughly disillusioned, penniless, and ragged, he made his way to Rome. There to his great good fortune the Prussian minister, Barthold Georg Niebuhr, rescued him. Niebuhr, who was one of the first great historians of the nineteenth century, trained Lieber in scientific historical methods and permanently impressed upon him the necessity for sound governmental institutions. The only means of obtaining freedom without lawlessness like that in Greece, he convinced Lieber, was through the orderly development of constitutional liberty within the bounds of law, such as could be found in England or the United States.

Through Niebuhr's intercession Lieber was allowed to return to Berlin in 1823, where he established himself in the highest intellectual circles. But the police again harried and imprisoned him, for although he had shed his early revolutionary ideas he would not inform upon his companions. In May, 1826, he fled to England. During his year in England Lieber became acquainted with young John Stuart Mill, the economist and philosopher, and with Jeremy Bentham and his Utilitarian followers. He did not become a Utilitarian, but one of them persuaded him to come to America to build the bodies of young Bostonians through operating a gymnasium and swimming school. The Utilitarians believed that a healthy body was essential for the housing of a competent mind; Lieber was able to put to use for them the gymnasium training he had acquired under *Turnvater* Jahn.

Lieber had the good fortune to arrive at Boston when it had reached a high level of prosperity as a commercial and textile center. Its leading citizens were aspiring to make it the Athens of America, and having recently discovered German scholarship, were ready to make much of Lieber with his fine letters of recom-

This was editing the first encyclopedia of the United States, the *Encyclopedia Americana.* At first he thought he would simply translate a good German encyclopedia, but soon realized that this would not suffice. He enlisted several American intellectual leaders to prepare articles for him, the most notable being Justice Joseph Story of the United States Supreme Court, who wrote the legal articles. As a result the *Americana* had distinction as a broad and elaborate contemporary appraisal of the nation in the Jacksonian period, and a cheap and popular exposition of the advance of knowledge to the 1830s. Tens of thousands of Americans bought the book as a means of self-improvement, and some of them were people who were later influential. In the 1850s the *Americana* was among the scanty store of books owned by a rather obscure Illinois lawyer-politician, Abraham Lincoln.

While editing the *Americana* Lieber became interested in prison reform, a highly controversial field in which Americans led the rest of the world. He became acquainted with two young French artistocrats, Alexis de Tocqueville and Gustave de Beaumont, who had come to America in part to study its prisons; Tocqueville became famous later for his classic *Democracy in America.* In addition he and Beaumont wrote a book on American prisons which Lieber translated, adding voluminous introductory remarks and notes encompassing the whole field of penology. In fact the word "penology" itself was one that Lieber subsequently coined. Some of what he wrote was not palatable to Tocqueville and Beaumont, but the work gained for him a wide and respectful hearing. Unfortunately he was in part defending what today would be considered barbarous—a system of solitary confinement in which no prisoner was allowed ever to communicate with any other prisoner. He was so able in his arguments for this that when Charles Dickens in his *American Notes* launched a sentimental attack upon one of the Pennsylvania penitentiaries, the reformers turned to Lieber to refute the criticism.

Out of writing of this sort in a variety of fields, Lieber gained much prestige but little compensation. He had edited the *Encyclopedia Americana* for a flat sum which was soon spent, and he constantly cast around for new projects that might be lucrative. His practical-minded friend Jared Sparks, later President of Harvard, explained to him why his schemes for scholarly journals and technical books on educational theories would not succeed in this country. He warned Lieber that he must not think in terms of Europe with its cheap labor, but of the United States, "where the young men crowd in throngs in active life, and fill up spheres in which intellectual attainment or culture is not necessary to success."

Fortunately for Lieber, he was able in 1835 to find a chair at South Carolina College. There for a period of twenty years he chafed over his isolation in a country town in the deep South, but there he was able to formulate his ideas about fundamental institutions of government. These he expounded in two lengthy treatises: *The Manual of Political Ethics* and *On Civil Liberty and Self-Government*. Neither is read today, but they had a significant effect upon the development of the social sciences in the United States. The *Political Ethics* examined the rights and duties of a citizen toward his government, and took such a broad view of society that to some extent it molded the thinking of the pioneer sociologist, William Graham Sumner, and, in its institutional approach, influenced the economist, Thorstein Veblen.

The *Civil Liberty* grew in part out of Lieber's disappointment over the drift of France into a dictatorship under Napoleon III and the failure of the Germans to build a constitutional government at the Frankfurt Parliament after the Revolution of 1848. Lieber had hurried to Frankfurt to participate, but had found himself a stranger in his native land. He concluded sadly that the British or American governmental systems would not work in Germany since "they presuppose a people well skilled, trained, and formed in the politics of liberty." In his book on *Civil Liberty* Lieber extolled the American government with its array of institutions, complementing yet checking and balancing each other.

Their "number supports the whole," he wrote, "as the many pillars support the rotunda of our capitol."

By the outbreak of the Civil War Lieber had moved from the uncongenial South to New York City, where he became a professor at Columbia University. His ardent nationalism and patri-

General and the General-in-Chief in Washington. Problems of international law involving the conduct of armies in the field especially concerned him, and led to his drafting a code—promulgated in 1863 as "General Orders 100." It was the first code of the international law of war actually to be put into operation, and it became the basis for the later regulations drawn up at The Hague Conferences.

After the Civil War Lieber continued to concentrate upon the relationships between nations. He was one of the leading promoters of private international conferences among experts on international law. These paved the way for the later Hague Conferences and the League of Nations and United Nations. Lieber had planned to attend the first of these private conferences in 1872, but died before he could do so.

Since his death, Lieber has not had the lasting fame to which he aspired. Nevertheless he had made a substantial contribution to his adopted land, by bringing to America many European ideas which later took root. Moreover, he had helped clarify and crystallize American thinking on individualism and nationalism. And he had not stopped at nationalism, but had gone on to emphasize the significance of its counterpart—internationalism.

Townsend Harris and W. W. Rockhill

American contact with the Far East dates from 1784, when the Baltimore-built, copper-bottomed, 360-ton merchantman, Empress of China, *reached Canton with a cargo of furs and cotton which she exchanged profitably for silks, tea, and chinaware. This success led quickly to the development of an immensely valuable trade. Lucky voyages often produced clear gains of one hundred percent, and even more fabulous returns were sometimes recorded. The Yankee skipper Edmund Fanning, for example, steered his 93-ton* Betsey *into Canton harbor in 1798 with a cargo of sealskins. He exchanged these for tea, silk, and other Oriental products which he sold in New York for more than $120,000. On a total investment of less than $8,000 he cleared some $53,000.*

Soon the Stars and Stripes became a common sight along the crowded Canton waterfront, and, after the Treaty of Wanghia in 1844, in other "treaty ports" as well. American missionaries bent on Christianizing and "civilizing" the Chinese followed in the wake of the merchants. Their influence was considerable and not always for the best, although it is difficult to measure it exactly. Soon Chinese laborers began migrating to the United States, where they were employed in the California gold fields and later in railroad construction. While immensely useful, these workers were the unwitting cause of much trouble, because their alien culture and low living standards led other workers to demand their exclusion.

Meanwhile Commodore Matthew C. Perry "opened" Japan (as Nathaniel Peffer explains, it was actually Townsend Harris who negotiated the treaty that brought the Nipponese into commercial relations with the rest of the world), and by the end of the nineteenth century American influence in the Far East was very great.

While Japan eagerly adopted western ways and grew strong, China proved a reluctant pupil, resisting westernization yet succumbing to its blandishments. As a result her culture—and her government—slowly crumbled, and the great European powers hastened to take advantage of her plight. At this point William W. Rockhill made his contribution to the history of American activities in the Orient. As Paul A. Varg describes it … *Rockhill probably prevented the total disruption* … *of the "Open*

…

mation of America's needs and …

Nathaniel Peffer is Professor Emeritus of International Relations at Columbia University and the author of many books, including The Far East: A Modern History. *Paul A. Varg is Professor of History at Michigan State University. In addition to* Open Door Diplomat, *a life of Rockhill, he has written* Missionaries, Chinese, and Diplomats.

". . . the basis for friendship and trust"

NATHANIEL PEFFER

WE SEEM to have come full circle in our relations with Japan. Fifteen years ago it would not have been credible that a few years later the United States and Japan would be on the most cordial terms, that they would be bound by a treaty that amounted to an alliance, and that the United States would be helping Japan with several hundred million dollars a year, money paid by American taxpayers whose sons had been fighting Japanese troops, and perhaps dying, everywhere in the Pacific. Yet so it is.

This is not really unprecedented, however. As a matter of fact, except for the years before the war that started at Pearl Harbor, relations between Japan and the United States always had been cordial. It was Japan's ambition to conquer China and America's exclusion of Japanese immigrants that produced strain and, later, conflict; but these accounted for only a small part of

warning. China was then at war with England and France, which had become impatient at China's evasion of the obligation to carry out her treaties permitting foreign trade. This, Harris argued, was what lay before Japan if it followed China's example, whereas if it established normal relations voluntarily, it could escape the impositions being forced on China. Again he dwelt on the fact that the United States was not a colonial power, that it wanted no territory but only trade, and if Japan made its first treaty with the United States it would get more favorable terms which would serve as a precedent.

Probably the argument drawn from China's experience was the most effective. The Japanese could see for themselves what was happening. They yielded. At the end of February, 1858, a treaty was drawn up much as Harris wanted it, with the provision that it be formally signed on April 21. This was but the beginning of another chapter. Influential nobles around the Shogun's court in Yedo and the Emperor's court in Kyoto sought by every kind of intrigue to prevent signature. The Shogun begged Harris for postponement. Harris, aware of the internal difficulties, resolved still to be patient. Then came news of China's crushing defeat and the harsh peace terms imposed. The Japanese saw the handwriting on the wall. It would be only a matter of time before combined Western fleets would be making for Japan. They signed the treaty July 29, 1858. It provided for exchange of diplomatic representatives, the opening of additional ports for trade and the stationing of consuls at open ports, extra-territoriality for Americans, and a uniform tariff fixed by treaty.

Thus Japan came into the world, ushered in by an American. But Harris had brought it in not by force or the threat of force but by persuasion, by conciliation, by demonstration that he had Japan's interest as much in mind as that of his own country. It was a unique victory by a unique diplomat, and it laid the basis for friendship and trust between the two countries broken later by a period of friction and war but now resumed.

His task accomplished, Harris resigned from his Japanese post late in 1860 and returned to the United States. Although a Democrat, he supported the Lincoln administration in the Civil War. He never entered official life again, but he retained his interest in public affairs. He was active in the temperance cause, in the work of church and foreign missions, and in discussions of international affairs. He died on February 25, 1878, having lived a long and useful life. He deserves a high place in American history.

"... *carving of the Chinese melon*"

PAUL A. VARG

mid-nineteenth century, a [illegible]
1, 1853, in Philadelphia. At the age of eleven his widowed mother took William and his brother to Paris for an education. Subsequently he graduated from St. Cyr military academy, the French West Point, and served in Algeria in the French Foreign Legion. While a student he developed an interest in Oriental languages and the history of Central Asia. After four years of military service he returned to the United States and married a childhood sweetheart. Without financial means or any training that fitted him for a suitable position, he decided to try his luck on the frontier. After three years he sold out and returned to France where he gave full time to his studies.

Long before he earned fame as a diplomatist Rockhill earned distinction among a small coterie of scholars as one of the world's leading authorities on Tibetan Buddhism. Although he later became involved in the turbulent diplomacy of the years before World War I, Rockhill remained first of all a student who much preferred the lonely life of the scholar to the gay social affairs of diplomats in the capitals of Europe and Asia.

Twice he made explorations in Tibet. These expeditions, carried out on the most meager of resources, involved no fanfare. The simplest of equipment and barest of necessities sufficed. Rockhill, the scientist, collected information on the social institutions and way of life of the Buddhists of central Asia. He traversed the most lonely and forbidding stretches on earth. The snow of the mountains blinded him. The shortage of supplies brought him to the edge of starvation. The frightful experiences he endured he scarcely noted. He concentrated on recording accurate observations of what he saw, and he collected material that would be invaluable to ethnologists for years to come.

At Berkeley, West Virginia, in the autumn of 1889 his wife and daughter, Dorothea, waited anxiously for him to return from his first trip of exploration. More than a year passed when finally a telegram laconically announced "Arrived in Shanghai."

When the wife and daughter met Rockhill at the railroad station, Dorothea recorded:

> He was emaciated and almost blind from the months spent in the snow, and it frightened one to see the condition in which his nerves were after his many hardships. He could hardly speak when he met us, and all the way in the train he sat quite still holding my mother's hand with the tears rolling down his cheeks.

This from Dorothea, but not from Rockhill himself, who never wrote about the hardships he endured.

When his close friend, Henry Adams, read Rockhill's account of his explorations, he wrote to him:

> I feel quite a new spring of self-esteem that I should be able to treat you with familiarity. It is as though I had lived on intimate terms with Marco Polo, and had Genghis Khan for dinner.

Adams scolded him for being overly modest in relating his story of adventure "as though it were a ramble in Pennsylvania Avenue" with Tibet "a kind of ornamental pleasure-ground somewhere near Georgetown."

Rockhill's long experience in Asia fitted him for a career in the foreign service. He was appointed chief clerk of the State Department in 1893, and rose to be assistant secretary in 1896. In the 1890s China came to the fore as the great theater of diplomacy. Africa had already been carved into colonies, but the great Manchu-Chinese Empire lay open and defenseless.

On the other side of the world the nations of Europe were on a search for markets and for opportunities for investment. After China's decisive defeat at the hands of Japan in 1895, the carving of the Chinese melon seemed to be underway.

In 1898 Russia, Germany, France, and Great Britain staked out their respective spheres of influence. Germany secured the rights to establish a naval base at Kiaochow in the province of Shantung, Russia obtained Port Arthur in the strategically important Liaotung peninsula, and Great Britain leased land for a naval base, Weihaiwei. Russia already dominated Manchuria thanks to her acquisition of railroad rights in that province.

Rockhill left his post as Assistant Secretary of State in 1897 to become the United States Minister to Greece, but in the fall of 1898 his close friend, John Hay, returned to Washington as Secretary of State. He wanted someone to advise him on Far Eastern

The notes called on each [illegible] equal commercial opportunity within its sphere of influence.

Rockhill inserted into the notes a provision that aimed at more than that. Chinese officials were to continue to collect the customs duties within the spheres. Rockhill saw in this a way to preserve Chinese sovereignty.

The replies of each of the powers had strings attached. Only the rivalry among the several nations saved China from partitioning. But the notes did commit the United States to a policy calling for China's independence and territorial and administrative integrity.

For the next twelve years Rockhill served the State Department as a China expert. In the negotiations at Peking following the Boxer Revolt of 1900 he represented the United States, and did what he could to mitigate the severity of the settlement. Rockhill hoped to use the opportunity to promote reforms in China's administration and to abolish the internal tax called *likin.* The final protocol signed at Peking on September 7, 1901, fell far short of American aims. Rockhill confessed that he had been "practically alone in the negotiations." "England has her agreement with Germany, Russia has her alliance with France, the Triple Alliance comes in here, and every other combination you know of is working here as it is in Europe," he wrote to his friend Hippisley.

In 1905 Theodore Roosevelt appointed Rockhill minister to China. That unhappy country now faced a new threat. Japan, as a result of her recent victory over Russia, assumed a new importance and compelled China to agree to her taking over the Russian rights in Manchuria and the reduction of Korea to a protectorate. The United States supported Japan, a nation still considered a diplomatic ally. During the crucial summer of 1905 Rockhill gave all of his attention to the Chinese boycott of American goods. The Chinese deeply resented their exclusion from the United States, and especially the ill treatment met by many of their fellow nationals in this country. Rockhill pursued a firm course with the Chinese government, but he urged patience on Theodore Roosevelt, who had proposed stern measures.

When William Howard Taft became President, he named Rockhill ambassador to Russia. Secretary of State Philander C. Knox was about to launch his scheme for the neutralization of railroads in Manchuria, and much depended on winning the support of Russia. The plan fell through because Japan and Russia would not agree to give up their interests in Manchuria, and these two nations gained the diplomatic support of their allies in western Europe. Rockhill had doubts about the plan's success from the beginning. When the negotiations failed, he strongly urged that if the United States were to win Russian support in Asian affairs, she must first recognize Russia's great interest in that area.

The Chinese Revolution of 1912 disturbed Rockhill. He knew China too well to be optimistic. Changing the name of the government in no way altered the fact that before a unified and modern state could develop, the strong local loyalties would have to be replaced by a nationalistic feeling. Reading the high-flown rhetoric of the revolution, Rockhill observed that an old mud scow could not be converted into a battleship overnight. He would have preferred a slower and more gradual accommodation of China to the twentieth century world. But he did not live to see the collapse of liberal hopes for China. On December 8, 1914, while en route to China, he died.

Sam Patch

Dorson, has christened "fakelore," such as Paul Bunyan, Sam Patch is an authentic folk hero, at once real and also the subject of a cluster of legends that have been passed orally from generation to generation in song and story. In the present account, Dr. Dorson describes first Patch's actual deeds, and then the legends that have clustered around his name since his spectacular end.

Richard M. Dorson is Professor of Folklore and History at the University of Indiana. Among his many books are Davy Crockett and the American Comic Legend, Bloodstoppers and Bearwalkers *and* American Folklore.

"... the American mock hero"

RICHARD M. DORSON

SAM PATCH was his name. The date of his birth is uncertain, save that it was before 1807, for he had passed twenty-two when he jumped to his death over a waterfall in 1829. He was born in South Reading, Massachusetts, son of a farmer, but his family soon moved to Pawtucket, Rhode Island. There young Sam worked as a mule-spinner, tending the machine that twisted and wound cotton thread in Samuel Slater's cotton mill, the first American factory. Surely this humble factory-worker in preindustrial America was one of the most obscure men in the United States.

But Sam was born at the right time for men of modest origins. He grew up in the decade of the 1820s, when brash young America was flexing her muscles and preparing for a mighty destiny. The War of 1812 was behind and the threat of European invasion safely removed; ahead lay the inviting reaches of the Louisiana Purchase and the shores of the Pacific. American statesmen looked for the prosperous rearing of a glorious civilization on this land blessed with natural wealth, among a people favored with democratic institutions. This was a dawning day for the common man. Andrew Jackson, narrowly defeated for the presidency in 1824, entered the White House in 1828 on a triumphant platform dedicated to the ordinary citizen. In this decade too arose a new breed of native American folk heroes, reflecting the rowdy humor and bumptious spirit of the times. Into this gallery of homespun heroes Sam Patch quite literally jumped.

He began simply enough. The Slater mill was located just above the Pawtucket Falls, and some of the hardier mill hands took to jumping into the river from the top rail of the bridge, or from the roofs of adjacent mills towering one hundred feet above the deep water of the falls. Thus Sam Patch found his career as a jumper over waterfalls before admiring townspeople.

On reaching manhood Sam went into cotton manufacturing for himself. But when his partner skipped off with the firm's funds, Patch left Rhode Island and found a job in the Hamilton cotton mills in Passaic, New Jersey. Here he made his first public jump to be reported in the newspapers, September 30, 1827, when a covered bridge was being laid across the scenic Passaic Falls. Dodging town constables, Sam appeared by a whitened oak at the edge of the precipice, just as a rolling pin slid from the guide ropes into the chasm, leaving the bridge teetering precariously halfway across. Sam jumped the falls, swam to the pin, took the trailing rope in his mouth and returned to shore. The pin was placed in position on the guide ropes and the bridge successfully pulled across the gap.

The publicity given this feat set Sam to jumping before electrified crowds throughout New York and New Jersey. On August 11, 1828, he jumped ninety feet from a platform erected on the masthead of a sloop moored off Hoboken in the Hudson River.

A year later Sam jumped over Niagara Falls for his crowning triumph. On a rainy Saturday, Patch boldly climbed the perpendicular ladder erected on Goat Island, a wooded islet dividing the American and the Horseshoe Falls. Before ascending, he shed his shoes and coat and tied a handkerchief about his neck. Atop the ladder, he mounted the narrow, reeling platform. It was barely large enough for a man to sit upon, and for ten minutes he displayed his poise and tested the stand, while the

Jumping Hero swam briskly to the shore, to inform his first onrushing admirer: "There's no mistake in Sam Patch!" Unanimously the surrounding group exclaimed: "This is the real Sam Patch!" The Buffalo *Republican* commented: "The jump of Patch is the greatest feat of the kind ever effected by man. He may now challenge the universe for a competitor."

Flushed with the publicity of press notices and the public excitement, Sam turned in November to Rochester and the Genesee Falls for a new conquest. By now the newspapers of the nation were playing up Sam enthusiastically, and his sponsors determined to provide a still greater, climactic feat, by erecting a twenty-five foot scaffold on a rock's brow to extend his jump to 125 feet. In the posters Sam announced, with unwitting irony: "*Higher yet! Sam's last jump. Some things can be done as well as others. There is no mistake in Sam Patch.*" Monroe and Ontario counties poured out for the Friday the 13th leap; schooners and coaches ran excursions; betting ran high in the local bars as to the outcome; nearby roofs and windows and both banks swarmed with the curious. But when Sam walked out on the grassy, tree-covered rock that divided the greater and lesser branches of the cataract, at two o'clock (his pet bear was to jump at three), and climbed up to the platform, some spectators thought he staggered and lacked his usual aplomb. Some would assert that the jumper was reeling drunk; others would deny that he took more than a glass of brandy to counteract the chilly day. Sam made a brief speech: Napoleon was a great man and conquered nations, Wellington was greater and conquered Napoleon, but neither could jump the Genesee Falls—that was left for him to do.

Then he jumped. But this time the descent lacked its usual

arrowy precision. One third of the way down his body began to droop, his arms parted from his sides, he lost command of his body and struck the water obliquely with arms and legs extended. He did not reappear before the horror-stricken assemblage.

Dragging for the body proved unsuccessful, perhaps because of pinioning branches on the river bed. Nor was it found until the following March 17, when a farmer broke the ice to water his horses at the mouth of the Genesee near Lake Ontario.

What manner of man was the true Sam Patch? Some comments indicted him as a "wharf rat" and ignorant loafer, a short, chunky sot who spent his days licking sugar hogsheads and pilfering from water craft. Others idealized him as an intrepid, debonair acrobat aiming to leap off London Bridge, and a devoted son who before his Last Leap stipulated that if he died all proceeds should go to his mother. But whatever his actual character, the real Patch speedily disappeared under successive coatings of myth applied by rhymesters, humorists, comedians, and storytellers.

Torrents of newsprint washed over the lifeless high jumper in a volume to match the waters of Genesee Falls. Newspaper editors praised his selfless heroism; ministers preached sermons against his vanity and folly. Some punster composed an epitaph filled with such double meanings as "*divers* times, a *drop* too much, untimely *bier,* this sad *fall,*" and concluding:

> There's none alive will ever match him—
> Ah, cruel Death, thus to dis-PATCH him!

Many refused to believe that Sam had really died. One widely printed newspaper story, signed by "Sam Patch," declared the Genesee jump to be a capital hoax, with a man of straw and paint, sand, and stones substituting for the Jumping Hero. Even after the finding of the body the jumper continued to be seen; there were those who at twilight perceived Sam sporting at the Falls, and repeating his fearful feat to a concourse of sea gulls and fishes.

To American poets and rhymesters of the 1830s searching for native themes, the heroics, tragedy, and humor of the Last Leap proved magnetic. A lengthy narrative poem by Thomas Ward, a Newark doctor, made an elegant Byronic hero of "The Great Descender, mighty PATCH—Spurner of heights—great Nature's overmatch!", and unblushingly likened him to Columbus, Franklin, Newton, Galileo, and Nelson in what must be accounted an overlooked curiosity of American literature. In Boston a printer ran off an anonymous news-ballad on the Last Leap, with a picture of Sam careening downward. Seba Smith, who

> He sought for fame, and as he reached to pluck it,
> He lost his ballast, and then kicked the buck-it.

If the versifiers mourned for Patch, the humorists promptly restored him to life and glory. Remolded by fabulists, he took on the outlines of the American mock hero. A Yankee whaler sighted the Jumping Hero in the South Seas. Amazed, he asked him: "Why, Sam, how *on airth* did you get here? I thought you was drowned at the Canadian lines." "Why," said Sam, "I didn't get *on earth* here at all, but I came slap *through* it. In that Niagara dive I went so everlasting deep, I thought it was just as short to come up t'other side, so out I came in these parts. If I don't take the shine off the sea serpent when I get back to Boston, then my name's not Sam Patch."

A spurious autobiography, riddled with misspellings and puns, narrated sensational feats of the super-jumper for comic-annual readers. The nation's youth learned about the illustrious aerialist in a brightly illustrated nursery book, *The Wonderful Leaps of Sam Patch,* tracing the saga in rhyme from precocious springs to adult transatlantic leaps between Washington and London.

In 1836 an aspiring comedian, already known for his Yankee roles, portrayed Sam Patch in Buffalo and found himself heir to Sam's fame. In western cities, and then in New York and Boston, Dan Marble exhibited *Sam Patch, or The Daring Yankee,* and its sequel, *Sam Patch in France, or The Pesky Snake,* year after year before enthusiastic audiences. After various Yankee capers, involving a courtship, an encounter with Mrs. Trollope, and a discussion of Steam Doctors, the stage Patch leaped tremendously over Niagara Falls, from a height estimated at between forty and seventy feet, to bob up triumphantly in a pool of spray and foam. The bills proudly announced: "Mr. Marble will leap from the extreme height of the Theatre, a feat never attempted by any one but himself, and prove that *'Cold Water won't drown love.'*" An open trap behind the water set, containing a spring bed piled with bags of shavings, caught Marble when he jumped from the flies, a performance that frequently cost him minor bruises and at least once a serious injury. The jumping mania affected the audiences. Clerks jumped counters, farmers jumped fences, boys and old folks vied in "doing" Sam Patch.

In its fruition, the Patch legend became a subject for literary and proverbial reference. Nathaniel Hawthorne, always receptive to somber American traditions, stirred eagerly to this one on viewing the Genesee Falls in the dusk. "How stern a moral may be drawn from the story of poor Sam Patch!" he wrote. "Was the leaper of cataracts more mad or foolish than other men who throw away life, or misspend it in pursuit of empty fame, and seldom so triumphantly as he?"

In a novel with a good deal of factual description of western New York, William Dean Howells had one of his characters express dismay because his wife had never heard of Patch. "Isabel, your ignorance of all that an American woman should be proud of distresses me." On the level of popular allusion, "Sam Patch" gained household currency: "Afore you could say *Sam Patch*"; "Why did you play *Sam Patch,* and jump into the river?" In 1891 a Senator from Vermont illustrated his point on the floors of Congress by quoting the overeager Patch.

By mid-century the interest in Patch had waned, as the nation turned to the ominous issues of slavery and sectional strife. But Sam never completely disappeared from view. Those communities with a claim to him, Pawtucket, Paterson, and especially Rochester, continued to do him honor in feature articles and centennial floats. In recent years the daredevil jumper has returned to the national scene. William Carlos Williams described Sam's Passaic plunge in the first volume of his extended poem, *Paterson,* in 1946. A new children's book, *Sam Patch the High, Wide and Handsome Jumper,* by Jack Conroy and Arna Bontemps, in 1951 depicted his spectacular leaps in competition with a villainous Westerner called Hurricane Harry. And a high school student in Rochester, David Coapman, fired by enthusiasm for the feats of Sam, cut the grass around Sam's unmarked grave at Charlotte and led a campaign which resulted in the decoration of the grave with a handsome granite marker and plaque. The marker was officially dedicated on November 12, 1948, one hundred and nineteen years almost to the day after the Last

Wilhelm Weitling

Wilhelm Weitling was a man whose career throws light on two related trends in the history of the United States during the pre-Civil War generation. One of these is the continuing role of America as a haven for the oppressed and dissatisfied of the Old World. Just as the reactions following the French Revolution led to the migration of men like Thomas Cooper, so the failure of widespread European revolutions in 1830 and 1848 brought many more outstanding liberals to our shores. The collapse of the German uprisings of 1848, for example, confirmed Weitling in his belief that, as Carl Wittke says, "he could find freedom only in the United States." Defeat also led many other Germans to the same conclusion, most notably Carl Schurz.

Secondly, Weitling's life illustrates the great interest of Americans of his epoch in utopian reform movements and in the establishment of ideal communities. The United States with its vast wilderness of cheap land provided a favorable environment, and many native-born Americans, such as Albert Brisbane and George Ripley (the founder of Brook Farm, probably the best known of the experiments in cooperative living), were influential in the development of the utopian movement. But the movement was chiefly European in origin and inspiration; Frenchmen like Charles Fourier and Etienne Cabet and Britons like Robert Dale Owen and Frances Wright were key figures in the conception and development of many American utopias. Weitling's Communia, on the Iowa prairie, was as much a European transplant as he was himself. Weitling's career also illustrates the close connection between these communistic societies and the labor movement, which, in the 1830s and 1840s, was deeply concerned with all sorts of cooperative ventures.

Carl Wittke, Dean of the Graduate School at Western Reserve University, is an authority on the role of immigrant groups in American history. He is the author of many books, the best known of which is We Who Built America.

"... disillusioned prophet of Utopia"

CARL WITTKE

languages, and stocked his
mind with an amazing amount of miscellaneous information. He learned the tailor's trade, and at eighteen began his travels as a journeyman through seven German states.

From 1837 to 1841 Weitling worked in Paris, and there he was deeply moved by the problems of the emerging city proletariat. He became a leader of the League of the Just, one of many radical, secret workingmen's societies which operated underground in the French capital, and for this society he wrote his first treatise on social reform, entitled *Mankind As It Is and As It Should Be.* This was an attempt to integrate the workers' movement with a program of communism based on Christian brotherhood, for although an agnostic and a severe critic of all institutionalized religion, Weitling always insisted on morality, ethics, and religion as a basis for social reform. The little book was replete with quotations from the Bible, and pleaded for a return to a simple life in which all property would be held in common. With the holy fire of a workingman's messiah, the author denounced the evils of private property, inheritance, banks, and the prevailing money system.

From Paris Weitling went to Switzerland to organize communist clubs and cooperatives and to publish a little journal. In 1842, *Guarantees of Harmony and Liberty,* his *magnum opus,* was secretly printed in Switzerland. It is the most complete exposition of Weitling's "system;" it went through a number of editions, was translated into several languages, and still has a place in the history of pre-Marxian socialism.

The *Guarantees* did not advocate the class struggle, but a religion of brotherly love. Its author equated communism with the

Gospel of Jesus, and expected man's religious feelings to provide the motivation for an elaborate system of social reconstruction. Weitling stressed a cooperative, handicraft system of production, a workers' utopia in which private property would be abolished, and a society reorganized in a hierarchy of families and industrial groups, managed by a complex system of representation, which would provide the perfect balance between what man desires and what he can produce.

In 1843 Weitling's *Gospel of the Poor Sinner* appeared. In it he elucidated what he regarded as the true doctrine of Jesus, whom he pictured as a revolutionary perpetually at war with the forces of Mammon. He was promptly charged with blasphemy, attacking private property, and inciting to riot, and was clapped into jail. In the long months that he spent in a Swiss prison, his mind nearly gave way, and his prison diary contains many references to suicide, delusions, and persecutions. In 1844 the Swiss got rid of their troublesome prisoner by handing him over to the German police, by whom he was pushed from place to place until he finally found safety among the London communists in England. Two years later, at a famous conference in Brussels, Marx read Weitling out of the communist party movement because of the irreconcilable conflict between Marxian materialism and the moral and religious emphasis of Weitling's brand of utopian communism.

On December 31, 1846, Weitling landed in New York, only to find that the German paper for which he was to write had suspended publication. In 1848, when revolution broke out in Germany, he hurried home, but he smelled no powder in that abortive uprising. He attended two workers' parliaments in Berlin and issued a small, radical journal, but when the Prussian military took control Weitling departed for Hamburg, where he continued his propaganda and established several workers' clubs. Finally, police surveillance convinced him that he could find freedom only in the United States.

In New York the prophet of Utopia promptly organized a Workingmen's League, and in January, 1850, he began publishing his *Republic of the Workers.* He got his first four hundred subscribers by ringing doorbells in the German section of the city, but circulation climbed to 4,500 and his readers were scattered over the country. The *Republic of the Workers* was not a newspaper, but an organ for its editor's theories of reform. It carried articles on politics, economics, and science, on a new bank of exchange and a new currency based on labor expended in the production of goods and services. It urged the founding of a communist colony where Weitling's system could be practically tested. Weitling managed to keep his journal alive for five years, although much of its content was a recapitulation of what he had

for a week of discussions and hammered out a program and a constitution of 270 paragraphs, which repeated Weitling's pet proposals, but also included demands for free land for settlers, direct election and the recall of officeholders, public libraries, free public schools, adult education, and a Pacific Railroad. Weitling's ultimate aim, of course, was to replace the existing order with a republic of the workers. Members of his League paid dues into a central treasury, established cooperatives and workers' halls in a number of cities, and created mutual insurance funds to pay sick, death, old age, and unemployment benefits. Weitling's plans encountered opposition from various sources, including the pulpit, and some members of his organization resented his messianic tactics and falsely accused him of financial irregularities, but Weitling believed in the ultimate triumph of an empire of the workers and predicted that his pension fund would reach two-and-a-half million dollars in ten years.

In 1851 Weitling had the misfortune to set foot for the first time in a little communistic settlement known as Communia, which had been started four years earlier by a band of enthusiasts on the prairie land of Clayton County, Iowa. The group were eager to affiliate with Weitling's Workingmen's League and use its funds for the development of their colony, and Weitling welcomed the chance to put his system into practice. The community pledged its assets as security for the funds which Weitling began to pour into the colony from the treasury of his Workingmen's League, and eventually he sank over $16,000 in the ill-fated venture.

In the beginning, Weitling's journal carried glowing accounts of the new utopia. Before long, however, the editor had to report the growing friction between members and their newly appointed leader. The funds for Weitling's whole program of pensions, cooperatives, and social insurance became hopelessly confused with those of the colony. To protect himself and his organization, Weitling demanded a deed of trust, or a mortgage on colony property, at ten percent interest, only to be charged with wanting to become a dictator. The community enjoyed several good harvests, and on one occasion the discovery of lead deposits, mistaken for silver ore, raised wild hopes for a new prosperity, but it soon became evident that Communia was doomed, and Weitling was accused of robbing the workers by using their League dues to keep the colony afloat. Frequent inventories were taken to determine what the assets of the community really were, and for months Weitling's paper chronicled the endless quarrels which marked the meetings of the settlers. In January, 1854, Weitling resigned as administrator. In 1857 the colony went into receivership and title to its real estate and other items was conveyed at a sheriff's sale to private owners. In 1903 the Post Office of Communia, Iowa, was officially discontinued.

The collapse of the colony pushed Weitling's League and his paper into bankruptcy, and convinced their founder that communism was impractical for the present and for the foreseeable future. The disillusioned prophet of utopia now said farewell to reform forever. He spent his last years at the tailor's bench, trying to support his poverty-stricken and growing family. He busied his restless mind with devising a new system of astronomy and a universal language, and perfecting several inventions for sewing machines.

The last meeting Weitling attended was a fraternal festival of the German, French, English, and Czech sections of the Workers' International held in New York in January, 1871. A few days later he died, virtually bankrupt; the tailor's union had to raise money for the funeral and the needy family. With the exception of the New York *Times*, German and English language newspapers paid little attention to his passing, and even the *Times* stressed his career as an inventor rather than as a social reformer. History has passed him by, although at one time his name was well known in radical circles on two continents. The Utopian Communist's eldest son became a New York industrialist and a bank president. Another son was successful in the South American export business, and a daughter was for years a respected teacher in the New York schools.

John Brown, Horace Greeley,

as bound servants rather than as permanent chattels, for the English settlers had no previous experience with slaves. Even when the true nature of the servitude was recognized and confirmed by law, the institution grew slowly; after six decades there were still but 3,000-odd Negroes in Virginia, and not all these were slaves. But thereafter the number of slaves increased very rapidly. On the eve of the Revolution Africans were being imported into the colonies at a rate of more than 7,000 a year, and in 1790 there were more than 750,000 Negroes in the United States, almost 700,000 of whom were slaves.

The "peculiar institution" spread widely in colonial times, penetrating every area from New Hampshire to Georgia, but only in the South did it flourish. The nature of southern agriculture rather than any fundamental difference of culture or morals accounted for this. The long growing season made it easy to keep slaves busy the year round, and the production of staple crops like tobacco, rice, sugar, and (later) cotton could be effectively carried out by using slaves in loosely organized gangs. It would be unfair to "blame" Southerners for the way slavery flourished in their domains.

Nevertheless, when the libertarian concepts loosed by the Revolution clashed with the institution of slavery, it survived in the South alone. Congress outlawed the fresh importation of slaves in 1808; meanwhile the northern states had passed legislation gradually abolishing the institution. Thus was developed a fundamental difference in the way of life of southerner and northener that led to the Civil War. Indeed, its effects are still being felt in the nation today.

There were always men of good will in the land who were

deeply troubled by the existence of a system that allowed one man to own another. Slaveholders like Washington and Jefferson, and—in later years—Henry Clay and James K. Polk, were frank in their criticisms although unable to suggest a practical means of doing away with the evil. However, after the invention of the cotton gin in 1793 and the expansion of cotton cultivation that followed, the demand for and thus the value of slaves rapidly increased. As they did, southern criticism of the institution declined; by 1840 it had practically ceased to exist.

As southerners stopped speaking against slavery and began, instead, to praise it, northern fear of slavery developed apace, and particularly with regard to its extension into the unsettled regions of the West. Economic arguments against it were reinforced by moral and humanitarian considerations. A hot debate developed. While few citizens in the free states could be said to like Negroes or to be willing to treat them as equals, the tendency to view slavery *as an unmitigated evil was irresistible. The position of Lincoln was typical of that of thousands of northerners. He spoke repeatedly of "the monstrous injustice of slavery," but he also said: "I am not . . . in favor of making voters or jurors of Negroes, nor of qualifying them to hold office, nor to intermarry with white people."*

But northern opinion was neither unanimous nor uncomplicated. It ranged from the extreme abolitionism of William Lloyd Garrison to the pro-slavery stand of men like James Buchanan and Mayor Fernando Wood of New York. The careers of the Unforgettable Americans in the following sketches represent some but by no means all of the varying reactions of northern leaders to the challenge posed by the expansion of slavery.

John Brown, of course, was an extremist. He sought not merely to check slavery but to destroy it, and to do so with fire and sword. Horace Greeley was less passionately involved in the slavery question than Brown, but as an ardent believer in the future of the American West and in free land he consistently opposed the extension of the institution into new areas. Stanton, on the other hand, became less *radical on the issue as the crisis deepened, but his patriotism was more profound than his Southern sympathies, and when secession became a reality he rallied powerfully to the side of the Union. In the following accounts the authors do not limit themselves to a discussion of the role of the slavery controversy in their subjects' lives. But each shows his man against the background of the time, and it was a time when the issue reached—and passed—its crisis.*

Boyd B. Stutler, a former newspaper and magazine editor, was for many years managing editor of the American Legion Maga-*zine. He has published some fifty articles about various aspects of*

"*. . . it was the curtain-raiser*"

BOYD B. STUTLER

"THREE men who will loom forever against the horizon of time as representative types of the Civil War era, like pyramids above the desert, or mountain peaks over the subordinate plains, are Abraham Lincoln, U. S. Grant and Old John Brown." Thus wrote Senator John J. Ingalls, of Kansas, many years ago at a time when there were probably more people in America who could sing "John Brown's body lies a-moldering in the grave" than any other song or hymn. And yet another historian, Dr. Frank H. Hodder, also a Kansan, wrote that John Brown's fame has been perpetuated through what he called the "accident" of the John Brown song. But the man must have done something to catch the imagination of the people or to smite the conscience of the nation to inspire the "accidental" popularity of a song so long remembered and so frequently sung. Who was this Old John Brown whose soul goes marching on?

The answer is short but not simple: he was a homely old farmer and tanner of Ohio and northern New York and wool dealer in Massachusetts who became the guerrilla captain of Bleeding Kansas and the raider at Harpers Ferry. And he is also one of the most controversial characters in all American history; there is today just as much divergent opinion about the man and his acts as there was in 1859 when the hangman at Charles Town, in what is now West Virginia, sent him plunging into his measure of immortality. His is a story of bloodshed and violence and of a one-man war against Negro slavery. He troubled his foes more than ever when they nailed his coffin down. John Brown, dead, was a more powerful force than John Brown living, and his old, dead hands reached out from his lonely grave at bleak North Elba, New York—high up in the Adirondacks—to turn the pages of history long after his sturdy frame had moldered into dust.

To flash back to the personal story of the man, John Brown was born May 9, 1800, at Torrington, Connecticut, the second of Owen Brown's sixteen children. He came of good New England stock, from a God-fearing pioneer family that traced its American lineage back to Peter Brown, the carpenter of the *Mayflower*. His grandfather, Captain John Brown, died while serving in the patriot army in the American Revolution.

At the age of five Brown was taken by his parents to Hudson, Ohio, and there he was reared. Following in his father's footsteps he became a farmer and tanner, with fair success in business in his early years. Also following his Yankee abolitionist father—as well as conforming to the prevailing sentiment in the Hudson settlement—he became a strong anti-slavery advocate in early youth. But he married at the age of twenty and children came into his home—one after another in quick succession until there were twenty of them—and for many years he had to scratch so hard to feed so many hungry mouths that there was scant time for anti-slavery activities.

In 1826 he removed to Randolph (now New Richmond), a few miles east of Meadville, Pennsylvania, where he hewed a farm out of the wilderness and set up a tannery. He establishd a community, organized a church and school in his own home, was the village postmaster and the recognized community leader. There he lived for ten years, and this was the most peaceful and prosperous period in the nearly sixty years of his turbulent life.

But the grass always looks greener on the other side of the fence. He was caught by the lure of the promise of easy money by trade and speculation in a boom town. Brown hurriedly closed his affairs at Randolph and removed to Franklin Mills, Ohio (now the industrial city of Kent), where he bought lands well beyond his means and laid out an addition to the village. For a time all went well; then the bubble burst and in 1840 he was thrown into bankruptcy. To add to his financial woes he had, in a desperate effort to save his property, taken for his own use $2,800 which had been entrusted to him by George Kellogg, agent for the New England Woolen Mills of Rockford, Connecticut, to buy wool for the concern from the Ohio sheep farmers. Fortunately for him, the woolen company was lenient and no prose-

the New England Mills became heavy buyers of their western wools. How much, if any, of the old debt was paid in these transactions is not known, but there was a balance still due when Brown came to his end at Charles Town—in his last will he bequeathed $50 to be paid to Kellogg on the debt.

To mend his broken fortunes after the debacle at Franklin Mills, Brown turned again to farming, tanning, and sheep-raising, without much gain in purse other than a bare living for himself and family. But notwithstanding his business reverses and the embezzlement of the wool-buying money, he still maintained a reputation for old-fashioned New England honesty and integrity, and his industry was unquestioned. So it was that in 1844 he was able to enter into a partnership with Colonel Simon Perkins, one of the wealthiest citizens of Akron, Ohio, to manage a large flock of sheep, and in 1846 the firm opened a wool depot at Springfield, Massachusetts, to dispose of wool for western sheep farmers. It was really a big business, involving thousands of dollars in the monthly transactions. Brown was in sole charge of the depot. But as the years rolled on he became more actively engaged in anti-slavery work, sometimes to the disadvantage of his commercial trade. After the passage of the Fugitive Slave Act of 1850, for example, he organized a group of fugitives at Springfield and counseled them to resist capture. A combination of circumstances, some of his own making, caused the business to collapse in 1850 and he, flat broke again, returned to Akron to help Perkins straighten out their tangled affairs. Brown was an acknowledged judge of wool and a good shepherd, but by nature he was not fitted for the management of a large business—he was a failure in the wool trade.

John Brown's life up to his fifty-fifth year was not above the commonplace. He had been a farmer, tanner, shepherd, real estate promoter, and whatnot, with most of his ventures ending badly. Now a new field of operation was opened to him. For twenty years, he said, he had prayed and planned for freedom of the Negroes held in slavery, and now cutting loose from all trade and commerce, even from his wife and small children left in the family home at North Elba, New York, he dedicated the few remaining years of his life to Negro freedom. Kansas was the testing ground, and there he was to come into national notice as a grim, relentless, ruthless crusader and Free State partisan.

Five of Brown's sons removed to Kansas Territory in the spring of 1855. It was then the battleground between the pro-slavery and anti-slavery forces. The South was determined to make Kansas a slave state, the North was equally determined that it should be free. Brown joined his sons in October, 1855, and almost coincident with his arrival became embroiled in the border war. With his own little company he made his name feared as a guerrilla leader of Free State forces all along the border. It was at the battle of Osawatomie, fought on August 30, 1856, where he made a losing defense, that he won his name by which he is popularly known—Osawatomie Brown. His one act in Kansas that has been most severely condemned by friend and foe was the summary execution—or massacre—of five pro-slavery men on the Pottawatomie on the night of May 24, 1856. Brown led his little company to the settlement at the dead hour of midnight, took the men from their homes and cut them down with broad-swords; it was a bloody business that spread terror in the ranks of the pro-slavery element, but at that time was only conditionally condemned by the Free State partisans. It must be remembered that in the Kansas troubles the embattled partisans fought a brutal guerrilla type of warfare in which murder was considered moral and theft pious. They made the rules as they went along.

Brown's name began to appear in the news dispatches published in the eastern newspapers, and as his reputation grew his plans for a one-man war on slavery expanded. Perhaps it was his ego exalted by exaggerated reports of his Kansas exploits, or perhaps it was his Old Testament sense of Christian duty to the bondmen. Even before the Kansas troubles were ended he was planning raids into slave states on a more extended scale. He was always a lone wolf in the field, and, distrusting the organized abolition societies, he kept his plans to himself. Even his closest associates who were asked to give money liberally for his "greatest or principal object" were not taken into full confidence. Better for them after the Harpers Ferry strike.

Kansas grew quiet. The North had won; Free State settlers

In the Spring of 1858 all things seemed to be in readiness for the big strike. Brown assembled the eleven men comprising the nucleus of his Army of Liberation and with thirty-five Negroes held a convention at Chatham, Canada, to adopt a Constitution and to organize a free government for the area to be taken over by liberated slaves. The plan seemed to be to move directly from Chatham at the adjournment of the convention to the yet undisclosed point of attack. But while the convention was in session word came that Brown's former military advisor, Colonel Hugh Forbes, a British soldier of fortune, had become disgruntled and had made disclosures of the plans as far as he knew them. In a panic the secret committee urged suspension of immediate action and tried to recall arms which had been furnished to Brown. He was sent back to Kansas for a cooling period, and there he added to his reputation by raiding into Missouri and liberating eleven slaves.

John Brown capped his militant career and won his greatest measure of fame or infamy—depending altogether upon the point of view—by virtue of his abortive raid on Harpers Ferry on the cold, drizzly Sunday night of October 16, 1859. That place was selected as the first objective in the one-man war because of the location there of a U. S. Armory and Arsenal; arms would be needed for the hordes of slaves expected to be liberated. The town was quickly taken, but Brown had not reckoned on the rapid mobilization of the Virginia militia of the neighboring town. After Monday noon he was ringed in by the militia and volunteer groups of citizens, and escape was impossible. At daybreak on Tuesday morning, October 18th, U. S. Marines under command of Brevet Colonel Robert E. Lee battered down the doors of the fire engine house in the Army enclosure in which the surviving remnant of the Army of Liberation had taken refuge. It was all over in a few minutes. The raid had failed and the Negroes were still held in bondage. Three citizens, a Marine, a free Negro, and two slaves were killed in the fighting, and nine militiamen and one Marine were wounded. But of Brown's little Army of Liberation of twenty-two men, including himself, ten were killed outright, seven, including Brown, were captured and later hanged at Charles Town, and five made good their escape. But not a single slave was liberated.

The Harpers Ferry raid was one of the momentous events in American history. Insignificant as it was in itself and in its immediate results, it was the one spark needed to explode the stored up hates and differences cumulating for years between the two sections of the country. Truly it was the curtain-raiser—though not the immediate cause—of the war between the sections which followed less than two years later. John Brown struck at slavery, the sorest point at issue between the North and South, in a way that he well knew could not fail to arouse both sections to frenzied and intemperate action.

John Brown lost the battle at Harpers Ferry, but as events shaped themselves within a few years, his cause was not lost. He was hurried into trial, and as hurriedly convicted of murder, treason, and conspiring with slaves to rebel—all capital crimes. Thirty days after sentence of death was passed on him, on the morning of December 2, 1859, he marched unflinchingly to the scaffold at Charles Town.

And so with flaming torch and blazing guns at Harpers Ferry, John Brown marked the beginning of the road that led to Lincoln's Proclamation of Emancipation of the slaves, and to the surrender of Lee's Army at Appomattox five years later. His "greatest or principal object" had been accomplished. And soldiers marched toward their homes singing: "John Brown's body lies a-moldering in the grave, But his soul is marching on!"

". . . a consuming desire to . . . elevate society"

was working as a woodchopper, and

stances Horace Greeley grew up. When he died in 1872, Henry Ward Beecher, the greatest pulpit orator of the times, preached his funeral sermon. "Today," he declared, "between the two oceans, there is scarcely an intelligent man or child that does not feel the influence of Horace Greeley." And Greeley rose to his position in his sixty years despite a rather unstable physical constitution, without any formal education beyond a few years of district school, and lacking the support of a happy and sympathetic home life.

Although his rise from poverty to power may seem to follow an American pattern, Greeley was quite as distinctively American in his variations from such a norm. In his eccentricities, his aberrations, his inconsistencies he was following an exploratory idealism which is one of the most precious phases of the American spirit.

Horace was a precocious boy, with an overmastering passion for print and facts. He could read almost anything in English by the time he was four years old, and before he reached his teens he had read the Bible through, most of Shakespeare, and all the books available to him in the neighborhood, as well as every newspaper he could lay hands on. His was not a bookish home by any means, nor were there any notably literary influences in the community—the drive to read and to know seems to have originated right inside the head of Horace himself.

Between the ages of four and thirteen this boy was able to attend the district school four or five months out of each year; but he began riding horse to plough when he was five, and work on the farm interfered with school. Besides, the schoolteacher said to Zack Greeley, Horace's father, one day when the lad was thirteen: "It's a pack of nonsense sending that boy of yours to school: he knows a sight more than I do a'ready." So ended the formal education of Horace Greeley. But not his self-education, for the fascination of print and facts was stronger than ever within him.

Moreover, he began teasing his father to let him go to town and learn the printer's trade, and when he was fifteen Horace was apprenticed to the editor of the *Northern Spectator*, in East Poultney, Vermont. He had come into his own. He was later to become a candidate for high public office, an author of books, and a lecturer of some note; but the newspaper was ever his true vocation, his school, his livelihood, his forum, his career.

The *Spectator* was a poor paper, and when it failed Horace rolled all his personal possessions into a bundle which he attached to the end of a stout stick. Carrying this over his shoulder he set out on foot for northwestern Pennsylvania, whither his father and mother had emigrated a few years earlier, and where they were now doing as badly as usual. He did not stay with them long, but found jobs at Erie, Pennsylvania, and across the line in New York towns. Those were the days when the brotherhood of "itinerant typographical artists"—better known as "tramp printers"—flourished, because nearly everything in the printing office was done by hand, work piled up, and a newcomer could almost always be used for a few days at least, to catch up. But this purposeless life could not hold Horace Greeley; and he soon set out for New York City.

It was an odd, gangling figure that entered the town on August 17, 1831. Horace was twenty years old, dressed in shrunken homespun with high country boots and a shapeless white hat; and he walked with a shambling gait. Possible employers were amused by the high-pitched whine of his voice, his mild little blue eyes in a round moon face, and his country manners; they refused him curtly, one after the other. There is a story that after Horace did get a job on the *Evening Post*, Editor William Leggett happened into the composing room. Seeing the new man he exclaimed: "For God's sake, fire him; let's have decent-*looking* men around here anyway!"

But Horace was a good workman. Moreover, he was extremely industrious and saving. After he had been in New York only about a year, he found a partner in another printer named Francis Story, who helped him get $200 together to set up a business of their own, based chiefly on credit, hard work, and ideas. One of the ideas was that of a penny paper; but this project had a run of bad luck—snowstorms that prevented street sales, bad editing, inadequate financing, and so on—and it lasted only two or three weeks. When Greeley's partner was accidentally drowned, he went on alone, founding a week-end miscellany called the *New* ... paper which seems to have

the Whigs ...
1838. This was called the *Jeffersonian*; it did its work ... was followed during the presidential campaign two years later by another called the *Log-Cabin*, in the picturesque log-cabin and hard-cider campaign which elected Harrison to the tune of "Tippecanoe and Tyler Too."

It was the great success of the latter paper which caused Greeley to resolve to start a Whig penny daily of his own in New York, which he did in 1841 under the name of the *Tribune*. Brilliant as this paper was, it had strong competition, and would doubtless have failed if its editor had not persuaded Thomas McElrath, a lawyer with publishing experience and a faculty for organization, to take a partnership in the venture. "Blessed is the Greeley who can find a McElrath!" exclaimed James Parton in the first biography of the famous editor.

Thereafter the *Tribune* was a striking success. Its daily edition never topped the lot in New York, but the *Weekly Tribune*, which circulated upstate and in New England, and along the path of the Yankee emigration to the West, had a phenomenal circulation. It served to crystallize thinking on the great issues of the time for that great segment of the population which may be called "Transplanted New England." Greeley was a part of that segment himself, and he became its spokesman. An Illinois farmer was listening to a political argument in the country store. Finally one of the disputants turned to him and asked: "Silas, what do you think about this?" The farmer scratched his head. "Wal, now," he replied, "what does Horace say about it?" It was not that he was delegating all his *thinking* to Horace, but he was willing to turn over the *saying* to his favorite editor because he knew that he and Horace thought alike on most things.

The chief Greeley "causes" may be enumerated:

1. *Antislavery.* Not originally a strict abolitionist, Greeley

eventually wrote a famous editorial, "The Prayer of Twenty Millions," urging Lincoln to sign the Emancipation Proclamation.

2. *Temperance.* His observation of the evils of intoxication among the poor made him a strong supporter of the Maine Law and other prohibitory measures.

3. *The Westward Movement.* His own boyhood sufferings and his observation of life in the slums of New York, as well as a "manifest destiny" philosophy, led Greeley to feature the advice "Go west, young man," and to urge enactment of the Homestead Law and the construction of a railroad to the Pacific.

4. *Social Amelioration.* Greeley was continually on the look-out for systematic reforms which would equalize opportunity in American society. For several years he was interested in the communal organization of life known as Fourierism, of which the most famous example in this country was the Brook Farm experiment, near Boston. He was for labor unionism, and active in the formation of the first effective typographical union; he was for joint-stock ownership of industry, and formed the Tribune Association to control his own business; he was for making the rich lands of the Midwest easy to acquire by farmers through homesteading.

Besides these major "causes," Greeley gave attention in the *Tribune* to many adventures in thought and life—what the conservatives of the time condemned as "isms." His greatness as a journalist is based upon his devotion to the business and art of the communication of important matters, upon a lucid and pungent style often infused with feeling, and upon his policy of presenting new ideas and fresh systems of thought.

Oddities of appearance and behavior marked Greeley throughout life. He was no poseur; he simply did not take the trouble to conform. His was a round, rather pallid face surrounded by a halo of tow-colored hair above and straggly under-chin whiskers. He always wore heavy boots such as he had been accustomed to in youth; outdoors he wore a white country hat and light, wrinkled coat. His clothes hung on him, rather than fitting him. His posture was always bad; standing, sitting, or walking, he always bent over. His gait was the shambling, uneven walk of the "clodhopper."

But this man of clownish appearance and squeaky voice could write like an angel. Always an idealist, he was caught and held by a consuming desire to give opportunity to the downtrodden, correct economic abuses, and elevate society.

What Greeley thought of as the climax of his career turned out to be final tragedy when, in 1872, he was nominated as the reform candidate for President and was decisively defeated. This [illegible] coupled with the death of his wife,

BENJAMIN P. THOMAS

EDWIN MCMASTERS STANTON, lawyer, cabinet member under three presidents, and one of the most controversial figures in American history, was born in Steubenville, Ohio, on December 19, 1814. His father, a physician, died when Edwin was twelve years old, and soon afterward the boy was apprenticed to a bookseller who allowed him time off to attend school. At seventeen he was admitted to Kenyon College, at Gambier, Ohio. But he was the chief support of his widowed mother, a younger brother, and two sisters, and after a year and a half at Kenyon he was obliged to go to work.

Unable to complete his college course, Stanton studied law in the office of his guardian, Daniel L. Collier, at Steubenville. At twenty-one he was admitted to practice. A tireless worker and a dogged courtroom fighter, he advanced rapidly in his profession. He also took an active part in Democratic politics. Although he never sought an important office for himself, he helped to formulate policy at county and state conventions and was an effective campaign speaker. A fervent Jacksonian Democrat, he was hostile to private banks and special privilege of all sorts. His parents had been abolitionists, and he detested slavery and southern aristocrats. He favored the Wilmot Proviso, which would have prohibited slavery in all territory acquired by the United States in the war with Mexico. Salmon P. Chase, one of Ohio's most resolute antislavery spokesmen, became one of his closest friends.

Stanton's boundless energy demanded that he be busy without letup. In 1847 he moved to Pittsburgh, where his legal talents would have a wider range. Nine years later he moved to Washington, where he had an extensive practice before the United States Supreme Court. In 1858 he was appointed special counsel for the government with respect to certain land claims in California, which had originated in questionable Mexican grants. The property at issue was valued at more than one hundred and fifty million dollars, and Stanton performed a signal service in unmasking the fraudulent nature of many of these claims.

Meanwhile, Stanton's attitude toward slavery had undergone a fundamental change. From the time he moved to Pittsburgh, where the business interests wanted harmony between the sections, he had avoided taking any action that might mark him as an antislavery man. Then, as the rift widened between North and South, he assumed a conservative position. He accepted the Dred Scott decision whereby the Supreme Court declared that neither Congress nor a territorial legislature could exclude slavery from the national domain. He supported President James Buchanan's proslavery policies in Kansas. He favored John C. Breckinridge, the most pro-Southern of all the presidential candidates in the campaign of 1860, believing that only through his election could the Union be preserved. This, in any case, was Stanton as he appeared to his Democratic friends; members of his family still considered him an antislavery man.

The election of Abraham Lincoln as President brought the nation to the brink of civil war, and President Buchanan found himself hindered and embarrassed during the last months of his administration by secessionists in his cabinet. Prevailed on to replace these southern sympathizers with men of unquestioned loyalty, he reorganized his cabinet and appointed Stanton Attorney-General. Stanton worked closely and effectively with his fellow unionists, Jeremiah S. Black, Joseph Holt, and John A. Dix, to counteract secessionist designs and stiffen Buchanan's backbone. Thus, the President determined to defend Fort Sumter in Charleston harbor, and attempted to reinforce it. He avoided taking any action that might be interpreted as granting legal recognition to the Confederacy.

Easily excited, Stanton suspected the Confederates of plotting to seize Washington, or to prevent Lincoln from taking office. Still fearful that Buchanan might fail to act decisively in a crisis, he secretly informed the Republican leaders in Congress of the dangers he apprehended, and of the administration's shortcomings. He was not alone in this activity; Secretary of War Holt was doing the same thing. But later, when Stanton's dealings with the Republicans became known, he was charged with betraying Buchanan.

During the early months of Lincoln's administration, Stanton

Cameron as Secretary of War.

Stanton brought financial honesty and tremendous energy to the administration of the War Department. Favoritism was abolished. New and efficient purchasing methods were introduced. Some fraudulent contracts were canceled and some thieving contractors were jailed. Stanton obtained authorization from Congress to take control of the railroads. He assumed control of the telegraph system and instituted a rigorous censorship. Internal security was brought under his charge; he put a host of suspected seditionists under military arrest. Many of the government's dealings with state governors, notably the administration of the draft, came within his jurisdiction.

Stanton became notorious for his brusque and arrogant demeanor toward officers and civilians alike. He was known as the "terrible Stanton" and the "black terrier." Yet he also performed many acts of kindness. Nothwithstanding the severity that marked his official conduct, he was warmly affectionate in his home life and devoted to his aging mother. He took his brother's widow, a divorced sister, and their numerous children into his home. As a matter of fact, his bad temper came partly from poor health. Asthma plagued him from the age of ten, and overwork brought on a liver ailment.

Stanton had been a close friend of General McClellan, the commander-in-chief of the armies, when he first entered Lincoln's cabinet. But he soon lost confidence in him. Stanton's dealings were often devious, sometimes downright deceitful, and while working for McClellan's removal he professed to be his friend. But he used the resources of his department unstintingly to keep the General's needs supplied. The War Secretary was accused of deliberately thwarting McClellan by withholding troops from him. The charge was untrue; for Lincoln was deciding how the troops should be disposed at this stage of the war. Stanton's intimacy with certain radical Republicans in Congress, who opposed Lincoln's policies, gave rise to suspicions that Stanton may have been disloyal to Lincoln, but the charge remains unproved to this day. Stanton often differed with the President, and was sometimes disdainful of him behind his back; but on the whole the two men respected and trusted each other and worked together effectively.

The passions growing out of war reanimated Stanton's early loathing for slavery and southern aristocrats. Perhaps this feeling had never been wholly absent from his mind. He was quite ready to believe that the slaveocracy had instigated Lincoln's murder, and he made every effort to implicate Jefferson Davis and other Confederate leaders in the plot. He had supported Lincoln's lenient reconstruction policies during Lincoln's lifetime, but he now aligned himself with the Republican radicals who planned to degrade the South.

Stanton stayed on as Secretary of War in President Andrew Johnson's cabinet, but when Johnson changed his attitude toward the South from sternness to moderation, Stanton became first his secret and then his open enemy. He worked hand in glove with Johnson's political enemies while continuing to hold a position of trust in his administration.

Stanton could plead patriotic motives for his treachery toward Johnson. He agreed with the radicals that the war would have been fought in vain if the unpunished and unrepentent Southern leaders, working in alliance with disloyalists in the North, were allowed to regain control of the government. Johnson finally decided to remove him from office, but Stanton stubbornly resisted. The radicals in Congress accused Johnson of illegal use of power in attempting to force him out, and brought impeachment charges against the President. When Johnson was exonerated by the narrow margin of one vote, Stanton surrendered his office.

During the presidential campaign of 1868, Stanton made a few speeches in support of Grant. After the election, his radical friends persuaded Grant to appoint him to the Supreme Court. But Stanton never wore the judicial robe. Illness and exhaustion had taken a heavy toll, and he died the day before Christmas, in 1869. He had just turned fifty-five. Had his public career ended at the same time Lincoln's did, and before he had deviated from the course that Lincoln set, he would hold a brighter place in history today.

[illegible] S. Grant

men under fire that defy easy [illegible] vestigation to evidence provided by our own Civil War, the variety of personality types that have produced excellent generalship is astounding. There was Robert E. Lee, for instance—quiet, reserved, aristocratic, conservative—yet a daring tactician, beloved of his men. On the Union side think of George B. McClellan, in nearly every way Lee's opposite. Fond of flashy uniforms and bold display, seen most typically clattering romantically through his camp on a spirited horse in the company of his handsome, worshipful aides, he was a fine strategist and equally as admired by common soldiers as Lee. Yet McClellan was cautious to the point of timidity in battle, where the placid Lee was bold.

Many other Civil War generals can be used to show how different outstanding soldiers can be and how mysterious the relationship between personality and battlefield performance. There was William Tecumseh Sherman, who believed that war was "all hell" but who made it particularly hellish for the citizens of Georgia. He was tense, testy, and overly forthright as a man, but possessed of as sound a military judgment as the War produced. Phil Sheridan, on the other hand, was a brave, dashing, reckless, almost careless leader in battle, but out of contact with the enemy a reserved, self-controlled man who devoted endless hours to caring for the routine needs of his men. "Stonewall" Jackson, to cite one more case, was in private life devout, deliberate, and unprepossessing, yet no more daring or imaginative commander ever lived.

The subjects of the two following essays were about as dissimilar as two men can be. Beauregard, the "Napoleon in Grey," appeared the very model of the perfect soldier. Grant, unable, as Bruce Catton says, to "quite manage to keep his uniform *buttoned," was as unsoldierly in appearance and in temperament as one could conceive. But of course, Grant was by far the greater soldier of the two.*

However, the stories of Beauregard and Grant belong together in these pages, and not simply because they were both Civil War generals. Both are representative of what so often happens to military heroes after they put aside their arms. Like Washington, Jackson, William Henry Harrison, and Zachary Taylor before him (and like a number of other soldiers, including Eisenhower, in later years), Grant became President of the United States. Beauregard could not, because of his position as a former Confederate general, be active politically, but he prospered as a railroad president. The American people have always rewarded their favorite generals handsomely. Beauregard flourished in his new career, and Grant, had he wished it, might have been the first three-term President in our history.

The sad aspect of such careers is that sometimes the hero is asked to perform tasks for which his talents and experience have failed to prepare him. There is something pathetic both in Beauregard's posing on the stage in his splendid uniform during the drawings of the Louisiana Lottery, and in Grant's stolid administration of the highest office in the land. Power and prestige, these two careers teach us, are not inevitably associated with happiness, or even with true dignity.

T. Harry Williams is Boyd Professor of History at Louisiana State University and a former President of the Southern Historical Association. He has written widely on the Civil War, his best-known works including, besides a biography of Beauregard, Lincoln and the Radicals, Lincoln and His Generals, *and* With Beauregard in Mexico. *Bruce Catton is the editor of the magazine* American Heritage. *His* A Stillness at Appomattox, *third of three volumes on the Union Army, won him the Pulitzer Prize. He has also written many other books about the Civil War, the latest of which is* Grant Moves South.

"... the South's first hero"

T. HARRY WILLIAMS

in his Creole orig[illegible]
suggested a more exotic environment than the South of J[illegible] Davis. A vague air of romance, reminiscent of an older civilization, trailed after him wherever he went. When he spoke and when he acted, people thought of Paris and Napoleon and Austerlitz and French legions bursting from the St. Bernard pass onto the plains of Italy. Even down to the last bitter hours of Confederate defeat, he seemed to carry with him the sound of bugles, the flash of martial swords, and an aura of magnolias and roses.

His military career was one of the most unique in the Confederacy. It was not confined to one narrow area like Lee's or interrupted by long periods of inactivity like Joseph E. Johnston's or cut off before the end of the war like Braxton Bragg's. Beauregard was in every important phase of the war from its beginning to its end. No other Confederate general served in as many different theaters. He fired the opening guns of the great drama at Fort Sumter. He commanded the Confederate forces in the first great battle of the war at Manassas. He planned and fought the first big battle in the West at Shiloh. From the West he went to Charleston, and there he conducted the war's longest and most skillful defense of a land point against attack from the sea. In 1864 he was called to direct the defenses of the southern approaches to Richmond. Later in that year the government assigned him to command a huge department with empty resources in the West. In the waning months of the war he tried vainly to halt the onward rush of Sherman through Georgia and the Carolinas.

He saw most of the war to preserve the Old South. When his cause crashed in defeat and the dream was ended, he was able to adapt himself to the ways of the New South. He was more successful than any other prominent Confederate general in making money in the hard postwar years. And that is why—for a time—he became a forgotten man in the southern tradition. In the southern myth, Confederate heroes, like other people in the reconstruction era, were supposed to live in honorable poverty. Beauregard did not conform to the legend. He ran railroads and, of all un-Confederate actions, presided over the drawings of a lottery company. When he died he left a fortune that in terms of the present dollar would be reckoned at half a million. It seemed very wrong to many people.

Beauregard was born on May 28, 1818, on a plantation called Contreras a few miles below New Orleans in St. Bernard Parish. His family was of the proud Creole aristocracy of south Louisiana. The Creoles were of French descent. They were Americans, and yet in many ways they were apart from all things American. They considered themselves as cultivated Europeans living in a crude new world. They tried to preserve their old culture against the American hordes who poured into Louisiana after the territory was purchased from France. Young Beauregard was raised a Frenchman, and in many respects he would always be a Frenchman. His father gave him a rich Gallic name: Pierre Gustave Toutant Beauregard. It would ring grandly in the future annals of fame. It would also always stamp its bearer as different outside the delta country. That resounding title would stand out in the Anglo-Saxon Confederacy like *pompano en papillote* in a mess of turnip greens. His French background was one of the paradoxes of his life. He was an ardent Southerner, but in the Confederacy he would always be viewed with a certain reserve. He was an alien—that queer Frenchman.

While yet a boy, Beauregard found a hero and decided on a profession. His hero was the great Napoleon, upon whom he would model himself for the rest of his life. And, like Napoleon, he determined to be a soldier. He asked his father to get him admitted to the United States Military Academy at West Point. Entering the school in 1834, he graduated four years later with high honors, second in his class.

Then followed a series of dull, routine assignments in the small peacetime regular army. Beauregard finally ended up in his native state directing engineering work around the mouths of the Mississippi River. He had time to visit in New Orleans and in the homes of Creole friends. At one plantation he met the beautiful Marie Laure Villere. He loved her at once, courted her overwhelmingly, and soon made her his bride. Three children were born to the marriage, two sons and a daughter.

Lieutenant Beauregard's first chance for fame came in the [illegible] He was one of the group of able young engineer

[illegible]

departures from the accepted rules of war. [illegible] signs of weakness in an otherwise fine soldier: a tendency to criticize his superiors and a conviction that battles must be fought according to a rigid pattern.

After 1848 Beauregard resumed his army duties in Louisiana, where he would remain until 1860. During these years his wife died, and he remarried—another Creole belle. He continued to rise in his profession, winning praises from the high brass and being rewarded with important assignments. Late in 1860, right on the eve of the secession of the Southern states, he secured one of the best positions in the Army: superintendent of the Military Academy at West Point. He went to Washington, informed his superiors that if Louisiana seceded he would go with his state, and then went on to West Point and assumed his duties. The directing heads of the Army, aware of the mistake they had made in placing an avowed secessionist in charge of the school, issued immediate orders for his removal. He gave up the office after a tenure of five days, the shortest superintendency in the Academy's history.

Beauregard returned to Louisiana to offer his services to the newly formed Confederate States of America. Largely because of his engineering reputation, he was named by President Jefferson Davis to command the Confederate forces in Charleston, the first general officer to be commissioned by the Confederacy. He was starting on the glory road. He captured Fort Sumter and became the South's first hero. Called to Virginia, he won the battle of Manassas, and was acclaimed as the South's first soldier. The public, especially the women, worshipped him. Five feet seven in height, weighing about 150 pounds, with dark hair and olive complexion, he looked like a French marshal or like Napoleon in a grey uniform.

Then the trouble started. Always inclined to question his superiors, he dared to criticize President Davis. He let himself get mixed up in a series of controversies with Davis and the Secretary of War. Finally the President shifted him to the Western theater, where he was second and then first in command. He was widely blamed for the failure of the Confederates to win a decisive victory at Shiloh. Now the glory road was about ended for him. Davis exiled him to the relatively minor command at Charleston, where he won some laurels that did not quite redeem his reputation. In 1864 he came back to Virginia in another secondary command. Then the government sent him to the West again as a kind of figurehead commander for the duration of the war. In between his many travels he found time to design the Confederate battle flag, the famous emblem which present Southerners and Yankees fondly mistake for the official flag of the Confederacy.

As a general, Beauregard was a paradox. He was given to turning out grand plans of large strategy. His plans would not work because they were not related to realities. They were too ambitious for the scanty Confederate resources. And they inspired distrust because of the excited Gallic manner in which he presented them. But as theatrical and impractical as he seemed before a battle, Beauregard was a different man once conflict was joined. Then he became a grim and purposeful warrior. He was a solid combat soldier. Had he been given the chance, he would have developed into one of the Confederacy's great fighting captains.

After the war Beauregard returned to New Orleans. While other Confederate generals struggled to make modest livings, Beauregard went from success to success. He became president of two railroad companies, and finally accepted a lucrative job as front man for the Louisiana Lottery, a gigantic gambling organization. He died in 1893, a rich man by the Southern standards of his time. The legal inventory made of his possessions revealed his wealth. It listed everything he owned, including property in Louisiana and three other states.

The final enigma of his life was in that inventory. There in the painfully listed columns was the sword which the ladies of New Orleans had presented to him after he captured Fort Sumter, and the little red-topped artillery general's cap which he had worn at Manassas and Shiloh, and the battle flag which a famous Southern belle had made for him from her own dress in the exultant days of 1861—faded and pathetic relics of the Old South. There, too, and more numerous and significant, were the

". . . what his country had to have done"

BRUCE CATTON

AMERICA in the early 1860s was a loose-jointed sort of place. It had strength where nobody would expect to find it, its strength always went hand-in-hand with weakness, and under everything there was a tough fibre which meant, finally, survival and a continuation of the great American dream.

So there was a little town on the Mississippi named Galena, Illinois—a boom town, in a way, making money out of the nearby lead mines and the Mississippi river traffic; nothing extraordinary about it, just a Middle-western town where people made a living and tried to have fun and didn't worry too much about appearances. In this town there was a harness shop, and back of the counter there was a slouchy, rather mildewed little man with an uneven beard and a pair of level clear eyes, who looked as if he had had a lot of hard luck but was maybe going to get the better of it some day—an under-sized and unimpressive person named Ulysses S. Grant, a former captain in the United States Army.

Grant had had his times, He grew up in southern Ohio, in the 1830s and 1840s, a lad with no especial aims in life except that he liked to ride horses and loved the sandy roads and the rolling, wood-covered hills of his native land. They sent him to the U. S. Military Academy, rather against his will; he was graduated in the exact center of his class, and in the Mexican War he made a good record (as did a great many other young officers) and he came out of it a captain by brevet.

After the Mexican War things had not gone well with him. While still in the service he married Julia Dent, daughter of a Missouri planter, which was the one thing in that decade that went right for him. She was literally the only woman in his life, and most of his troubles came on later when they were apart. When she was away, Grant seems to have been a little less than whole. But the Army sent Grant out to the west coast, where he could not take his wife and children, and he wasted his time doing boring military chores on God-forsaken Army posts in the desolate wilds of the northwest coast. He brooded, felt unhappy, took to drink, and finally had to resign from the Army.

Then came lean years. He tried to farm in Missouri, and failed; tried to sell real estate in St. Louis, and failed; got down on his uppers, wound up as back-of-the-counter man in his father's leather-goods store in Galena, and looked like a middle-aged man who had failed at everything.

Along came the Civil War: and suddenly it developed that slouchy little U. S. Grant, who could never quite manage to keep his uniform buttoned and who disliked military life intensely, was a born soldier and a great commander—the one man who could take the Armies of the United States (made up of young men very much like himself) and win a great war with them. Grant went off to war as colonel of the 21st Illinois Volunteer Infantry. He served in Missouri briefly, got promoted to brigadier general through rank favoritism (his Congressman was allowed to nominate one brigadier, and he could not think of anybody he liked better than little Colonel Grant) and after that things started to happen.

In the winter of 1862 Grant led an expedition which captured Fort Henry and Fort Donelson, in northern Tennessee. Fort Henry was easy, but Fort Donelson was tough. Grant penned 15,000 Confederates in it, and when their commander, General Simon Boliver Buckner, sent him a note asking what terms he would offer, Grant wrote a note that became famous: he would offer, he said, no terms but "immediate and unconditional surrender." Although the Confederate complained that these terms were rough and ungenerous, he finally accepted them, and Grant was "Unconditional Surrender Grant" all across the North.

Then Grant drove south. He fought and won the terrible battle of Shiloh, got in bad with his government because it was falsely

reported that he was drunk at the time, came close to resigning from the Army once again because he was being ignored by high authority, and then snapped out of it, put on one of the
... of the Civil War, and in the early sum-

crippling invasion of Georgia the following spring. ...
was clearly tagged as a winner. He never had much to say, he never struck any lofty attitudes, and that fondness for drink seemed to stay with him—although it is notable that he never indulged it when the chips were down: his benders always took place in dull periods, when nothing much was going on—and yet somehow he had a quality that all other Union generals lacked. In his quiet way he was a driver; he seemed easygoing, but when he showed up things happened, and the dull work of preparation and organization got done; and so in March, 1864, President Lincoln made him lieutenant-general and gave him top command of all of the country's armies.

That was the beginning of the end for the Southern Confederacy. Grant sent Sherman down into Georgia, and himself took the Army of the Potomac into Virginia against Robert E. Lee. Lee was a matchless strategist, and nobody up to now had ever been able to cope with him; Grant simply kept crowding him, robbed him of the chance to use his strategic ability, pinned his army against the wall in the squalid trenches around Petersburg, Virginia (the key to the Confederate capital of Richmond), and waited while Sherman tore the heart out of the Confederacy. His strategy was non-spectacular and it did not give the newspaper boys much to write about—and it cost a very large number of lives, to boot—but in the end it worked. By the spring of 1865 it was time for the payoff. Lee had to retreat from Petersburg and Richmond, Grant pursued him and caught up with him, and on April 9 Lee surrendered his "unbeatable" army at Appomattox Courthouse. A little later the other Confederate armies surrendered and the war was over. It had mostly been the doing of Ulysses S. Grant.

Grant's career after the war was spotty. He had never wanted to be a soldier, and yet it was only as a soldier that he could use his capacities to their fullest extent. When the war ended, his chance to use himself the way he was meant to be used came to an end. He wound up, inevitably, as Republican candidate for President, in 1868. He was elected, served two terms, and somehow gave his great name to one of the unhappiest periods in American history.

Probably no President could have done very well in the eight years beginning on March 4, 1869. The war had blown the lid off everything. Old moral standards had been discarded and new ones were not yet formed; industry was on the prowl, every man was out for himself, the terrible problems of reconstruction of the Union were coming up for settlement in an era when nobody except the vengeful men with axes to grind wanted to think about them. The "U. S. Grant era," as it is known, was a pretty sorry time.

There was corruption in government—bribery, favoritism, and an unabashed atmosphere of every man for himself and hang the appearances. Reconstruction became less a business of putting the Union back together than of finding a way by which grasping politicians could remain in office. The Negro, whom Grant more than any other man (except Lincoln himself) had freed from his shackles, became a mere pawn in a political struggle, and neither he nor his former masters fared well in the turbulent years after 1869. It is not possible for any American, North or South, to take much comfort from a study of those years.

Grant did his best. He was honest, patriotic, and well-intentioned. He had saved the Union, he wanted it re-cemented again, he wanted the Negro kept free and given a fair chance, and he hoped that peace could mean prosperity and good times for all Americans. His mind was never an analytic one, and in the intricacies of American politics he was a babe in the woods; and he was used, finally, by some of the worst elements in the country—used, simply because the mental and emotional qualities that had made him a great soldier were precisely the qualities that were of no use to him as President of the United States.

He left the White House, at last, toured the world, got into an odd Wall Street bucket-shop sort of firm in which he lost all of his money and much of his reputation—and then found that he was doomed to die of cancer. This last challenge was one that he could meet. This man, under whose command so many soldiers went to their deaths, could in his turn die well. But first he had to make some money, to leave his family a stake; and he [illegible] of his life to the writing of his memoirs,

city making [illegible]

Except that it was not quite the end. For Grant is more and more remembered for what he did, not for what he failed to do. If his failures were sad, his successes were magnificent. He was, in the end, one of the great Americans; great because he met a supreme challenge as it had to be met, great because in his strength and his weakness he perfectly expressed the America of his day. He did what his country had to have done, in a way no one else could have managed. There was no malice in him, and no overweening pride. He was the Middlewest, called on to step out and make a bit of history. He made it. Pile his faults high as you will, in the last analysis there was something quite unconquerable about him—unconquerable, and essentially American.

Abner Doubleday

The name of Abner Doubleday is probably known to more people than that of a majority of these unforgettable but not always well-remembered Americans. For baseball is "the national game," and, although the legend has been questioned, every fan associates Doubleday with its invention. Sportswriters can refer to him as casually and with as little need for further identification as they do to Babe Ruth, Ty Cobb, or any of the other great figures of the game.

Yet most people know little about his life outside baseball, or even about the problems he had to solve in standardizing the sport. It was Doubleday who achieved the perfect balance of offense and defense by determining the distance between the bases, and between the pitcher's box and home plate. As Robert S. Holzman explains, Doubleday had a passion for orderliness and arrangement; this was what made him such a fine rule maker. It is no mere accident that the rules of baseball have escaped the constant alterations and revisions that those governing basketball and football have been subjected to. Holzman also describes Doubleday's career as a soldier and engineer, showing that his memory deserves to be preserved in these fields as well as in the archives of sport.

Dr. Holzman is Director of the Budget and Professor of Taxation at New York University. He has published more than a dozen volumes, including General "Baseball" Doubleday *and* Stormy Ben Butler.

". . . problems of position"

ROBERT S. HOLZMAN

UNLIKE most of our sports and pastimes, baseball is not an imported product; it is as American as maize or tobacco. Ball and bat games had been played for thousands of years in all quarters of the globe. But these sports bore the same superficial resemblance to our national pastime that the toga does to the tuxedo. Prior to 1839 the game was utterly different from what it is today; [illegible] each contest engaged in was different from [illegible]

[illegible] of one-old-cat, stick ball, scrub, or other [illegible] rules, authority, or—in many instances—even a name. This man was Abner Doubleday.

It all started in 1839. That spring, a twenty-year-old West Point cadet named Doubleday spent a vacation at his home in Cooperstown, New York. Doubleday was a serious-minded young man whose chief characteristic, then and always, was orderliness. As a youth his hobby was map-making; as a young man he was so much interested in problems of position that his parents sent him to the United States Military Academy to get an engineering education.

The confused and haphazard ball games that were played at Cooperstown—and at every other place—disturbed the orderly mind of the West Pointer. He saw the disadvantage of engaging in a contest where the most stubborn man could win any point, because there was no authority to say the contrary. He noted the dangers of engaging in a game without a clearly-defined playing area. People who had learned their game in one town were not able to follow the sport as played in the next community, for a different custom of play was practiced there. Even the number of players varied from place to place. The cadet concluded that the first requirements for the game were orderliness, uniformity, and rules. He provided them.

Doubleday outlined a diamond-shaped playing field. He filled in the positions to be occupied by the players, who, in this first plan, numbered eleven men to a side. He provided a simple, uniform set of rules. Basically they are the rules of today. It does not appear that the young cadet was instantly hailed as a wonderful inventor; such on-the-spot recognition is rarely accorded in any field. But apparently the players saw the advantage of having a single standard of play within a prescribed frame-work, for the game now known as baseball began to be developed as of that time.

Doubleday was graduated from West Point in 1842, in the same class with Pope, Longstreet, D. H. Hill, and several other men who were to become famous Civil War generals. In that same year the game of baseball reached New York City for the first time. The Knickerbocker Baseball Club was formed, the first ball club that ever was organized, as teams up to the point had been selected just prior to each game. It was not until 1846 that a second baseball club was organized, the New York Nine. The first inter-club match was played in that year at the Elysian Fields in Hoboken, New Jersey.

In 1850 another team, the Washington Club, was formed in New York. The Washingtons lost a famous match the next year to the Knickerbockers, who almost caused a riot when they appeared as the first team to wear baseball uniforms: long blue trousers, white shirts with full sleeves, and straw hats. By this time baseball teams had been reduced to the present nine-man size, an innovation introduced by Alexander Jay Cartwright, Jr. Cartwright left for the California gold rush in 1850, and he took the new game with him. Up to this time baseball had been played only in New York and New Jersey. It was not until 1860 that the first baseball tour took place, when a Brooklyn team journeyed to Pennsylvania, Delaware, and Maryland.

Until the outbreak of the Civil War, Abner Doubleday got around the country much more than his game was able to do. He saw service in Maryland, South Carolina, and Florida, and he distinguished himself in the Mexican War. It does not appear that this serious young man attempted to popularize his game while on army service; his militiary career occupied him completely.

It was the Civil War which really made baseball the national sport.

Boredom is the worst enemy of soldiers, and there was little to do in camps, on bivouacs, or in prison compounds. The soldiers learned baseball in camp; and when the war was over returning veterans took the game back with them to their homes all over the nation. The mustering out of the troops brought baseball to tiny communities everywhere. For the first time the nation had a national game.

But Doubleday was too busy during the Civil War to be much

concerned with the wild-fire spread of his game. When South Carolina sought to secede from the Union in December 1860, Captain Doubleday was second in command of the Federal [illegible] in Charleston harbor. One of President [illegible]

[illegible]

fired against the Rebellion," he later recalled, [illegible]
of self-reproach, for I fully believed that the contest was inevitable." Eventually the fort ran out of supplies and had to surrender.

Doubleday next served in the field, where he participated in several battles. He earned several promotions, and received the temporary rank of major-general in November 1862. He was distinguished in appearance, dignified and courteous in manner. Unlike certain other generals of that time, he did not drink, smoke, or swear, and his men were puzzled at this officer who frequently recited poetry aloud while on the march. At one point during the Battle of Gettysburg, General Doubleday commanded the Union troops for seven decisive hours before he was relieved by a higher-ranking officer. Later in the war he served in the forts that protected Washington. At the end of the war he was at Fort Sumter again when the United States flag was hoisted over the ramparts.

When peace was restored, Doubleday served at various army posts until 1871, when he resigned. He had been trained as an engineer, and his first civilian post was in San Francisco. As always, he was interested in problems of position, and he turned his orderly mind to the problem of getting trolley cars up and down the steep hills that horses could not navigate in poor weather. He suggested and obtained a charter for the first cable car street railway in the United States. His cables remained in use until the great earthquake of 1906.

Doubleday's life after retirement was uneventful. As is the case with so many retired generals, he wrote his memoirs. He began the study of Sanskrit. And—the problem of position again—he spent much time playing chess. He died in 1893.

By the turn of the century baseball had reached full maturity. The first World Series was played in 1903. Two years later, with Big League baseball at substantially its present status, people began to wonder about its origin. Many persons believed that Abner Doubleday was the inventor of the game, but others felt that later rule-makers and writers, such as Alexander Jay Cartwright, Jr., and Henry Chadwick, were the real fathers of the game. Others believed that the sport actually was of English origin and that it had existed long before Doubleday's time.

The presidents of the National and American Leagues appointed a commission of experts to look into the evidence. In 1907 the commission reported as follows: "First—That Baseball had its origin in the United States. Second—That the first scheme for playing it, according to the evidence obtained to date, was devised by Abner Doubleday, Cooperstown, New York, in 1839."

Some people never have accepted Doubleday as baseball's author. But far more people never have accepted Shakespeare as the author of those greatest of plays; in fact, Shakespeare has far more rivals than has Doubleday. The evidence in Doubleday's favor is strong. First, there is the report of the commission formed to investigate the game's origins. Second, one of the persons present at that historic laying out of the game in 1839 gave his direct statement as to what had occurred, and he even produced a battered ball which had been used upon that occasion. Third, the methodical Doubleday with his preoccupation with problems of position was just the sort of man who would have invented the game. Fourth, there were no baseball teams prior to Doubleday's invention of the game; but in the year of his graduation from West Point, the first club unquestionably was formed in New York City.

On the hundredth anniversary of the invention of baseball, in 1939, the Hall of Fame and National Baseball Museum was dedicated at Cooperstown. Messages to honor baseball and its founder were sent by many of the nation's great personages. The President of the United States wrote:

> We should all be grateful to Abner Doubleday. Little did he or the group that was with him in Cooperstown, N.Y., in 1839, realize the boon they were giving the nation in devising baseball. The rules of the game may have changed since Doubleday and his associates formulated them a century ago, but baseball through all the changes and chances has grown steadily in popular favor and

remains today the great American sport, with its fans counted by millions. General Doubleday was a distinguished soldier both in the Mexican and Civil Wars. But his part in giving us baseball [illegible] at the time—shows again that peace

George Frederick Root, Jonathan Letterman, Thaddeus S. C. Lowe

The Civil War has been a source of unending interest to Americans for nearly a hundred years. The list of novels, biographies, and histories dealing with it is interminable. There is a Civil War Book Club, a Civil War Round Table, a great horde of Civil War "buffs" who are fascinated by every possible aspect of the War's history. Indeed, the study of the conflict is one of the great popular intellectual interests of our times, perhaps the most popular of all.

The tremendous concern of so many Americans with this subject is not hard to account for. The War, to begin with, was extremely dramatic and is therefore exciting to study. Coming after a series of tense crises, it sundered the nation geographically, economically, socially, and emotionally, tearing families apart, literally sending brother into battle against brother. Many of its individual engagements rank among the fiercest in history. One thinks of the "Bloody Angle" in the Wilderness Campaign, where great trees were felled by concentrated rifle fire, of Shiloh, where nearly a quarter of the hundred thousand participants were casualties, and of Cold Harbor, where Grant lost 12,000 men in a single day. Some campaigns were also of great importance from a technical military point of view. Ever since the War ended students of tactics from all over the world have been coming to America to study battlefields like Gettysburg and Chancellorsville first hand.

The Civil War also appeals to Americans because of its decisive influence on our own times. So many of our modern dilemmas can be traced at least in part to those dreadful, stirring years: the Negro problem and school desegregation, sectional jealousies, the conflict between farm and factory, state versus *federal power, to name only some of the most obvious. As Lincoln said (and his saintly yet mysterious personality is itself another reason that the Civil War is so popular), the War was fought to prove that the principle of majority rule could not be arbitrarily*

disregarded by a selfish and ruthless faction. "Our popular government has been called an experiment," Lincoln reminded the nation. "It is now for [the people] to demonstrate to the world
... fairly and constitutionally de-

Revolution scarcely knowing that it was taking place, ...
relative handful were deeply affected by the War of 1812 or by the brief Mexican campaign of 1846-7. The Civil War left its mark on an overwhelming majority of the people: on farmers and industrial laborers, on southern slave and northern freedman, on western pioneer and eastern merchant.

Such a struggle was fought on many battlefields, and not all of them the obvious sites marked today by statues, bronze plaques, and rows of antique cannon. A war involving millions demanded many varieties of service, employed many kinds of talents besides those strictly military. Thus Paul M. Angle examines the life of George Frederick Root, a peaceful singing teacher employed by such institutions as the Rutgers Female Academy and Union Theological Seminary. The Civil War caught him up and inspired him to write songs like "The Battle Cry of Freedom," worth many regiments to the Union cause as a morale builder. Thaddeus Lowe, a typical "harmless" inventor, became involved in the conflict when he floated from Cincinnati to the Carolinas in a balloon. His purpose was purely scientific, but the Southerners took him for a Yankee spy, and this, as Waldemar Kaempffert suggests, may well have led Lowe to develop the idea of the observation balloon. Kaempffert's sketch of Lowe shows how important this was to the Northern army. Dr. Jonathan Letterman was a professional soldier. In a sense, therefore, his contribution was more in the line of regular military duty. But the heroic scale of the Civil War affected his work, too. His earlier experience had been limited to small posts in remote areas; seldom was a doctor in such a position called on to deal with more than a dozen or so casualties at one time. The challenge posed by the thousands who fell at Antietam and the other great clashes between the Army of the Potomac and the Army of Northern Virginia led Letterman to the important reforms described in Charles M. Wiltse's account of his life.

Paul M. Angle is Director of the Chicago Historical Society and the author of the Lincoln Reader *and many other books about the Civil War. Charles M. Wiltse, Chief Historian of the Army Medical Service, is the author of* The Jeffersonian Tradition in American Democracy *and a three-volume biography of John C. Calhoun. The late Waldemar Kaempffert, former science editor of the New York* Times, *wrote the* Popular History of American Invention *and many other books.*

". . . the part played by music"

PAUL M. ANGLE

In the summer of 1862, with the Civil War more than a year old, the Union faced a grim prospect. After months of preparation General George B. McClellan had launched a full-scale attack against Richmond, only to be fought to a standstill within sight of the city. From the White House Lincoln called for more troops—300,000 volunteers to fill the wasted ranks of the army and build a force that he hoped would overwhelm the South.

George Frederick Root, a new resident of Chicago, heard of the call for troops while he lay on a sofa in the home of his brother, who was a partner in the enterprising music publishing firm of Root & Cady. For more than half of his forty-two years Root had been a professional musician—he had been a choirmaster, organist, singing teacher, and composer. He had written a number of songs, but only one, an evangelical hymn called "The Shining Shore," had received more than casual notice.

But on this summer day in 1862 a rhythm began to pound through Root's mind. With it words took shape and dropped into sequence:

> Yes, we'll rally 'round the flag, boys,
> We'll rally once again,
> Shouting the battle cry of freedom!

And then the chorus:

> The Union forever, hurrah! boys, hurrah!
> with the star!

meeting.

Within an hour Jules Lumbard was "lining out" the song. His brother led the chorus once, twice, three times, until at the fourth stanza a thousand voices shouted out the refrain:

> *The Union forever, hurrah! boys, hurrah!*

A blasé generation, remembering a world war so devastating that it was fought almost without song, can hardly comprehend the part played by music between 1861 and 1865. Yet testimony to the popularity of the Civil War songs is overwhelming. Soldiers sang them around the camp fires, rallied to their stirring tunes in the heat of battle, and with them kept up their spirits as they lay in the hideous prisons of both armies. At home many a family bore separation and often sorrow the more bravely because of the solace its members found in music which everyone played and sang.

Something of the influence of Civil War music comes out in an incident that took place in Richmond a few days after Lee's surrender. A group of Union sailors on shore leave found that they made up a quartet, and decided to spend the evening singing. Since a number of paroled Confederate officers had rooms next door, the sailors refrained from any music that might offend their neighbors. The Confederates asked if they could come over and listen. They came, and the quartet continued with college and glee club offerings.

"Excuse me, gentlemen," said one of the visitors, "you sing delightfully, but what we want to hear are your army songs." The Northerners responded with "The Battle Hymn of the Republic," "Tramp! Tramp! Tramp!", "We'll Rally 'Round the Flag, Boys," and other favorites. One of the visitors, a major, spoke up.

"Gentlemen, if we'd had your songs we'd have whipped you out of your boots!" He continued. "I shall never forget the first time I heard 'Rally 'Round the Flag.' 'Twas a nasty night during the 'Seven Days' Fight,' and if I remember rightly it was raining. I was on picket when, just before 'taps,' some fellow on the other side struck up that song and others joined in the chorus until it seemed to me the whole Yankee army was singing. [A man] who was with me sung out, 'Good heavens, Cap., what are those fellows made of anyway? Here we've licked 'em six days running, and now on the eve of the seventh they're singing, 'Rally 'Round the Flag'!"

George F. Root was perhaps the leading contributor to the music of the war. "Tramp! Tramp! Tramp! the Boys are Marching"—the song of the ragged, despondent, but unbeaten Union soldier in a southern prison camp—swept the North when it came out in 1864. "Just Before the Battle, Mother," and "The Vacant Chair," both published in 1862, were enormously popular. To our jaded taste both songs drip with sentiment, but at the time of the Civil War people were not ashamed of their emotions, and the songs expressed perfectly what millions felt.

Only one other song writer—Henry C. Work—could have challenged Root's claim to first place, and it was Root who gave Work his opportunity. Root related that early in the war a quiet, shabbily dressed young man appeared at the store of Root & Cady, with the manuscript of a song. "Did you write this, words and music?" Root asked. "Yes." "What is your business, if I may inquire?" "I am a printer," the young man replied. "Well," Root said, "if this a specimen of what you can do, I think you may give up the printing business."

The song was "Kingdom Coming," the lilting taunt of the slave to the master chased from his lordly plantation by the "Linkum" gunboats. Work would handle the slavery theme again, this time in more serious manner, in "Wake Nicodemus," but today he is best known for the triumphant "Marching Through Georgia." The song was published too late in the war to achieve great contemporary popularity, but the Grand Army of the Republic marched to its stirring strains from 1866 to its last encampment. It is safe to say that if a person today knows only one song of the Civil War, that song will be "Marching Through Georgia."

The composing of Civil War music was, of course, only an interlude in the life of George F. Root. His principal occupation was that of music teacher, or rather a teacher of music teachers. Several years before joining his brother in Chicago, Root had held his first "Normal institute." Each institute was a convention ... learning the newest methods of in-

Normal institutes to tell him how "We'll Rally 'Round the Flag, Boys," or "Tramp! Tramp! Tramp!" had cheered them in dark hours of the war. But Root died ten years too soon to witness the most touching testimonial of all. That came in 1905, when Jules Lumbard, then eighty years old, was invited to give an "old-timers" recital in Chicago. The old man's voice was gone, yet the audience applauded politely until the last song. With the words, "We'll Rally 'Round the Flag, Boys, we'll rally once again," a thousand auditors forgot the cracked and quavering voice, and a thousand throats roared out the chorus in a crashing tribute to a once-great singer—and to a composer who had caught in words and music the martial spirit of a people.

". . . to reach and treat the fallen"

CHARLES M. WILTSE

No ASPECT of modern warfare is better organized or more smoothly run than the battlefield evacuation of the wounded. But this has not always been true. The man more responsible than any other for the prompt and orderly care of battle casualties was born in Canonsburg, Pennsylvania, on December 11, 1824. His name was Jonathan Letterman.

The son of a country doctor, there was never any doubt as to the career young Letterman would follow. He graduated from Jefferson Medical College in Philadelphia in 1849, and after passing the required examinations was appointed an assistant surgeon in the army. For the next ten years he served in various frontier posts in Florida, Minnesota, and New Mexico. He was in California when Fort Sumter fell, and came east late in 1861 with a levy of troops from that state.

Letterman's intelligence, directness, and boundless energy quickly brought him to the attention of the Surgeon General. Though only a captain, he was named medical director of the Army of the Potomac in the summer of 1862, and reported for duty on the Fourth of July. The army Letterman joined was a beaten army. For weeks the men had been fighting in swamps and sleeping in mud, when they slept at all. Twenty thousand were in the hospital. All were bone weary, dirty, discouraged; and medical supplies and hospital tents had been abandoned in the retreat from Richmond. There were not enough doctors; there was not enough food, not enough shelter, not enough time.

Undismayed, Letterman took hold. He asked General McClellan for more authority than any American army surgeon had ever held before, and he got it. He had already exercised a measure of it on the way to his post. Finding the telegraph wires cut, he had ordered drugs and dressings from the main army depot on his own responsibility, and had started hospital ships supplied by the Sanitary Commission and by the State of Pennsylvania moving toward the Harrison's Landing encampment. From the commissary he requisitioned "large supplies of potatoes, onions, cabbage, tomatoes, squashes, and beets" to combat scurvy. With McClellan's backing he enforced a rigid sanitary discipline that went far to wipe out typhoid, malaria, and dysentery. By the middle of August all of the sick and wounded had been moved to general hospitals in the northern cities, and the Army of the Potomac was back in health and fighting trim.

That would have been enough for most men, but for Letterman it was only the beginning. The army was in bivouac, but soon it would take the field again and there would be a new wave of casualties. With the single-minded purpose that characterized everything he did, Letterman went straight to the heart of the problem. He conceived it to be his responsibility to keep the army at maximum fighting strength. The first objective was to reach and treat the fallen as quickly as possible. The second was to provide hospital facilities close to the front for all who might fight again within a reasonable time. The long-term cases and the permanently disabled were to be moved promptly to base hospitals outside the combat zone.

There were no precedents for what Letterman did; certainly there was nothing to foreshadow it in his earlier career. American army surgeons had no experience with great field armies, or with the kind of war that produced thousands of casualties in a single

rades, who seized the opportunity to escape [illegible] selves; some made their own painful way back, and thousands of others were left for days where they fell, many to die of neglect or thirst. The jolting, two-wheeled carts that passed for ambulances were seldom at hand when needed. They were freely commandeered by footsore officers, and they disappeared with alarming rapidity. Even when they were available, quartermasters would not—and surgeons could not—order ambulances up to the fighting lines.

Letterman's first reform, made within a month of his appointment, was the creation of an ambulance corps. It was a model of simplicity. Vehicles were assigned to regiments, divisions, and army corps. They were commanded by line officers, drawn from the formations they served, and were under the complete control of the surgeons. Light, four-wheeled wagons replaced the uncomfortable carts. Each had a driver and two attendants, detailed from among the line troops, and each carried two litters. Only the men of the ambulance corps were allowed to assist the wounded from the field; and to divert an ambulance to any other purpose whatsoever was made a court-martial offense.

The ambulance corps of the Army of the Potomac was organized and equipped on the march. It saw its first action at the battle of Antietam, on September 17, 1862—still one of the bloodiest days in American history. Ambulances followed the shifting lines, and litter-bearers carried their human burdens while bullets whined overhead. The small, dynamic Letterman was everywhere. Within twenty-four hours the field was cleared of ten thousand Union wounded, and almost half as many Confederates left behind by the retreating Lee.

In the course of the next six weeks Letterman added all that was needful to complete a unified system of front line medical care. Hospitalization and medical supply were centralized at the division level, to cut down waste and to conserve professional skills. The basic unit became the divisional field hospital—large enough to keep a staff of surgeons fully employed, small enough for rapid movement. Each division pitched its hospital tents behind its own lines. Every ambulance driver knew where he was to go and every surgeon and wound-dresser knew what he was to do. At Fredericksburg, Chancellorsville, Gettysburg, the Letterman system was put to the test, and in every particular it measured up. At Gettysburg the field was cleared each night of the three-day battle. More than fourteen thousand Union casualties and thousands of Confederates were cared for without a hitch.

By the fall of 1863 Letterman's reforms had been extended to the entire army, and he felt that it was time for others to carry on. In October of that year he married Mary Lee, who had served him at table in a Maryland farmhouse after the battle of Antietam. In January 1864 he was relieved of duty at his own request, and in December, with the issue of the war no longer in doubt, he resigned his commsision.

For a time Letterman tried his hand at business in southern California; then he settled in San Francisco to practice medicine. He gave freely of himself, and many honors were bestowed upon him, but his health was failing. Mary died suddenly late in 1867, and Letterman never fully recovered from her loss. He died on March 15, 1872, at the age of 47.

Jonathan Letterman was a man of clear vision, great courage, selfless devotion to his profession, and an almost childlike gentleness that was remarked by all who came in contact with him. Today Letterman General Hospital in San Francisco stands as a living memorial to his fame. A less tangible but more enduring monument exists in the system of field evacuation now followed by every army in the world. The springless wagons have long since been replaced by streamlined motor ambulances, jeeps, and helicopters, but the principle remains as Letterman laid it down in 1862. Countless thousands of fighting men since that time have owed him their lives, though they may never have heard his name.

"... industrial evolution of the United States"

interested in all the physical sciences, though he had no more than a common school education. He was born in 1832 in New Hampshire, died in 1913, and was therefore a contemporary of Thomas A. Edison. The two men had much in common—Edison was the more prolific inventor but, like Edison, Thaddeus Lowe founded industries on his inventions.

For the greater part of his life Lowe was called "professor," a title usually given to aeronauts in the nineteenth century, and Lowe was an aeronaut before he was thirty. His first balloon ascent was in 1858 at Ottawa, to celebrate the laying of the first Atlantic cable. His interest in ballooning was at first purely scientific. Like others before him he was convinced that there are currents at different altitudes and that advantage might be taken of them to travel great distances in a balloon, so he began with the scientific project of exploring the upper air. Lowe needed a balloon to prove that there were currents in the upper air, but he had no money. A hotel proprietor in Springfield was his salvation. "Come to Springfield and give us an ascension on the 4th of July, and we'll pay you well," read the invitation. Lowe accepted at once and, using this guarantee, constructed a balloon with which he made a successful ascent. Other ascents followed, and his reputation grew. It was not fame as a balloonist that he wanted, but scientific information about the winds at high altitudes.

Next Lowe built an enormous balloon, 350 feet high with a capacity of 720,000 cubic feet of coal gas, to try to cross the Atlantic. No gas bag of that size had ever been made. There were so-called "revolving fans," designed to push the vessel up or down rather than to propel it horizontally, for Lowe wanted to reach the favorable upper currents as rapidly as possible.

Joseph Henry, secretary of the Smithsonian Institution and one of the most distinguished scientists in America, lent him scientific instruments. These were to be used by two scientists who would accompany Lowe, along with a "historiographer" who was to keep the records.

Lowe intended to float up from what is now Bryant Park, in New York City, but attempts at inflation in New York and later in Philadelphia failed and the transatlantic venture came to an end. Probably Joseph Henry had something to do with the abandonment; he suggested that an attempt at a long distance journey be made in a balloon of less heroic proportions. And so, one night in April 1861, Lowe rose from Cincinnati. The wind on the ground was blowing from east to west, but Lowe was certain that higher up it was blowing steadily in the opposite direction. When he received the news that conditions were seemingly favorable he was at a banquet. He rose at once and, in full evening dress, high hat and all, he rushed to the balloon. Seated in the basket, the man in evening dress rose and drifted westward to the great delight of skeptical onlookers. But soon the balloon changed its direction and traveled 800 miles to the Atlantic coast at about 100 miles an hour. When he saw the ocean Lowe wisely decided to come down. He landed at Pea Ridge, close to the boundary of North and South Carolina. The Confederates took him for a Yankee spy and arrested him, but luckily a witness had seen an earlier ascent of Lowe's from Charleston, South Carolina. This man came forward and vouched for Lowe as a scientist who had no interest in military matters. Lowe made the most of the arrest whenever he told about it in later years—he always maintained that he was the first prisoner to be taken in the Civil War.

His arrest as a Yankee spy may have put ideas into Lowe's head. After making several captive balloon ascents from the grounds of the Smithsonian Institution in the early stages of the Civil War, he received an appointment as an aeronautical engineer in the army and went to the front to do some reconnoitering from the air. He made an ascent on June 6, 1861, and sent Lincoln a telegraphic message from midair, using an ordinary telegraph wire connected to lines strung on the usual poles.

These were not casual performances of Lowe's; he rendered valuable military service. He made sketches and even took photographs from the air, he observed the enemy's disposition of troops and preparations, and then telegraphed them to the Union artillery.

Lowe did much to save the Army of the Potomac in its retreat from before Richmond, Virginia, during the battle of Fair Oaks. He had three balloons from which he made observations. At night, [illegible] told him much, and by day his observations

reconnaissance.

Lowe's example was not lost on the Confederates. General James Longstreet has written that the Confederates could not but admire Lowe's balloons floating high out of the range of Confederate guns, but the South was so poverty-stricken that it found it hard to match Lowe. "A genius arose," Longstreet wrote, "who suggested that we gather silk dresses in the Confederacy and make a balloon." And a balloon was made. It was a patchwork of many hues. There was no gas except in Richmond, so that each time it was used the balloon was inflated there, lashed to a locomotive, and taken along the York River Railroad to its destination. On the last occasion a steamer was used, which was left high and dry on the James River when the tide ran out. "The Federals gathered the balloon in," Longstreet recorded, "and with it the last silk dresses in the Confederacy."

Even if he had done nothing more than engage in ballooning, Lowe would have gone down in military history for having demonstrated the usefulness of aerial reconnaissance in war. But he did much more. After the Civil War he became interested in making artificial ice. He built the first shipboard ice machine and refrigerating plant in this country, and shipped fresh beef on a steamer from Texas to New Orleans. The beef was in good condition when it arrived—a remarkable achievement for 1866. So Lowe must be regarded as the father of cold storage.

Though he had given up reconnoitering from midair for military commanders, the lessons learned as a balloonist brought forth other inventions. As a military balloonist Lowe had to supervise everything himself even to generating the hydrogen gas that he needed to inflate his gas bags on the battlefield. After the Civil War it was natural for him to examine the business of making the coal-gas which he used for ascents in Washington, D. C., and which was used in cities and homes for illumination. Widely read in science, he knew that Antoine Lavoisier, the distinguished French chemist who was guillotined during the Reign of Terror in the French Revolution, had pointed out that water could be decomposed by intense heat. Lowe saw the point and developed a method of making what was called "water gas" by blowing steam over incandescent coal. But if water gas were to be used as an illuminant, it had to burn with a bright flame; Lowe enriched it with partly refined petroleum, known as light oil, and thus achieved his end. Lowe's water gas, or blue gas, was a tremendous success. It displaced coal gas because it was both cheaper and better. If we do not hear about water gas or blue gas nowadays, it is because of the remarkable growth of the natural gas industry. We used to waste natural gas in the reckless way that we wasted all our natural resources fifty and more years ago. It may be that Lowe's water gas had something to do with the recklessness, for coal was cheap and water gas plants were highly efficient. But as the price of coal rose with the years, it paid to tap and exploit natural gas resources.

Here it must be mentioned that Lavoisier's suggestion of decomposing water by intense heat made as deep an impression on a Frenchman as it did on Lowe. That Frenchman was Tessie du Motay, who did in Europe what Lowe did in the United States, though neither man had heard of the other until water gas began to be written and talked about. This phenomenon of simultaneous and independent invention and discovery is, of course, well known to sociologists and historians of technology. Leibnitz and Newton developed calculus independently; Alexander Graham Bell and Elisha Gray filed patent applications for the telephone on the same day in Washington, D.C. Given a similar environment, many minds hundreds of miles apart will think along the same lines. So it is not astounding that Thaddeus Lowe and Tessie du Motay thought of water gas at about the same time.

Lowe spent the last ten years of his life in working out plans for a plant which was to reduce anthracite to coke and at the same time make water gas. The coke stood up well in metallurgical processes, such as smelting ore, because it was harder than ordinary coke. The plant was intended not only to make anthracite coke and water gas but also to generate power and manufacture ice. It was a grandiose plan only part of which was ever carried out.

Despite his importance in the industrial evolution of the United

States, no formal biography of Thaddeus Lowe is available. All that we have are brief notices. So it happens that, though a mountain is named after Lowe, few Americans know very much about him and his inventions. He made no millions for himself, but he

James B. Eads and Grenville M. Dodge

Our next two Unforgettable Americans might well have been included in the last group with Root, Letterman, and Lowe, for both were engineers who made important contributions to the winning of the Civil War. But they are better treated separately from the others, for their most significant achievements came after the War and in the field of transportation.

If transportation was a vital problem before 1861, it was even more crucial after 1865, when the last wave of settlement swept across the Great Plains and destroyed the frontier. Without fast and efficient transportation and communication, the Rocky Mountain area and the Pacific Coast could never have been integrated into the economy of the East. This need was provided for by the railroads, the expansion of which after the War was phenomenal. In 1865 there were 35,000 miles of track in operation; by 1890 there were over 166,000 miles.

Because of the distance involved and the weight and volume of the products to be carried, it was not enough merely to lay out tracks and set locomotives and cars to running along them. Trains had to be heavier, faster, and more specialized in order to meet the new demands. This called for all sorts of improvements and inventions, and they were not slow in coming. The development of the Bessemer process of refining steel made possible the manufacture of cheap steel rails which, because of their strength and durability, could support far greater loads and withstand the stress of high speeds. The air brake, invented by George Westinghouse, also permitted the manufacture of heavier equipment which could be operated at high speeds. Mighty steam locomotives weighing 150 tons came into being. In the sixties a 15,000-pound freight car was considered heavy; by the end of the century cars with a capacity of 100,000 pounds were normal. At the same time travel was being made more comfortable. George Pullman designed his first sleeping car, the Pioneer A, *in 1864; three years later he organized the Pullman Palace Car Company, and soon the railroads of the country were using his luxurious dining and parlor cars as well.*

The chief contribution of James Eads to this technological revolution was the design and construction of the first railroad bridge across the Mississippi River. Together with his work in improving the navigation of the Mississippi, the Eads Bridge, a

Society, is the author of Missouri: A Guide to the Show Me State *and of many articles about the Missouri region. Robert Self Henry is a retired Vice-President of the Association of American Railroads. His many books include* The Story of the Confederacy, The Story of Reconstruction, Trains, *and* Portraits of the Iron Horse.

". . . victories over ignorance and selfishness"

CHARLES VAN RAVENSWAAY

From the time that white men first settled on the fringes of the continent, the Mississippi has been a legend, a shining and living thing that has stirred imaginations and made men sing songs and tell stories to express their wonder of it. For three hundred years the river has seen the parade of American history: explorers, fur-trappers, pioneers bound for new homes, the movement of armies and the flow of commerce. For the most part, the river's uncertain temper has shaped man's use of the stream. For a few, like James Buchanan Eads, its power has been a challenge.

During the middle years of the last century, Eads spent his life on or under or near the river, studying it and battling with it, until he knew more about its moods than anyone else. His use of that knowledge shaped our history. Today his victories over the Mississippi are well remembered, but perhaps his greatest victories were against those who said the river couldn't be tamed, and who fought with the river against him.

Eads first saw the Mississippi in September 1833, as a thin, tousled youngster of thirteen with blue eyes and blonde hair. With his mother and sisters, he was moving from Louisville to St. Louis. His father, a gentleman who had never quite made a success of anything, planned to follow them. Their boat took fire as it neared the St. Louis wharf, and though the passengers escaped ashore, all their possessions were lost in the flames.

Mrs. Eads opened a boarding house, and young Jim got work in a dry goods store. In the evenings he pored over books on science and mechanics, and through these he began to glimpse a new world of order and power. He built models of river boats and explored with his hands and his mind the workings of the engines. When he was eighteen, he signed up as a steamboat clerk, where his duties left him time to study the river currents and shifting sandbars, the winter ice floes and spring floods. He heard river men talk about the wrecks of sunken boats. If a way could be found to salvage their cargoes, they said, a man would get rich. Eads, wondering if that were possible, began sketching and figuring. Perhaps a diving-bell boat would do the trick.

One morning, when he was twenty-two, Eads visited a St. Louis boat-building firm and startled the two owners by offering to take them into the salvage business if they would build the boat he had designed. He had a quiet way of explaining things that made men listen, and in time his queer-looking boat was built. It proved such a success that others followed. To locate wrecks under the surface, Eads employed a "diving suit." When he first began his salvage work, he brought in a Great Lakes diver who worked with only a "diving harness." But the currents buffeted the diver about so that he could not work on the bottom, and Eads was forced to convert the old diving-bell technique to his needs. This consisted of a heavy iron shell controlled from a boat, under which the diver could move about. Later Eads used an armored diving suit and helmet with glass windows. He walked miles along the river bottom, learning about the wild currents, sudden canyons, and shifting sands in that grey, eerie world. Still hungry to learn, he continued his studies.

When Eads married he sold out and left the river, and for a few years tried the less hazardous work of developing a St. Louis glass factory. It was a sensible idea and he made good glass, but the business failed and he went home again to the river and to his salvage boats. After ten years he had made a fortune but was physically exhausted, and after a trip to Europe, where he studied boats and locks and river engineering, he came home to retire at thirty-seven. He wanted to be with his family, he said, and

the idea was approved and bids for seven boats were received, Eads won the contract.

To build these boats Eads had to create everything overnight. Within two weeks 4,000 men were at work in his St. Louis shipyard, and factories and lumberyards, mills and tool shops throughout the Union were scoured for materials. Although Government engineers changed the design and Treasury officials held up funds, the work continued. Within 100 days the seven boats were finished. Others followed, and with their help by 1863 the Union forces had opened the Mississippi to the Gulf.

When peace came again St. Louis had become a great city. There were more steamboats than ever before, but the railroads were reshaping the nation's thinking along lines running east and west. Only the Mississippi remained as a barrier, for rail freight and passengers had to cross the stream on ferries which floods and ice and storms often delayed. People had talked of a bridge for years, but everyone said it was impossible—the distance was too great and the current too strong. Piers would have to be sunk through fifty feet of water and several hundred feet of mud and sand to reach bed rock.

When a bridge company was formed, Eads was made chief engineer, but during the six years of construction he was more than that to the project. He created a new type of bridge, designed new kinds of steel for its lacey arches, invented new ways of sinking piers and of protecting men against the strange new disease which came from working under heavy air pressure. Always there was the battle of wits against those who for one selfish reason or another didn't want the bridge built. But when the bridge was finished in 1874 it was not only a marvel of science, but a work of art, beckoning the East to the new West.

Eads then turned to another problem that had stumped river men for years. The mouth of the Mississippi was divided into many channels, and the weakened current dropped its silt to form bars and shallows which blocked deep sea vessels from the port of New Orleans. Eads insisted that with dykes and revetments the channel could be narrowed, the current increased. Then the river would scour its own channel. Opponents called the plan impractical, insane, visionary. When work began at South Pass, the channel was eight feet deep. Four years later, when Eads work was finished, the river had dug itself a 30-foot channel and New Orleans had become an ocean port.

Eads now turned his thoughts to the whole problem of the river, its perennial floods, and the shifting of its channel. He insisted that with the means he had employed at South Pass, the whole river could be tamed. Time, of course, has proved him right.

While fighting for approval of this project in Washington, his interest was attracted to the scheme of Count Ferdinand de Lesseps, the great French engineer of the Suez Canal, to build a canal across Panama. Eads pointed out that instead of building a canal it would be easier and simpler to haul ships across the isthmus of Tehuantepec on a giant railroad. After obtaining a concession from the Mexican government, he introduced a bill into Congress asking that the government guarantee him a dividend of six percent for fifteen years after his railway had been proved practical. He offered to build the railway at his own expense. Again the familiar cry arose—fantastic, insane, impossible! In his clear, patient, often humorous way, Eads wrote and lectured tirelessly to present his facts. Meanwhile awards and distinctions came to him from distinguished groups in Europe and America. He was famous and honored, and from everywhere came requests to consult on problems of harbors and rivers, and other engineering needs. But even with all these demands he found time to continue urging the ship railway project. While de Lesseps' work sank to failure in the jungles of Panama, and Eads' bill suffered delay and attack in Washington, the feeling of exhaustion he had known before returned. He sailed to Nassau for a rest early in 1887, but he had waited too long. Just before the end, he murmured: "I cannot die . . . I have not finished my work."

The ship railway across the isthmus was never built, but the idea remains. Engineers today find it neither fantastic nor impossible. His great bridge still soars above the river at St. Louis, still beautiful, and now carrying traffic far greater than even Eads had ever intended for it. The Mississippi flows to the sea, disciplined and controlled very much as he suggested. New

ROBERT SELPH HENRY

When Grenville Mellen Dodge was born in Danvers, Massachusetts, in 1831, the United States was a very young country, with its wild and vast frontier still awaiting development. By the end of his life, which came in 1916, the frontier was gone: the railroads Dodge had helped to build linked cities and towns from coast to coast, and the Union he had fought gallantly to preserve had become one of the great nations of the world.

In the mid-years of the nineteenth century, railroads which had been building westward from the Atlantic seaboard for twenty years reached their trans-Allegheny goals on the "Western Waters" of the Great Lakes and the Mississippi Valley. Other railroads were building even into the vast area west of the Mississippi which President Jefferson had obtained from Napoleon only half a century earlier, not thinking to see it settled by civilized man for another thousand years. Into these great transportation events young Grenville Dodge graduated from Norwich University in 1851, as a civil engineer.

There was in the America of that time a peculiar need for the kind of engineer whom A. M. Wellington described as one who "knew how to do well with one dollar that which any bungler can do after a fashion with two." Distances were great, population was sparse, capital was scarce, and those who would locate, build, and operate railroads had, therefore, to make their limited means go as far as they could be made to go.

But the American West was exuberantly confident of the

future, and to that West went young Dodge, to become one of that great brotherhood of engineers whose genius was to leave its marks upon the face of the land. He worked with a surveying party on the new Illinois Central Railroad, and then on the even newer Rock Island line across Iowa. Pushing westward, he took up a claim to lands in the Platte Valley in Nebraska, but Indian troubles forced him to relinquish his homestead and to settle in Iowa at Council Bluffs.

When the Civil War broke out, Dodge was chosen Colonel of the Fourth Iowa Infantry Regiment, with which he was sent to St. Louis and thence over the hundred-mile line of railroad leading to the forward outpost of the Union forces in Southwest Missouri. The railroad being in an advanced state of disrepair, the Iowa Colonel with railroad experience was called upon to put it in shape to supply the armies which, by a narrow margin, held Missouri for the Union.

The nature of this first military service foreshadowed the dominant note in Dodge's Civil War career. He fought gallantly, receiving wounds at Pea Ridge and in the siege of Atlanta. He commanded ably, rising finally to the rank of Major General commanding one of Sherman's army corps in the Atlanta campaign. But it was as the rebuilder and operator of war-worn railroads in the South that he made his greatest reputation. By his feats of railroad rebuilding he helped maintain the essential supply lines that made possible the Union victories in the West, and for that service he received the highest commendation from General Sherman and General Grant. In the course of the Civil War—the first war in which railroads were extensively used—there had to be developed, without previous experience, a system of operating military railroads.

After the war, the combination of construction engineering, railroad operation, and soldiering—three arts in which Grenville Dodge was trained—made him the ideal man for the immensely difficult and immensely important work as Chief Engineer of the Union Pacific, being built westward from the Missouri River to meet the Central Pacific, then being built eastward from the banks of the Sacramento. Here was a new kind of engineering and construction, calling for new concepts and practices. The base of operations was far up a tortuous, shallow, and shifting river; to this base there had to be brought all the things needed for building a railroad: across plains and through mountains, for more than a thousand miles. From this base, everything had to be hauled over the line as it moved westward, following engineering locations which often had to be sought out and surveyed under armed protection. One critical location, indeed, was found only when a war-band of Indians chased the surveying

manded and improved finances permitted,
were relocated and rebuilt. But, as the engineer in charge of this rebuilding said: "Taking into consideration the existing conditions of the 1860s, lack of maps of the country, hostility of the Indians . . . difficult transportation, excessive cost of labor, uncertainty as to probable volume of traffic, limited amount of money, and the necessity to get the road built as soon as possible . . . the line was located with very great skill."

Grenville Dodge's life reached its dramatic high on the tenth day of May in 1869, when two locomotives touched head to head on a newly joined track in the mountains north of the Great Salt Lake, and the Atlantic and the Pacific were joined by rail. Yet he still was under forty years of age, and ahead of him were long, useful, and honored years in which, as engineer and constructor, as financier and executive, he laid his mark upon the railroad map of the West.

Besides his connection with the Union Pacific, extending through half a century, his engineering skill, organizing ability, and dynamic driving force helped to build, in the 1870s, the Texas & Pacific. He had a part in building the International Great-Northern, reaching the border of Mexico, and also lines south of the border. He was one of those who created the line between Texas and Colorado. The Fort Worth and Denver City Railroad, to give it its original name, was so distinctively a Dodge achievement that it was long nicknamed "the Dodge Road." When the road fell into receivership during the panic of 1893 it was reorganized without foreclosure, largely because confidence in the capability and integrity of Dodge himself caused the financial community to provide the necessary funds.

In his day General Dodge saw the continental network of rails filled in. He saw the rails change from iron to steel, and grow in weight from forty pounds to 100 pounds to the yard. He saw cars grow from a capacity of ten tons to a capacity of fifty tons, and locomotives grow from a weight of thirty tons to a weight of 150 tons, with an even greater increase in power and dependability. He saw the introduction of automatic signals and the universal use of automatic safety couplers and air brakes. He saw the standardization of track gauge and the standardization of time accomplished by the railroads. He saw the setting up and working out of a variety of inter-railroad arrangements which make it possible to ship freight from any railroad point to any other on the continent, in cars which move freely on the tracks and in the trains of all railroads—a system of universal interchange of cars which is at the very foundation of our great national markets and our continent-wide commerce.

All these things Grenville Dodge saw in a long life, extending into the early years of this century—a life in which he applied his great abilities to the defense of the Union and, through his pioneering in the building of railroads in the West, to the vast enrichment of the nation. He died on January 3, 1916.

Cochise,

… found on nearly every page of the history of the dealings of white men with red.

There have been two basic ways of looking at this stark and sordid story. One is to stress the inevitability of the march of civilization from Atlantic to Pacific. The Indian, a creature out of the Stone Age, simply had to make way before the advance of the white man's superior culture, this line of reasoning runs. As William Henry Harrison asked when he was Governor of Indiana Territory: "Is one of the fairest portions of the globe to remain in a state of nature, the haunt of a few wretched savages, when it seems destined by the Creator to give support to a large population and be the seat of civilization?" Although the Indian was the original possessor of the soil, the argument continues, he should have accepted the wave of the future, recognized the superiority of the white man's ways, and allowed himself to be absorbed and "Americanized."

The other view sees the Indian as a noble savage: brave, dignified, owning a culture and way of life suited to his environment, and intrinsically as worth while as any other. Having innocently greeted the white settler, he was rewarded, according to this interpretation of the facts, by being robbed, treated with contempt, and ruthlessly exterminated when he dared to protest. The white men should have recognized the Indians as equals, treated them fairly, and, at the very least, made sure that those who wished could preserve their tribal ways on reservations.

Something can be said for both these points of view, but the main ingredients that were lacking in relations between the races were efficient management once policy was established, and in-

telligent understanding on the part of all involved. The Indian was neither completely noble nor utterly despicable. His complex culture was interesting and worth preserving, but also capable of profiting from much of what the "invader" had to offer. Yet the United States government, while seldom dishonorable in its intentions, could not control the behavior of the actual settlers, and many minor government officials dealing with the Indians were ignorant and venal. Nor could the tribal chiefs, by and large, control the actions of their braves and make them understand the real questions at issue. As a result this tragic tale unwound, reaching its inevitable conclusion in the almost total destruction of the weaker race.

The moral of the two following accounts is neither that white understanding could have preserved the red man's culture nor that greater Indian adaptability would have made for a completely smooth absorption into the culture of western civilization. Cochise, despite his pacific intentions, was not willing to submerge his tribe's individuality to keep the peace, and Richard Henry Pratt never claimed to be able to make over every Indian in the image of a middle-class citizen of Pennsylvania. But the stories of both these men show clearly how intelligence and understanding could soften the strident clash of alien ideas, and ease the burden of adjustment between totally different ways of life.

Elliott Arnold has written Blood Brother, *a novel based on the life of Cochise, and many other works of fiction. Charles Coleman Sellers, Professor of History at Dickinson College, is the author of a three-volume biography of the artist Charles Willson Peale.*

"... *personally responsible for his people*"

ELLIOTT ARNOLD

COCHISE, chief of the Chiricahua Apaches in Arizona from the mid-1830's until his death in 1874, never had more than two hundred warriors to command. Yet he laid waste to the Southwest, and for twelve years fought to a standstill the finest soldiers and the most brilliant generals the United States could send to do battle with him. He laid down his arms only when a President of the United States pleaded with him to name his own terms of peace.

The tragedy was that Cochise was a man of vision who wanted to be a man of peace, and that he was driven into hi

hired professional killers—American bounty hunters—to collect them. It is a matter of historical truth that the Apaches never practiced scalping until they were tutored in this grisly art by white men.

Just before the middle of the century the situation changed suddenly. The United States fought a war with Mexico and won from her the great Southwest. Then in 1853, chiefly to acquire a desirable route for a railroad to the Pacific, the United States bought another strip of land from Mexico—a section south of the Gila River called the Gadsden Purchase. In 1856, from his great stronghold in the Dragoon Mountains, Cochise watched United States soldiers come across his land for the first time and enter the sleepy, walled Mexican city of Tucson.

Of all the Apache tribes the Chiricahuas were the deadliest warriors, and of all the Apache leaders Cochise was acknowledged the most dangerous. Yet, as he saw the American newcomers swarm into his country, and as he heard by means of his incomparable intelligence network of the American activities and the American approach to this new world, he made a revolutionary decision: he would change the warlike ways of his people. He would make peace with the Americans. He would live by their sides and work with them and learn from them.

This decision was not made because of any upsurge of altruism. It was made because Cochise was a leader, and man enough to face new and harsh realities. These newcomers, these tough, seasoned soldiers, these ranchers who cut up the earth with a rifle in their hand, these were hard men—and there was an endless number of them. They were there, he knew, to stay. With a blinding clarity he saw that in the end any struggle between his two hundred poorly armed warriors and the white men who were pouring into the land with the newest guns could be resolved only in one way: the extermination of the Apaches. Cochise felt himself personally responsible for his people. He wanted them to live and multiply and prosper. From a deep, instinctive vision he knew the only way this could be achieved was by peace.

To make this move he first had to impose his will on the hotheads of his own tribe. It was not easy. The Apaches had had their own way, with other Indians and with the Mexicans, for many years. But because his people loved and respected him beyond all men, most of them followed him down the path of peace. A few did not. They left to continue their old ways on the other side of the Mexican border. They were led by a Chiricahua medicine man named Gokliya, who became better known by the name given him by the Mexicans: Geronimo.

But with the bulk of his people Cochise had his way. He journeyed to Fort Buchanan, the first military establishment set up by the American troops in the newly acquired territory, and there he made a treaty of peace and pledged to maintain that peace with his honor. More than anything, Cochise loved truth—he could steal, he could torture, he could kill. But he could not lie.

And so there was peace. The great hot desert bloomed and prospered with ranches, farms, mines. The Butterfield Stage Line was built through dreaded Apacheria to Tucson, and far from opposing this intrusion into his very heartland, Cochise gave the line his protection. To the amazement of all people, Apache fighting men served as guards, and not infrequently travelers witnessed the fantastic spectacle of Chiricahua Apaches fighting other Apaches to protect white men. A stage coach station was built in Apache Pass, the deepest part of Cochise's country. He welcomed it and persuaded his warriors—for the first time in Apache history—to work for the station employees, supplying them with firewood.

All this came to an abrupt and somber end when, in October 1860, a half-breed child of six named Mickey Free was kidnapped from the ranch of a settler named John Ward. Ward stormed into Fort Buchanan, and although Cochise had been for five years a friend and protector to the white man, he named the Chiricahua chief as the kidnapper. Since Ward was a man disliked by the other white settlers, who knew him for his viciousness and violent temper, his accusation might have been judged by its source and the war to come averted. However, unfortunately for the history of the Southwest, there happened to be stationed in Fort Buchanan a brand new second lieutenant named George Nicholas Bascom, just in from West Point on his first military assig-

word no Chiricahua Apache had raised a weapon in anger against a white man. Bascom ordered them to be silent. In his rigid code enlisted personnel, no matter how experienced, gave no advice to commissioned officers—no matter how inexperienced.

Bascom arrived with his troop at the Butterfield Station in Apache Pass, erected a tent, and from it hung a white flag—traditional symbol of peace and guaranty of protection during parleys between white men and Indians. Then he sent word by means of the station attendants that he wanted to talk with Cochise. The Indian leader, with members of his family, came to the tent in confidence. Ironically, they were engaged at the moment in bringing firewood into the station. They were half naked, covered with dirt and sweat, and as Bascom looked at the grimy chief his contempt rose. In his childish mind an Indian chief should wear feathers and warpaint and ride a great horse. He was about to make this concept come true.

Cochise entered the tent without hesitation, followed by his wife, his young son, his brother, and two nephews. With a covert signal, Bascom had the tent surrounded on the outside by soldiers, and then, without preamble, charged Cochise with the kidnapping of Mickey Free and ordered the Indian leader to produce the child. Cochise recoiled as though struck, but he fought to control himself. Calmly, he denied the kidnapping. He asked for more details about the abduction of the child and offered to help recover him. Many years later it was proved that Cochise had not lied—the child had been stolen by Pinal Apaches, another tribe altogether.

Bascom lost his temper. He told Cochise he would hold him

prisoner until the child was returned, a direct violation of the white flag that was still fluttering over the tent. And in final insult, he called Cochise a liar. With a wild cry of rage, Cochise whipped out his knife and slashed his way out of the tent, calling upon his family to follow him. Soldiers knocked down his brother, bayonetted a nephew, grabbed all the others—except Cochise himself. Cochise dodged and swerved up the hillside. He was wounded by bullets—but he got away.

Cochise captured several white men and held them as hostages and then, backed by his warriors, he took a position on the hill above the station. There he appeared as Bascom had envisioned an Indian chief—armed and mounted and covered with streaks of paint—a man far removed from the dusty, friendly Indian who had come to visit with Bascom in his tent. Still trying to avert a major rupture, still clinging to his belief that white men and red men could work side by side and live in peace, Cochise offered to exchange his white hostages unhurt for his own people. And he again offered to use all his influence to obtain the release of Mickey Free from whomever had taken him.

Bascom refused curtly. He would not release any Indians until the boy was returned. A sergeant argued with Bascom, pointing out Cochise's mania for truth. Bascom arrested the soldier and ordered him held for a court-martial. Then one of Cochise's white prisoners tried to escape and was killed. Bascom hanged Cochise's brother and nephews. Cochise ordered the rest of the white prisoners put to death. The peace was ended.

Bascom returned to Fort Buchanan and there turned loose Cochise's wife and son. After many days of hardship on the desert, the woman and small boy found their way back to Cochise's camp. Cochise, as soon as Bascom departed from the Butterfield Station, went down and cut down his brother and his brother's sons. He brought the bodies up to his stronghold and covered his face with black paint. He mourned for twenty-one days, and then he gathered his small band of warriors around him and put on his red turban of war. He raised his head and he spoke to his god: "There will be war to the end with the white-eyes. There will be ten white-eyes slain for every Indian slain. There will be no end to this war and there will be none spared from it. This I pledge! This I pledge! This I pledge!"

Again he was as good as his word. From one end of the land to the other he spread death and destruction. Ranches were abandoned. Farmers fled from their homes. Mines were left to gather water. Settlers huddled for safety in towns like Tubac and Tucson. When the Civil War started, the soldiers were recalled to the East; then there was nothing to stand in the way of Apache wrath.

[illegible]

[illegible] even to the point where, in superlative arrogance, he laid siege to Tucson itself—surrounded it with warriors and cut off all communication from the outside world—and broke off his siege only when it pleased him to do so.

When the Civil War ended, the cavalry and dragoons returned to Arizona. Military leaders who had won great names in the battle between the States were sent out to find and destroy the implacable Apache. Still with no more than two hundred warriors, Cochise took on and defeated again and again the best the army could put up against him. He became a legend—a legend of death. Army leaders ruefully saluted his brilliance and called him the "Red Napoleon."

At this time a strange white man appeared in Tucson. Thomas Jonathan Jeffords had been at one time a riverboat captain, a miner, a dispatch rider during the Civil War, a lawyer, a surveyor. Now he took over the management of the mail line between Fort Bowie and Tucson. His riders were slain relentlessly as they rode across Apache country. He paid his men $200 a month—enormous money for that time and place—and he used to say almost nobody ever collected it. He saw how helpless the army was to give protection to his men, and he made a momentous decision: he would seek out Cochise, speak to him, and try to work out some way for the mail riders to perform their duties unmolested. If arms could not subdue Cochise, perhaps understanding might.

This decision made by Jeffords called for incredible courage. Since that terrible time in Apache Pass, no white man had looked upon Cochise and lived to tell of it. For years Indian and white men killed each other on sight, with no mercy asked and none offered. Against this, Jeffords had only one thing to go by: at one time Cochise was a man of honor. Perhaps he still was.

Jeffords set about his task with care. He spent weeks learning the Apache language from a "tame" Apache who worked in Tucson. He studied the customs of the Apaches, their religious beliefs, their ceremonies and rites. During these weeks he must, many times, have thought about what he was risking. He must have spent many nights lying awake wondering whether he was a fool to attempt to get to Cochise. After all, he had no personal stake in the matter. The Government operated the mail and the Government should have protected the riders.

Nonetheless, after a long preparation, Jeffords set out, alone, on one of the great personal courses of valor of all time. He rode for days, deeper and deeper into Apache country, and with the feeling that shock tactics alone might keep him alive until he could face Cochise he sent out smoke signals several times each day, telling the Apaches he was coming alone in peace to parley with Cochise.

His hunch, on which he was gambling his life, paid off. The Apache vedettes who watched every inch of the Arizona desert were piqued by his boldness. When they reported on it to Cochise, the chief himself was interested, and he ordered that the white stranger be allowed to proceed.

Then, one day, Jeffords rode into the camp of Cochise. He instantly was surrounded by Apache men, women, and children. Calmly he climbed down from his horse, and he slowly took off his gun belt and handed it to a woman.

"Hold these for me," he said in perfect Apache. "I will need them when I leave."

From the mass of people there came a deep voice: "What makes you think you will leave here alive?"

Jeffords turned toward the voice. He looked upon Cochise and Cochise looked upon him.

"It is known that the chief of the Chiricahua Apaches is the greatest Indian leader," Jeffords said, his eyes full upon Cochise. "It is known that he respects bravery as he respects truth."

Cochise was silent for a long time. At last he said: "You are a brave man. I will listen to you."

The men spoke through the night. Jeffords appealed to the Indian to let his riders pass in peace. Cochise listened thoughtfully. His eyes, which seemed to look into a person's soul, never left Jeffords, and as he listened to the white man he came to recognize in Jeffords a man like himself—honest, forthright, courageous. As day came to the Indian camp, Cochise laid his hand on Jeffords' shoulder and gave his word—the mail drivers could pass in safety. He would continue his war against all other

... now could pass anywhere in safety, the war between the other white men and the Chiricahua Apaches never abated. It grew so savage that finally it came to the attention of President Grant, who saw that his army was accomplishing nothing. In February 1872 Grant sent General Oliver Otis Howard out to Arizona to find Cochise and try to make peace with him. For the good fortune of the country, Grant chose the right man.

Howard, who had lost an arm in the Civil War, was a bearded patriarch who was known as the "Christian General." A man of vision and faith, and of understanding, he lived by the words of his beloved Book, and he believed that all men were children and brothers in the eyes of God.

In New Mexico Howard sought out Jeffords and asked him to bring him to Cochise. Jeffords, sensing Howard's piety and his honor, agreed—but on one condition: Howard must go with him alone. No troops. Not even a bodyguard. Other army officers protested, but Howard silenced them. If that was the only way it could be done, he would do it.

Together the two men went up to the stronghold and Jeffords presented Howard to Cochise. The Apache chief asked his blood brother if he could trust this man, and Jeffords replied that he believed he could. Then Howard said he had come from the highest authority in the land to make peace on whatever terms Cochise demanded—the United States was admitting it could not conquer an Indian with 200 warriors—and was suing for peace.

Cochise named his terms. He set out the boundaries of the land he wanted for his people. Howard agreed. Then Cochise made his final demand: Jeffords was to serve as Agent on the reservation that was to be established for the Chiricahua Apaches,

Jeffords refused flatly. But when Cochise then refused to make the peace without him, he accepted. He too, however, made a condition: there were to be no soldiers on the reservation. The Apaches would be kept under control by one thing alone: the honor of Cochise. Although this was an unprecedented demand, and there was no reserve in the country that was not policed by soldiers, Howard agreed to this too. Cochise at last laid down his arms, and the mistake made many years before by a young officer—who, it must be added, himself died a hero's death in the Civil War—was finally corrected.

Because men believed that truth and understanding could accomplish more than guns and bullets, peace returned to the terrible and beautiful land of the Southwest.

". . . there is no better plan"

CHARLES COLEMAN SELLERS

As one of his grandsons said not long ago: "It all began when the rattlesnake crawled over Grandfather's neck." That must have been about 1869 or 1870, when Lieutenant Richard Henry Pratt was leading a detachment of the 10th United States Cavalry in pursuit of a band of hostile Indians. The 10th was a Negro regiment, former slaves commanded by white officers. At nightfall the Plains had become one vast reach of darkness; the horses were tethered close by the wagons; the men lay on the ground protected only by their blankets from the sharp wind. Lieutenant Pratt was awakened by the cold body of the snake moving across his neck. He knew at once what it was and lay still. The snake, happily, did not linger near the warmth of the blanket. It moved on, the faint, sinister sound of its body lost in the blackness, but it was a long time before the lieutenant could sleep again.

His thoughts went back over the years of the Civil War, hard fighting and narrow escapes, and the tremendous movement of armies. At the heart of it had been the status of the Negro, whether slave or citizen. Now it was the Indians, these "domestic dependent nations," wards of the government, and the succession of little wars battering them into submission and holding them roughly there. He thought of what fine fellows his Negro troopers were, how well they responded when treated as men among men, and of the good response which that same treatment had brought from the little force of Indian scouts under his command. From

as a weaver and printer's devil, toiled on the new railroad, split rails, and cut firewood.To his mother he was always a steady, loyal, affectionate son. Mary Pratt was what they called in those days a "singing Methodist," and the boy sang with her and absorbed from her the warm, heart-felt religion of the countryside. The war broke out, and he was singing still as a tall, broad-shouldered young trooper of the 2nd Indiana Cavalry. He fought at Shiloh and Chickamauga and a score of other battles and skirmishes, rose from private to sergeant, lieutenant, captain. Twice his horse was shot under him, but he came through unscathed.

He was married while on leave toward the end of the war. After its close he re-enlisted in the Regular Army and was commissioned a lieutenant in the 10th Cavalry. His wife, Anna Laura, with their two children, joined him at the western army post. There had followed those years of swift pursuits, of sharp and often cruel fighting, but by 1875 the tribes had been starved and beaten into submission. There the end—and the opportunity for a new beginning—came. By General Sheridan's orders, seventy-two young warriors, so-called "ringleaders" of the conquered tribes, Comanches, Cheyennes, Arapahoes and Kiowas were seized and accused of a long list of "crimes." Then, without trial, chained together in gangs, they were taken by wagons to the railroad, and by railroad across the continent to Saint Augustine, Florida, where old Fort Marion was to be their prison. There was but one concession to humanity—the officer who had expressed friendship for the Indians was placed in charge.

Saint Augustine watched the arrival of the wild and sullen

prisoners with excitement and alarm. Alarm continued as word came from the Fort that the officer in command had removed the chains, and then that he had released the prisoners from strict confinement. After a few months it was learned that the guard of soldiers had been dismissed and that the Indians, now dressed in trim army uniforms, were mounting guard upon themselves. Visitors to the Fort found prisoners making souvenirs for the tourist trade and, for the first time, feeling the independence that comes from profitable labor. Friendly people came forward with enthusiastic support of the plan. Soon the Indians were learning to speak and write English, mastering trades, going to school. They went swimming and boating between their hours of work. No one felt the wonder of the transformation as much as they themselves.

Thus the Pratt idea first took form. If the government would support him, Richard Henry Pratt felt sure that he could solve the whole "Indian problem" within a generation. He would take young Indians far from their home environment, give them the education and all the opportunities of white men. They would become a part of American life as readily as the immigrants swarming in from Europe. The reservations, the idle waiting for a government dole, must go. Instead of feeding civilization in small doses to the Indians, the Indians themselves would be fed into our civilization. Pratt would let their native culture pass into history. Obliterate all that. "Get them out of the curio class," the big soldier said. "Let them be men and women with ourselves."

The government was sufficiently impressed to send Pratt and some of his pupils to the Hampton Institute in 1878, and then, a year later, to give him the unused army post at Carlisle, Pennsylvania, and a small appropriation. Here, with the arrival, on October 6, 1879, of a hundred and thirty-two girls and boys, Sioux, Pawnees, Kiowas and Cheyennes the famous Carlisle Indian School came into being. Again there was a difficult start and again loyal friends appeared as from nowhere to help the officer carry out his plan. Carlisle is a college town, the home of Dickinson College, and the college people were with Pratt even before the students arrived. Soon after they came, a Dickinson professor began to lecture at Carlisle on science. It was strangely dramatic. He spoke through an interpreter, showing experiments in chemistry and physics, to them wildly exciting. This is the white man's magic, the secret of his greatness, the professor told them. But it is not really magic, nor secret; everyone, he said, can learn these things, and we are here to teach them.

For twenty-five years the School prospered as a personal expression of Pratt's ideal. The "Outing System," under which he sent young Indians to live in neighboring homes, going to
schools, earning

farmers, tradesmen,
doctors, lawyers, artists.

Those were years of work and battle both. Pratt knew that the Indian Bureau had been with him at first simply because it wanted Indian children held as hostages. He knew that the Bureau of those days was unidealistic, often corrupt, and that it shared the public's belief that the Indian was "born a savage." Said Pratt: "He was born a blank, like the rest of us," and only his environment makes him a savage. He proved it in his pupils. He fought officialdom with a soldier's blunt defiance, with all his tremendous energy, his ringing voice, and always with, in his own words, "the fundamental truth that all men are brothers." In 1904, soon after his promotion to Brigadier General, he was summarily dismissed from his post at the School. In a public address in New York he had called the Bureau "a barnacle to be knocked off sometime." The Bureau took over, gradually lowering the standards of the School, and finally abandoning it in 1918.

The old soldier watched with dismay, but fought on for his plan. At the last he wept, knowing that he must die with his dream unfulfilled. His death came at an army hospital in San Francisco in 1924. His daughter tried to comfort him with the hope that God would find a better plan. He turned his face away from her, saying: "There is no better plan." They were his last words, and the years, turning now to decades, have not proved them wrong.

Ignatius Donnelly, Henry George

From the earliest beginnings of the time of the Civil War the "typical" American was a farmer. During the colonial period about ninety percent of the people had been engaged in agricultural pursuits, and it was natural, therefore, that the farmer was portrayed everywhere as the symbol of industry and civic virtue. "Those who labor in the earth," Jefferson boasted, "are the chosen people of God."

But in the generation after 1865 the farmer suffered an eclipse. Rising industrialism inevitably reduced his significance in American life, and the particular circumstances of that time seemed to threaten to destroy his place in society completely. During the Rebellion, when demand and prices were both high, northern farmers tended to borrow heavily to buy more land and machinery and thus increase production. But after the restoration of "normal" conditions, agricultural prices fell precipitously. For example, wheat had sold as high as $2.50 a bushel in the sixties. In the nineties it dropped to as little as fifty cents a bushel. Farmers were badly stung by this decline, and the injury was compounded by the fact that their expenses did not decline proportionally. Fixed charges like mortgage and installment payments remained unaltered, and indeed were made more burdensome by the general decline of prices resulting from a post-war deflationary cycle. Farmers who pushed west discovered that the cost of transporting and storing their products went up accordingly, and they came to believe, with good reason, that monopolistic railroads and grain elevators were charging them exorbitantly for services performed. Then, about 1890, the disappearance of the frontier caused further concern. Although it did not mean that no undeveloped land remained for farmers to exploit, it seemed, psychologically, to mark the end of the time when cheap land and a new start lay always at hand for those dissatisfied with their present lot.

These conditions made radicals out of thousands of essentially conservative American landowners. A wave of reform movements and third-party political organizations swept across the Missis-

sippi Valley and the Great Plains. "Greenbackers" demanded paper money and a managed currency, "Grangers" insisted upon state regulation of railroads and public utilities, "Populists" campaigned for a graduated income tax, the regulation of big business, and the direct election of the United States

Much of this

significantly aided the cause of social and economic justice in the United States.

Ignatius Donnelly was perhaps a typical agrarian reformer of the period. Aggressive, unorthodox, and far from disinterested, he was associated with all the major movements of the era. George, on the other hand, was not directly concerned with the post-war farm uprising. But his whole system was based on land and its use, and his thinking was clearly marked by what was happening to land values in his day. Both men reflect the conditions that caused so much dissatisfaction among American agriculturalists between 1865 and 1900.

John D. Hicks is Professor Emeritus of History at the University of California. Among his many publications are The Populist Revolt *and* Republican Ascendancy: 1921-33, *a volume in the New American Nation series. Herman Ausubel is Associate Professor of History at Columbia University. He has written* Historians and Their Craft, The Late Victorians, *and other works.*

". . . an apostle of reform"

JOHN D. HICKS

"THE great interest of agriculture is almost voiceless in the nation. It is tongue-tied by parties and gagged by tricksters. Let it organize itself. If it can achieve success, all lesser interests can cling to it and be carried forward with it to prosperity. If it perishes, the nation sinks." So Ignatius Donnelly declared in 1870, when he sought election to Congress from a Minnesota district as the People's Independent candidate.

Born November 3, 1831, in Philadelphia, the son of a successful physician, Donnelly had emigrated to Minnesota during the boom of the 1850s, had made and lost a fortune in real estate, and, as a young Republican, had then risen spectacularly in politics, first with two terms as Lieutenant-Governor and then with three terms in Congress. During these early years his political orthodoxy was unimpeachable; he saw eye to eye with his party's leaders not only on the issues of slavery and reconstruction, but also on matters that pertained primarily to the welfare of business and industry. A high tariff and hard money advocate, he took a particular interest in easing the way for the innumerable new western railroad projects that depended for their success upon obtaining generous land subsidies from the national domain.

But eventually Donnelly aroused the misgivings of his political superiors. Despite his regularity, he talked too much and he thought too much; so, in 1868, just as his career was nicely under way, Donnelly found himself deprived of renomination and relegated to the political sidelines. By 1870, when he ran for Congress as an independent, he had revised his thought and reshaped his course. No longer was he to be the willing tool of business and industry; it was the cause of the embattled farmer that henceforth he meant to plead. Not that he overlooked the problems of the city laborers, for he recognized and understood them too. But the depressed farmers were closer at hand; they were his potential constituents, the voters to whom he must appeal; their cause was more directly his.

From this time to the time of his death, Donnelly played a leading role in every third party movement that broke across the New Northwest in which he lived. He was in turn a Liberal Republican, a Granger, a Greenbacker, a Farmers' Allianceman, a Populist, and a Middle-of-the-Road Populist. Between times he might lapse temporarily and uneasily into the Republican or the Democratic party, but old party leaders never trusted him nor did he trust them. It was indeed not so much political organizations that interested him, although he seemed never to give up hope that sometime, somehow, a real party of the people would rise to power. What concerned him most was the grim contest that went on between the rights of property on the one hand and the rights of men on the other, "between the few who seek to grasp all power and wealth, and the many who seek to preserve their rights as American citizens and freemen." He regarded poverty as an unmitigated evil, and someone's fault.

More specifically, as Donnelly saw it, the farmer was getting a raw deal. The government was rigged for the benefit of industry. The protective tariff

Donnelly changed his mind, too, on the money question, for he saw in the hard money policies of the financial magnates another device for keeping down farm prices, while at the same time pushing up the real value of debts. From the Civil War until nearly the end of the nineteenth century the United States experienced chronic deflation, instead of the chronic inflation we now know so well. This meant, among other things, that if a farmer borrowed $750 when wheat was worth a dollar a bushel, and paid it back five years later when wheat had dropped to seventy-five cents a bushel, it would take a thousand bushels of wheat instead of seven hundred and fifty to discharge the debt. So Donnelly and many other reformers embraced Greenbackism, and then the Free Silver "heresy," as a means of at least keeping the value of the dollar relatively constant, or perhaps raising prices a little.

As for the railroads, Donnelly denounced them now for their high and discriminatory rates, and demanded governmental regulation. He upbraided all "trusts," railroad and otherwise, for their monopolistic practices, told off the bankers for the unreasonably high interest rates they demanded, and charged middlemen and merchants with greedily exacting exorbitant profits.

After his early years Donnelly never again held high public office, although he served repeatedly as a member of one house or the other of the Minnesota legislature. He was primarily an apostle of reform, and as such he had two strings to his bow. He was superb as an orator, almost a match for the matchless Bryan, and he could write political polemics that made the efforts of his adversaries seem childlike in comparison. He was always in demand for the lecture platform, and he twice edited weekly newspapers, first the *Anti-Monopolist,* and later the *Representative,* both of which served as vehicles for his political writings. He reached possibly his highest eloquence in the preamble he wrote for the Populist platform of 1892: "We meet," he said, "in the midst of a nation brought to the verge of moral, political and material ruin. . . . A vast conspiracy against mankind has been organized on two continents, and is taking possession of the world . . . ." And much more in similar key.

The function of third parties in American politics is to call attention to issues that the older parties dodge. The fate of third-party politicians is usually dismal, for only rarely are they taken over into the old party even when it accepts the principles they have defended. The Populist party of the 1890s, which fell heir to the political heritage of so many preceding third party movements, lost its life when the Democrats nominated Bryan in 1896 on a Populistic platform, Although Donnelly voted for Bryan, he found himself outside the Democratic pale. Later he and others whose fate was similar tried to rebuild the Populist party on the anti-fusion principle, "Keep in the middle of the road." But they failed.

Donnelly was much more than a third-party politician. During one of his earlier periods of political eclipse he had decided upon a literary career, and in his first book, *Atlantis: the Antedeluvian World,* published in 1881, he undertook to prove that Plato was right in thinking that originally civilization developed in a great Atlantic island opposite the mouth of the Mediterranean Sea. The book sold amazingly well, and inspired its author to another endeavor, *Ragnarok, the Age of Fire and Gravel,* published in 1883, which explained geological formations on the earth by the impact during prehistoric times of a mighty comet. Quite in character with his political irregularity, he sought to prove that Bacon wrote Shakespeare, and in a two-volume work, *The Great Cryptogram,* which appeared in 1888, convinced those who wished to be convinced. Donnelly's books made his name known the world over, and sold well enough to make him comfortable financially. His most successful book was a political novel, *Caesar's Column,* published in 1890, which reversed the optimism of Edward Bellamy's *Looking Backward* and anticipated twentieth century fascism. He incorporated his views on the money question in a book entitled *The American People's Money,* which was published in 1896.

Donnelly's enemies sized him up as both a political and a literary crackpot. But despite his many strange notions he was in most ways a delightful person. Round-faced, smooth-shaven, and well-groomed, he was the complete antithesis of the average gaunt, bewhiskered, and disheveled Populist. His

"... *saintly* ... *dangerous as dynamite*"

HERMAN AUSUBEL

In 1939, a few days before the outbreak of the Second World War, delegates from all over the globe arrived in New York City to celebrate the one hundredth anniversary of the birth of Henry George. Except for Hitler's Germany and Mussolini's Italy, every major country was represented at the conference, and so too was a host of minor countries. The American hero in whose honor the celebration took place had been buried in Brooklyn for more than forty years—since 1897. If he had been alive, however, little would have pleased him more than the world-wide character of the festivities. Anything but parochial in his aims and aspirations, George was never content to be merely an unforgettable *American;* he was determined to be an unforgettable citizen of the world.

The reason for George's lack of provincialism is not far to seek. God, he believed, had singled him out to discover certain absolute truths about wealth and poverty and about man's economic relations in general. More than that, God had chosen him to propagate those truths not only among Americans but among all the peoples of the world. George saw himself as a modern soldier of Christ, a latter-day crusader whose activities made national boundaries both anachronistic and absurd. This, in fact, is what set him apart from many of his contemporaries in the turbulent reform movements of late nineteenth-century America. He had none of the anti-foreignism of the Grangers, Populists, bimetallists, and tariff reformers.

George wrote a great deal during the fifty-eight years of his life, but he owed his reputation to a single book, *Progress and Poverty*—"P and P," as he affectionately called it. He brought the volume out in 1879, hoping that it would enable him, after the fashion of Lord Byron, to awaken one morning and find himself famous. A few years passed before the book attracted the attention that George longed for. But the fame—indeed, the notoriety—did come, and not only in the United States but in England, Ireland, and other parts of the world. To his admirers George became as saintly a figure as graced the late nineteenth-century world. To his detractors he appeared to be at best a quack and at worst as dangerous as dynamite.

Forty years old at the time of the publication of his masterpiece, George thought of his life up to that point as simply a preparation for the formidable task that God had given him. The great poverty he had known (and the little progress) had equipped him admirably for the seminal work. All the important facts of his life fell into perspective as parts of God's design: his devout parents who had taught him to love God; his passion for reading and self-education in the years after he ended his limited schooling in Philadelphia; the stark poverty that he saw in places so diverse as New York and Calcutta; the revolting instances of land speculation that he witnessed in booming California; the humiliating unemployment that he knew as a teen-ager; the even more humiliating poverty he suffered as a young married man trying to support a growing family; his discouraging experiences in the printing and publishing business and the world of journalism; and the domestic security that enveloped him as the result of the determined efforts of a devoted wife and dedicated children who had boundless confidence in him. For the rest, as George confessed to an Irish priest and disciple, "Once, in daylight, and in a city street, there came to me a thought, a vision, a call—give it what name you please." That was the formal beginning of *Progress and Poverty*, and after the publication of the book the feeling never left him that the fate of his work was in the hands of God. Clearly, George was closer in some ways to the age of the Puritan Revolution than to his own Gilded Age.

George's central ideas were not complicated. Property rights, he argued, were based on God's unmistakable and absolute com-

mand: "Thou shalt not steal." Yet since God, not man, created the earth, no individual could legitimately claim an exclusive right to own land. On the contrary, since all men were in the world with God's permission, all had an equal and inalienable right to the earth. To be sure, people who used the land needed to hav-
security in ord-

..., and he expected almost unbelievably beneficial results to flow from it. The single tax would make possible an enormous growth of wealth as well as a more equitable distribution of wealth. It would solve the staggering unemployment problem and make the undeserving poor simply memories of a barbaric past. And it would raise dramatically the moral and cultural standards and achievements of society. In short, the single tax would prepare the way for the kingdom of abundance, righteousness, justice, and happiness for which Christ told his disciples to pray and work.

If George considered his first forty years a preparation for the great and good book—the Bible of ethical economics—that God had him write, he viewed his remaining years as designed by God to spread the truths that he had been permitted to discover. George accordingly wrote and lectured endlessly; he organized clubs to disseminate his principles; and he hunted tirelessly for converts, especially rich ones. He himself remained poor, eking out a meager existence from his lectures and writings. He ran for mayor of New York City in 1886, and though he lost, he won more votes than the young Republican candidate, Theodore Roosevelt. He ran again for the mayoralty in 1897, but just a few days before the election took place he died of a stroke.

As a prophet with a world outlook, George did not confine his missionary efforts to the United States. Ireland, with its notorious system of absentee landlordism, was an ideal proving-ground for his ideas, and George became deeply involved in the Irish struggles of the age of Charles Stewart Parnell and Michael Davitt. But George was particularly concerned with the fate of his message in England, which he steadfastly and reverentially regarded as "the center and radiating point of Anglo-Saxon thought." It is not surprising, therefore, that he hastened to distribute copies of his book among British celebrities who might be able to publicize it. Nor is it a surprise that he eagerly awaited the publication of an English edition of his work.

In January 1881, the English version of *Progress and Poverty* appeared, but it got off to a disappointingly slow start. George, impatient for fame and a mass audience, fumed at British critics who stigmatized his book as incendiary and communistic, and he reveled in every flattering comment he could find. At last, in February 1882, his publisher told him what he had been anxiously waiting to hear—that *Progress and Poverty* was "the most astonishing success he *ever* knew."

Although George recognized that he had accomplished something without precedent in the history of economic writing, he remained insatiable. He lectured indefatigably in England, Scotland, and Ireland in the hope of winning new single taxers; and he complained angrily that the English press did not pay sufficient attention to him, his book, and his lectures. Always George was convinced that if his movement caught on in England, its success would be furthered in other countries—including the United States. Indeed, as he ended his first visit to Britain, he assured his leading American financial backer that he had "done a bigger work (or rather started bigger forces) than any American who ever crossed to the old country."

George was only one of many reformers in the period of the worldwide price and profit depression of the late nineteenth century who tried to offer a solution to the economic difficulties of his generation. But he had at least one advantage over many of his fellow-reformers, whether American or British: the hyper-intensity of his convictions. It was characteristic of him, for example, to try to persuade the English Marxist leader, H. M. Hyndman, that he had been misled. Hyndman, as George put it, "has been lately a good deal under the mental influence of Karl Marx; but I think I have already shaken him in this, and will get him out of it before I get through." The joke of it all was that, while George was attempting to make a single taxer out of Hyndman, Hyndman was trying to win George to Marxian socialism. He had the Georges as house guests in London, and after many discussions he thought that he had brought George around to believing that the first thing to do was to replace capitalism with socialism. When neither converted the other, their friendship cooled. What a pity it was, George wrote with his superb self-confidence, that a man of such gifts as Hyndman should follow so slavishly such a shallow thinker as Karl Marx!

By his own standards George was a failure, but he was a failure only because he set such high standards for himself. It is true that no gover

when he wished that he could do for Americans of the early twentieth century what Henry George had done for the British of his youth.

J. Pierpont Morgan

Most of the Americans described in these pages are unforgettable because of their ideas and achievements. The subject of the following chapter is no exception, for surely J. Pierpont Morgan was the greatest banker in America for two generations after the Civil War as well as one of the most important of all American collectors of art. Although contemporary critics made him a symbol of evil wealth and arrogant privilege, most students today would grant that, on balance, his contribution was constructive and his motives above reproach.

In this sense the image of Morgan has changed over the years, reflecting corresponding changes in American society. But as Allan Nevins points out, it is primarily as a great personality that Morgan is remembered, and in this there has been no change since he first rose to prominence. Those who knew him were simply overwhelmed by his determination and inner force. As the photographer Edward Steichen once said, looking at Morgan was like gazing into the searchlight of an oncoming locomotive; one was either awed or terrified depending on whether or not one was standing in his way.

Allan Nevins is beyond question the most prolific and versatile, and probably the most judicious and penetrating of all our American historians. No period and few subjects have not been covered in his dozens of major books. At present he is engaged on a massive history of the Civil War era, The Ordeal of the Union, *the sixth volume of which has just appeared.*

". . . largeness of action . . . largeness of idea"

[illegible] his second duty to promote the growth of the country; the greatest banker, with all due deference to George Peabody and Jay Cooke, in American history.

And what is J. Pierpont Morgan chiefly remembered for? He ought to be remembered for his services in 1886 in getting important railroads to stop the competitive rate-cutting that was ruining some of them; for his skilful reorganization of important railway lines after the Panic of 1893; for his great bond syndicate of 1895, which banded together the important New York banks and dealers in foreign exchange to protect the Treasury's gold reserve, bring in gold supplies from abroad, and prevent the nation from losing the advantages of its existing financial situation; for his creation of the United States Steel Corporation in 1901; and for his courageous action in stopping a disastrous run on the large trust companies of the land in the Panic of 1907. Actually, he is remembered chiefly for his personality.

For his personality was so arresting and dominating that most people have fixed their eyes upon it to the neglect of his labors. Here was a magnate, born in 1837 to wealth and power, for his father was an important international banker, who vastly increased both during a long life that lasted until 1913, and who lived as a prince of finance, a magnifico among capitalists, was expected to live in that Victorian era. He moved in a glittering, spacious world, giving a luncheon at Kiel to Kaiser Wilhelm, sitting in Westminster Abbey at the coronation of Edward VII, holding audiences with popes, queens, and premiers, and looking upon presidents as equals. He was equally at home in New York, London, Monte Carlo, Rome, and Cairo. The note he struck was not of display, not of splendor, but of a largeness of action that impressed people as magnificent.

Thus when he requested Judge Elbert Gary to become head of his Federal Steel Company, he made a regal gesture: "You can select the directors, name the executive committee, and fix your own salary." When the Harvard Medical School asked various rich potentates for gifts, John D. Rockefeller characteristically arranged for a six-month study before he made his donation. But Morgan welcomed the Harvard representatives with watch in hand, remarked "I am pressed for time and can give you but a moment," glanced intently over the plans, and pointing his finger said: "I will build that, and that, and that. Good morning, gentlemen!" And most people have heard of his advice to another multimillionaire who enviously asked what it would cost to maintain a vessel like Morgan's *Corsair:* "If you even have to think about the cost, don't keep a yacht."

It was because of his largeness of idea, his magnificence of gesture, that people have thought of him first of all as a personality. It seemed right and fitting, in his era, that he should have a mansion on Madison Avenue, a country house, "Cragston," on the Hudson, a camp of a thousand acres in the Adirondacks, a "fishing box" at Newport, a place on Jekyll Island, a mansion in Prince's Gate, London, and a country house outside that city; fitting that he should move in imposing fashion from one to another. It was fitting that he should have sharply individual, even eccentric, tastes, and thus express a character as versatile, unpredictable, and human as it was aggressive and imperious. He was a pillar of the Episcopal Church, with so literal a faith that like William Jennings Bryan he accepted the story of Jonah and the whale as true. He found relaxation in solitaire, and even when he gave evening parties for important people sometimes drew coldly apart to play by himself at a little table. He was a passionate collector of rare books, fine paintings, antiques, and other exquisite objects, and gave many of them with Maecenas generosity to public collections; his own Morgan Library of books and manuscripts, and the Pierpont Morgan wing of the Metropolitan Museum, stand as monuments to his taste.

If Morgan had the personality of a great aristocrat, he had the character of a business leader of oaken integrity. Even close associates like Dwight Morrow were afraid of him: afraid of his cold, steely eyes, his grim frown, his abrupt, dictatorial, and sometimes harsh words. His "Well?" could be terrifying. But when he gave his word, men relied implicitly upon it. The important part of the bond syndicate operation in 1895 in protecting the United States Treasury lay in the personal guarantee that he gave to President Grover Cleveland. He declared that he could restore and maintain the gold [illegible]

him and his chief partners that they tried to be fair in their transactions. As Dwight Morrow put it, a hard bargain was always a bad bargain.

Beyond integrity, other qualities supplied the solid foundation for the success of the House of Morgan. They included imagination, dominating power of will, and courage. Together with a great deal of detailed financial and legal planning, imagination went into the building of the prosperous Southern Railroad system out of a clutter of small lines and other properties. Imagination of a somewhat colossal sort was the basis of the United States Steel Corporation, a more than billion-dollar creation which lesser men would have deemed impossible. As for courage, Morgan showed it from the time in 1869 when he fought the piratical Jay Gould and Jim Fisk for control of the Albany & Susquehanna Railroad to the time at the end of his life when he met with undaunted vigor the thrusts of the razor-minded counsel of the Pujo Committee, Samuel Untermeyer. Most memorable of all was his courage in the sale of United States bonds for European gold in 1895. When this hazardous transaction was completed, his New York office cabled his London office: "Heartfelt congratulations. You cannot appreciate the relief to everybody's mind, for the dangers were so great scarcely anyone dared whisper them."

His imperious will kept his partners, including such men as Robert Bacon and Charles H. Coster, completely under his sway, overawed such lesser financial magnates as James Stillman, H. H. Rogers, and George F. Baker, and impressed senators and governors. Now and then he met more than his match. Theodore Roosevelt scornfully refused to bow to his urgent demand that the government call off its Northern Securities Company anti-trust suit. Once Dr. William S. Rainsford, Seth Low, and various vestrymen overruled him when he tried to halt Dr. Rainsford's democratization of St. George's Episcopal Church in New York. But his will generally carried everything before it. It was evident, for example, when in a succession of conferences he compelled balky railroad presidents to submit to the decent rate practices prescribed by the Interstate Commerce Act of 1887, and to stop such suicidal competitive policies as those which had led the Pennsylvania Railroad to invade New York Central territory with the West Shore line, and the Central to invade the Pennsylvania's domain with the South Pennsylvania. He arranged for an exchange of these cut-throat subsidiaries.

Most of all was his imperious authority in evidence when his determined intervention stopped the 1907 panic among the trust companies. At the crucial moment he laid before the trust company heads an agreement to raise another $25,000,000 to halt the runs. "There's the place," he said to one hesitant banker, "and here's the pen." The banker signed. One of the financial leaders came to Morgan at the worst of the panic to say he was sick with worry because he was below his legal reserve. "You ought to be ashamed of yourself," growled Morgan. "What's your reserve for at a time like this except to use?"

Morgan's virtues were inescapably matched by great faults, his achievements by striking failures. The "gentlemen's agreement" that he effected among railway heads in 1886 did not stay the subsequent slip of many lines into bankruptcy. While his reorganization of some of these lines in the 1890s was almost miraculously successful, it was also miraculously efficient in putting their control into the hands of the House of Morgan, and contributed greatly to the aggrandizement of his interests. He built his own railway empire, and shared with James J. Hill the control of another. He made serious errors in the initial organization of the Steel Corporation, paying bloated prices for some properties. His creation of the International Mercantile Marine, a shipping trust, in 1901-02 could be called an error altogether. The most unfortunate of his later ventures was his share in controlling and expanding the New Haven Railroad, which had a long succession of financial troubles, wrecks, and other disasters. More even than Rockefeller and Carnegie, Morgan failed to understand the importance of public opinion, or to comprehend that a new era was dawning in which the government must and would control finance and industry.

Yet his massive character, keen mind, and expert skills were on the whole a national asset. In times of trouble his authority and leadership inspired confidence, while his judgment found the best way out of difficulties. His organizing talent increased the efficiency of the national economy. As our ablest international

Brooks Adams

Congress, says the Constitution, may not grant titles of nobility, nor may any citizen accept a title from a foreign power without special permission. Our democratic system of government has consistently rejected the idea of power or even prestige based on hereditary right. Each man must prove himself on his own; he cannot rely on the achievements of an illustrious ancestor to win him place or status.

Yet there has always been a "hereditary aristocracy" of sorts in America. In part this is inevitable and based on wealth. Great fortunes accumulated in the past have assured at least economic power to generations of duPonts and Astors and other old families. But political power has also been remarkably subject to inheritance. President Benjamin Harrison, for example, was the son of a Congressman, grandson of a President, and great-grandson of a signer of the Declaration of Independence. Surely his own political success was the result in large part of family reputation, for Harrison was far from being a statesman of the first rank. (Theodore Roosevelt once called him a "timid old psalm-singing Indianapolis politician.") And it has not proved a political disadvantage, in our own times, to be named Roosevelt, Taft, Lodge, or La Follette, to cite merely some of the most obvious examples.

The greatest of all American families by a wide margin was the clan fathered in the eighteenth century by an obscure Massachusetts farmer named Adams. For five generations his descendants were Presidents, cabinet ministers, diplomats, successful businessmen, and writers. Surely more first-rate intellects have never been centered in one family over so long a span of time.

In the sons of Charles Francis Adams (1807-86), himself the son and grandson of Presidents, the family produced three remarkable personalities: Charles Francis, Jr., Henry, and Brooks. Of these Brooks was the least well known, but he was possessed of perhaps the most original mind of the entire Adams family. What he believed and what was the significance of his career are described here by Charles Vevier, Associate Professor of History at the University of Wisconsin—Milwaukee. Professor Vevier, a specialist in diplomatic history, is the author of The United States and China, 1906-1913.

BROOKS ADAMS often complained that he suffered from boredom, yet he lived seventy-nine years and wrote innumerable magazine articles, at least four major books, and a series of legal briefs that were books in themselves. He delivered uncounted speeches on major public issues, traveled throughout the United States, Europe, and Asia, served for some years on the faculty of the Law School of Boston University, and contributed a good portion of personal correspondence to the papers of the Adams family. When he died at the Adams family home in Quincy, Massachusetts, in 1927, he believed himself a failure. Until recent years, critical opinion has tended to agree with him, relegating him to an unimportant place in American intellectual and social history. In a certain sense, this oversight is quite understandable.

For Brooks Adams had no manners; he was brusque, aggressive, stubborn, quarrelsome, and assertive. At times he had been a problem child to his famous father, Charles Francis Adams, Lincoln's Minister to England during the Civil War, and he often exasperated his brilliant brother, Henry, one of the few men whom Brooks could talk with and learn from. His cantankerous habits alienated people. Much of the time he was a lonely man, whose only friends were the ideas that he developed about history.

It was this trait of intellectuality that made him an Adams. The traditional family qualities of self-doubt and introspection, of devotion to duty and individual righteousness, of suppressed emotion that made cold intellectual brilliance even colder, had not raised a warm emotional response in many Americans for the Adams folk. Brooks, however, was proud of his family and its contribution to the life of America.

After the Civil War, American history was the story of the growth of a nation. Industrialism, the transportation boom, the expansion of cities, and the exploitation of mineral resources—all these occupied the increasing number of American people for almost forty hectic and exciting years of national progress. But by the end of the nineteenth century it was clear that the process of material expansion at home had outdistanced social institutions, governmental processes, and political thought. Action outran caution, while serious problems arising from this free-wheeling growth were shunted to one side. Labor clashed with capital. The farmer protested against falling prices, drought, and high transportation costs. Overcrowded cities, the demands made on government for extended social services, and drift and corruption in politics revived the reform tradition in the United States.

1893 was a confused year in American history. Chicago held a huge exposition of progress that exalted the achievements of science, but some men warned of the decline of the frontier and the opportunities identified with it. A college professor named Woodrow Wilson spoke of the need for higher quality and unifying principles in education in a maturing society. Moreover, 1893 was a year of depression, and it was this event that interested Brooks Adams.

Brooks was a philosopher of history, seeking meaning in events of the past for the education and advantage of the people of the present. He believed that the overwhelming complexity of the new industrial civilization could not be understood unless society had a unifying principle that would link together the many details of modern life. Confusion bred disorder, and the hostile lines between economic interest, political party, and social class in the United States would never be removed, Brooks argued, unless the people would agree to a standard that overcame fear and greed, which set men against each other.

Adams found his great principle in the life of the American nation. He always regarded the welfare of the entire country as the most important end to which Americans should aspire; he was one of the first critics in American history to attempt to map out an organized explanation of history in order to suggest solutions for the problems of the twentieth century.

In 1894 he published *The Gold Standard,* a study of the controversial currency question that had influenced the Populist revolt. His most important book, *The Law of Civilization and Decay,* came out a year later, and was followed by three others:

America's Economic Supremacy, The New Empire, and *The Theory of Social Revolutions.* Taken together they revealed Adams' conviction that the United States stood at the apex of the history of world civilization. He made a remarkable effort to bring this idea to the attention of his readers in order to warn them of [illegible]

[illegible] would always be contending for favored position. The result would be a disastrous clash, perhaps even revolution. Adams criticized businessmen for not restraining their efforts for excessive profits, but he also attacked socialists for advocating the confiscation of private property. Both groups, he insisted, were short-sighted and selfish.

Although his views were too strong and independent for the reformers of the Progressive movement in the United States between 1896 and 1916, he did exert a strong influence on President Theodore Roosevelt, whose administrations attempted to mediate between big business and the general public through government regulation of trusts and railroads.

Domestic matters were all-important to Adams, but when the United States became more heavily involved in world affairs at the turn of the century, Adams called for a vigorous policy of imperialist expansion, and welcomed the outbreak of the Spanish-American War in 1898. He admired military virtues, and felt that the American acquisition of the Philippines would give the United States an economic foothold in Asia. Like Captain Alfred Thayer Mahan, a leading advocate of the need for a large American navy, Adams believed that a country's international policies had to be shaped by the realities of geography if it was to be powerful. This idea has now been more formally crystallized in the study of geopolitics in our own day, and Adams has been given credit by European thinkers as one of the early exponents of this outlook.

Above all, Adams, like many thinkers before and since his time, puzzled over the question of efficient and effective government. He considered the best government to be administrative government. The level of public discussion in a democracy, as he judged it at the time, had serious limitations. It prevented action in an emergency; it often obscured the issues by appealing to emotionalism; and it left the power of decision in the hands of voters who were too preoccupied with their own concerns to judge carefully about matters of general importance.

Accordingly, Adams merged two American traditions, the strong exercise of executive leadership and responsibility personified by George Washington and the old democratic notion that proper education would teach people not only the facts of specialized knowledge, but the way to think about those facts in a broad way. If these related goals were achieved, congressional government and the use of regulatory commissions might be dropped in favor of programs drawn up by the President for presentation to the voters in a national referendum.

But Adams suffered the frustration of having his ideas rejected both by liberals, who felt that he was really preaching authoritarianism, and by conservatives, who did not enjoy hearing that they were not sufficiently conservative. The result, at least as far as his ideas were concerned, was that Adams' function became that of a pessimistic prophet. His extremism was too unpopular for men in public life to accept, even though it did provide a point of reference in thought from which men of liberal, conservative, or moderate positions could assess their own ideas.

It was Adams' tragedy that some of his best friends were men who were in partial agreement with him but who could never bring themselves to take him as seriously as he took himself. Theodore Roosevelt made much use of the stimulation that Adams provided; Henry Cabot Lodge corresponded with him frequently; and Justice Oliver Wendell Holmes thought that Adams was a provocative writer and thinker who stripped away some of the illusions of political, social, and legal institutionalism in order that men might see again with freshness and clarity.

Adams tended to think about comprehensive generalizations that frequently did not deal with practical problems facing American society. Convinced of his own intellectual position, he preferred to condemn the partisans of the political parties that were more cautious, perhaps more immediately practical, than he was. In a modern and mechanized mass society Adams stood alone, somewhat like the Romans of the early Republic, preaching simplicity, responsibility, honor, and service. But he never could quite reach mass opinion because he lacked the power of public office and was unable to translate his ideas into an acceptable contemporary idiom.

He was, in fact, Democracy's Roman, proud of his country but disgusted by its ostentation and the corrupt political performance of its citizenry, and painfully fearful for its future. His inabili

Lafcadio Hearn

The growth of America in the late nineteenth century was chiefly a material development. Morally and intellectually progress was, at best, limited, and for many sensitive souls the nation's headlong rush for wealth, and the glorification of matter over mind, were very dismaying. This was especially true of artists of all sorts, and, as a result, many of them sought more congenial surroundings in foreign lands.

The novelist Henry James, who became a British subject, is perhaps the best known of these expatriates, but there were many others, such as the painters James Whistler and Mary Cassatt in England and France and the sculptor William Wetmore Story in Italy. Such persons were more often than not held in contempt by the majority of Americans. Theodore Roosevelt, for example, called Henry James "a miserable little snob," and expressed gratification when he heard that James was being thought of as a British *writer. But such Philistine attacks merely confirmed the expatriates in the wisdom of their actions.*

Europe was the logical haven for these people, but some, such as Lafcadio Hearn, settled in Japan. That country was rapidly accepting Western industrialism, but it sacrificed neither its ancient faith nor the simplicity, beauty, orderliness, and quiet subtlety of its civilization, and these qualities appealed to the expatriate type. Men like the architect John LaFarge were able to love Japan and profit from the study of its art without ever becoming expatriates, but Hearn, William Sturgis Bigelow (who adopted Buddhism and acquired a magnificent collection of Japanese art), and a few others were completely captivated. Hearn is particularly interesting because, while accepting Japanese citizenship and becoming an expert interpreter of its civilization, he never lost his essentially Western point of view. Indeed, he never even bothered to learn the Japanese language!

Professor Alfred Crofts of the University of Denver's History Department has studied Hearn's career both in the United States and in Japan, where he interviewed some of Hearn's students. An expert on the Orient, he is the author of A History of the Far East.

"... bridge between East and West"

ALFRED CROFTS

the lovely island (Leukas to the ancient Greeks and Santa Maura to the Venetians) of his birth; the record was made in Greek script by an Orthodox priest.

Detached from Mediterranean duty, Major Hearn established his family in Dublin; there the son remained while his father accompanied his regiment to the West Indies and subsequently to the Crimea. In 1856 Hearn's marriage was dissolved, and next year he was remarried to an early sweetheart, who accompanied him on duty to India. He died a decade later, without revisiting Europe. The dark-haired, half-Levantine child of his first union had been left in custody of a well-to-do grand-aunt. "Paddy" Hearn (he was sensitive as a child about using his exotic middle name) attended a Catholic school in Yorkshire; during holidays in Ireland his companions included Celtic country people who lived on intimate terms with the native banshees and leprechauns, and seamen returning from many lands.

Young Hearn's formal education ended at the age of sixteen, when his guardian lost most of her fortune. For about twelve months thereafter he lived in London; he may also have spent some time in Paris during the decadence of the Second Empire. In 1869 Lafcadio (he now preferred this name) was packed off by the aunt to New York, and two years afterward he moved to Cincinnati.

Few less promising immigrants entered America during the brawling post-bellum decades than this friendless nineteen-year-old, who was half-blinded and disfigured by a playground accident, and almost morbidly sensitive. As a reaction against the primness of a Victorian public-school, he had adopted pagan beliefs. In a society of brawny pioneers he stood only five feet three inches, and was of slender build. To the end of his life he admitted that he knew nothing of "a boat, a horse, a farm, or an orchard," and as to the ways of finance he said he would rather burn a greenback than try to invest it.

Hearn's assets were a command of schoolboy French and a poetical appreciation of the English language. Yet Cincinnati proved generous to the shy immigrant, though this "Porkopolis" of the Ohio Valley had often been satirized by British literary Brahmins. To Hearn it gave a newspaper copy desk and police beat, on which he produced some classics of crime reporting. But his fullest satisfaction came in translating the French decadent authors—Baudelaire, Flaubert, and Gautier; and his admiration for Edgar Allan Poe was so great that he nicknamed himself "The Raven." His feature articles found no lack of readers in the frontier city; editors paid him well for his copy and winked at his bohemian ways. He was finding a mission in life: to explore "the odd, the strange, and the exotic."

The search led him, almost inevitably, downriver to fabled New Orleans. Regarding himself as a Latin, he revelled in the Creole civilization about him. Hearn was wiser than his age in his complete lack of race snobbery: Negro laundresses with their erect carriage and graceful gait appeared to him as classic divinities. He fraternized gladly with octoroon sailor-folk, loved the "Cajuns," haunted the waterfront cafés filled with Cuban exiles, and wrote lyrically of the relics of Bourbon France—its plantations, salons, and cemeteries—and especially of the mouldering palace where he roomed. Besides turning out newspaper sketches, young Hearn attempted books, mainly translations, followed by a novelette titled *Chita,* whose climax portrayed a carnival-ball inundated by a hurricane tidal-wave. *Harper's Weekly,* impressed by his work, commissioned him to write a travelogue on the French West Indies. He spent two years in Martinique, but when he had fulfilled his contract and the charm of the island began to pall upon him he returned to New York. Here *Harper's* presented another proposition: that he visit and describe Japan.

The project delighted him, but at the end of a slow passage by rail and water Hearn quarreled with his publishers and accepted a position as professor of English in the new Japanese national school system. He was forty, and he had lived for twenty-one years as an American. Now he took up duties on the coast of Izumo on the Japan Sea, a province as charming and exotic as a silk painting. His delight was unbounded. For years his studies had directed him to Oriental writings, and while in New Orleans he had published a collection entitled *Some Chinese Ghosts.*

Hearn's affinity for Japan was in part mystical. He was entranced by Ambassador Percival Lowell's book, *The Soul of the*

Japanese Mahayana Buddhism. The successive transmigrations of the Buddhist soul, achieving higher forms of incarnation in the struggle toward truth, represented the course of evolution. Karma, the fate of each sentient being, exactly compounded of the merit acquired in previous existences—was only Mendelian inheritance. Spencer asserted that "ancestor worship is the root of all religion"; this the Japanese too affirmed. Had not the Greeks, Hearn's own progenitors in the Ionian isles, followed a cult of aesthetic and military virtue almost identical with Shinto, the Way of the Gods?

Glimpses of Unfamiliar Japan, the next book Hearn wrote, is an elfin, beautiful rhapsody about the new land. He had already acquired a Japanese wife, whose impoverished *samurai* relatives lived opulently with him in a miniature compound with three gardens, on his $50 monthly income. A vagabond before, he now settled placidly into the security of the Oriental family system.

Glimpses of Unfamiliar Japan was followed by eight books of literary sketches and folklore—treasuries for the artist and anthropologist. Hearn wrote no more fiction and attempted no original plots; many of his stories were recited to him by his wife. His early ecstasy became tempered with sadness as he was moved from Izumo to other assignments in raw, hybrid-western communities. Everywhere advising his students to "respect the gods of their fathers," he carried on a running feud with the Christian missionaries. An escapist from the Philistines, he watched the harsh, expanding commercialism of the treaty ports—the march of an industrialism more ugly than the one he had left behind. "Evil winds from the West," he sighed, "are blowing over Horai, and the magical atmosphere is shrinking before them."

He continued to write of mystery and beauty, love and death, themes inherited from his French masters and the connecting threads of his work from first to last. He was writing once more for money—dollars from overseas to eke out an inadequate salary.

His final work, *Japan, An Attempt at Interpretation,* was a bid for literary immortality; in this book he endeavored to portray a civilization in twenty-two carefully drafted lectures. As the title implies, he was addressing the Western world; perhaps he was also justifying his new Oriental personality to his older, European self. He carried his study through millennia of history, and drew upon all that he had learned of Japanese life. The people he portrayed seemed no longer naive; he did not deplore the sabotage of their political constitution by feudal clansmen, and he rejoiced in their new Western-style militarism—even when a third of his earnings were withheld to help pay for the new Japanese navy. The time was 1904, when brilliant victories over Russia were launching Admiral Togo along the paths of glory.

Hearn's own fortunes were ebbing. To protect his children he had declared himself a Japanese subject, taking his wife's family name of Koizumi with the prefix Yakumo or "Eight Clouds." But he consorted with the American colony, wore foreign clothes at times, read English books, and warmed himself at an iron stove. Above all he retained his individuality, the pride of the western man—a social offense in the East. He was *chigai,* that is "different"; the Japanese have no other word for "wrong." His university chair was taken from him on suave pretexts. Unemployed at the age of fifty-four, he hoped fruitlessly to return to his own race and rear his eldest son as an American. And so death found him in 1904.

History has been kind to Lafcadio Hearn. To the fifteen works he published have been added shelves of posthumous commentary and biography. His lectures, transcribed from student notes, are literary texts; "Hearniana" are treasured at both Tulane and Tokyo Imperial Universities. Any American commentator on the East can be flattered by being called a "second Lafcadio Hearn." But the first one remains, in the view of the Japanese, incomparable. He was not their Homer; much more significantly he was their Hans Christian Andersen. He built the most enduring bridge between East and West—a rainbow-arch of fancy. Even while Tokyo burned under American fire-bombs, fresh flowers appeared unfailingly on the grave of Lafcadio Hearn.

Ida M. Tarbell, George W. Perkins

of the century 512,000 companies were producing thirteen billion dollars worth of manufactured goods a year. Steel production, a mere 68,750 long tons in 1870, reached 10,188,000 tons in 1900 and 20,000,000 only five years later. Cotton factories in 1900 consumed over 3,800,000 bales; in 1870 they had used less than 800,000 bales. Other industries show comparable growth rates. Indeed, by the 1890s the country was a productive giant, the greatest manufacturing nation in the world.

Increased production meant wealth and power, but the nation paid a price for this expansion. Efficient industrial growth depended upon the massive use of machinery and the development of huge corporations. Monopoly suddenly became a problem, not only for the consumer but also for the worker, whose individual bargaining power declined to nothing when a single employer hired tens of thousands of men, and when expensive machinery destroyed the need for human craftsmanship.

Naturally these changes led to social protests of many sorts. There was much talk of "busting" the "trusts" that came to dominate most of the major industries. The Sherman Anti-Trust Act of 1890 was a response to the widespread urge to break up the new monopolies, and it remains today a bulwark against the exploitation of the public by big business.

However, from the start there were many who believed that monopoly, or at least oligopoly, was unavoidable in modern industry and that the public would be better served if great corporations were regulated rather than destroyed. As early as 1886, in the Interstate Commerce Act, a federal commission was set up to supervise the railroad industry. On the principle thus established, modern commissions control not only railroads and other means of communication and transportation, but other businesses too.

The line between these two means of attacking the monopoly problem has never been clearly drawn. Economists and reformers argue endlessly about their relative merits. In the 1890s Henry Demarest Lloyd urged the destruction of trusts in his Wealth Against Commonwealth, *and in the early twentieth century Louis D. Brandeis assailed them in* The Curse of Bigness. *In our own day economists like Walter Adams and Horace M. Gray have carried on the battle in their* Monopoly in America. *But regulation has always had its defenders, too, from the early socialists (who wanted to carry regulation to the point of government ownership) down to modern experts like John Kenneth Galbraith, with his argument that trust-busting is unnecessary because various "countervailing" forces will prevent big business from becoming too strong.*

Ida M. Tarbell was one of the most influential of the early advocates of trust-busting, whereas George W. Perkins, with his intimate experience as a manager of industrial colossi like U. S. Steel and International Harvester, was a powerful advocate of government control. Miss Tarbell eventually came to change her views, but her History of the Standard Oil Company *remains a classic illustration of the literature of trust-busting.*

Adele deLeeuw is a prolific writer of books and stories for children and adults. Perhaps her most notable volume is The Story of Amelia Earhart. *John A. Garraty is Associate Professor of History at Columbia University. He specializes in biography, having written* The Nature of Biography *and lives of Henry Cabot Lodge, Woodrow Wilson, and Silas Wright. His most recent book is* Right-Hand Man, *a life of George W. Perkins.*

". . . a dent on the national consciousness"

ADELE deLEEUW

THERE was a purpose behind everything Ida Minerva Tarbell did. She told the story on herself that when she was a small child she wanted to know if her baby brother "belonged to the category of things which floated." The only way to find out was to throw him in the brook that ran near their home. So she did. Fortunately, a workman rescued the small brother in time, but Ida Tarbell could never feel too badly about the experiment. She found out that her brother, held up by his spreading dress,

the oil that meant gold to thousands of seekers; Titusville, where they moved when prosperity crowned her father's efforts, where their home was built from the timbers and ironwork of the bankrupt hotel; Pithole, with its gambling and shootings, its derelicts, and sudden fortunes made and lost.

When, forty years later, in 1904, she wrote the monumental *History of the Standard Oil Company* she had a background that made the story vivid, and she had a personal angle—rigidly suppressed—for her father had been one of those forced to the wall by the increased and discriminatory freight rates and the absorption of small companies by the growing monopoly. And she had the determination to interview, to research, to study, and to combine her findings in such a way that even in the heat of controversy that followed its publication, no single fact of hers was ever successfully denied.

The search for knowledge was perhaps the guiding passion of her life. At college, a microscope and the worlds it revealed to her made her decide that biology would be her major work. But there was the need to earn money, and after graduating from Allegheny College she took a teaching position at Poland Union Seminary in Ohio. Then came the opportunity to annotate the books on the four-year-old Chautauqua reading lists. The Chautauqua movement had got under way and was growing apace, and she stayed with this work for seven years.

She went to Paris—a great adventure, and done on a shoestring—to study the French method of writing biography and to work on her *Life of Madame Roland*. The Paris days were filled with new experiences, a broadening of her outlook, and a certain amount of success in her new field, for she did innumerable articles on French people, past and present, which she mailed home to magazines.

She had every intention of returning to Paris after a short visit to her parents, but when she was in New York S. S. McClure persuaded her to do a short life of Napoleon Bonaparte to be published in his new *McClure's Magazine.* Now she was started on her life work. The *Story of Napoleon Bonaparte* was so popular that she was persuaded to do a life of Lincoln. One of her most vivid memories as a child was the stricken silence that had fallen on her family when her father brought home news of Lincoln's assassination. She went at this life with a zest that never left her, for in the course of her career she did *He Knew Lincoln,* and then *Father Abraham,* and next *In Lincoln's Chair, In The Footsteps of Lincoln* and *A Reporter for Lincoln.* A project of hers, never before attempted, was the painstaking tracing of the Lincoln family tree. And, too, she wrote an introduction to the *Uncollected Letters of Abraham Lincoln.* This combination of works established her as one of the most astute and penetrating—and understanding—biographers of the Civil War President.

The standards of big business in Ida Tarbell's day were often in striking contrast to the ideas and ideals that had actuated Lincoln. The wideness of that contrast made her study of the Standard Oil Company a vivid one. She had a genius for portraying not only economic movements and for analyzing existing conditions, but for portraying people, their backgrounds and motives. It was this which gave all her work its immediate interest and its lasting quality. She had a strong moral sense herself, and when she spoke of moral issues it was in the voice of conviction. "As for the ethical side," she said, "there is no cure but in an increasing sense that a thing won by breaking the rules of the game is not worth the winning."

Three years after the publication of the *History,* the Supreme Court of the United States dissolved the trust of the Standard Oil Company, marking the end of the monopolistic era, and due in no small part to Ida Tarbell's gigantic work. It was of deep satisfaction to her that no statement she had made was ever successfully denied or disproved.

McClure's Magazine found her an able and stimulating contributing editor. But later, when she and John Phillips, the managing editor, could no longer see eye to eye with "S.S.," they resigned, gathered a few others to them, and used most of their capital to buy *The American Magazine,* which they ran according to their own ideas. Those were seven happy years, she always said, searching out new writers, encouraging them, and bringing political and economic and national problems to the attention of an increasingly aware public. Funds gave out, however, and the magazine had to be abandoned. But not before her work and

them. She drew them out, and pictured them against their backgrounds and the issues with which they were involved. Her interviewing took her across the country many times, and her articles and books led to a demand for her as lecturer, too. Although she at first disliked the idea of platform speaking, she set herself to master it—learning how to present her topics, studying breath control and voice placement in order to make herself clearer and more compelling. This was typical of Ida Tarbell's approach to anything she undertook.

Strikes, labor questions, coal mining, unions, economic balances: all these became her province, and she made them clear to others. She talked to miners and farmers, to college presidents and union leaders, to clubwomen and salesgirls, to chairmen of the board and lowly factory sweepers. When she wrote or spoke, she knew her material in all its facets and she made it fascinating.

Colleges honored her, clubs fought for her presence and her leadership. She was on countless committees, but she never took on anything she could not study and finish, or that she did not believe in. She was never just a "name-lender." She refused to go abroad on Henry Ford's Peace Ship because she did not believe that it could accomplish its mission. Instead she went abroad to do work for the Red Cross.

In a day when women were fighting for their political rights, she exhibited a "man's mind" while she gloried in being a woman. Her country home in Connecticut was her cherished retreat—for which she had little time but to which she always looked forward. She pointed with pride to her sows, her vegetable garden, her fruit trees, and the glasses of jelly in her cellar. Friends from all over the world came and were renewed in outlook and spirit. Magazines demanded articles, publishers wanted books—every new day brought new requests. Only once did she attempt fiction, and that was not a success. "I am not a fictioneer at heart," she said frankly. "I am an analyst and a researcher." But she was more than that, she was an interpreter and bringer of light.

Later in life she undertook a story of Judge Elbert Gary and the steel industry. Here was a business as wide-spread and important as the oil business, and she was curious to know more about the man who headed it. Nevertheless she approached her task with misgivings and reservations. "If I find practices which seem to me against public policy as I understand it I shall have to say so," she told him. "I appreciate your efforts to make working conditions for labor as good as you know how to make them, but it does not follow that I can stand for your financial policies. It is not your humanitarianism but your ethics I suspect."

Judge Gary said: "If you find anything wrong in our doings I want to know it. So do your worst."

He was as good as his word. He had made a steady and successful fight to strip the businesses which he was putting together of certain illegal practices, as well as to set up an entirely new code of fair practice called, in Wall Street, the Gary Code, and it was this Code and his efforts to put it into practice that reconciled her to her task. During the year she worked with him she found him frank and helpful, and he himself was amazed at how a man's mind unravels when he is urged to remember things chronologically by skillful questioning.

Out of her probings and investigations Ida Tarbell became convinced that the Gary Code was genuine, not mere window dressing, and her respect for the man grew as her book progressed. She felt that he was a true industrial statesman and said so . . . and as a result her favorite newspaper, under the heading of "The Taming of Ida Tarbell," declared that she had become a eulogist of the kind of man to whom she had sworn eternal enmity.

Her interest in the industrial life of the country led to a second biography—that of Owen D. Young, then president of General Electric Company. She believed that he was a new type of industrial leader—his work with the President's Second Industrial Conference had shown that—a man who was urging a broad, fair program, who was strong and firm, who kept his head under all circumstances, and who had warm human sympathies. He was a man, she felt, to handle the difficult tangle in labor relations that was more and more disturbing industry.

Her book came out in 1932 and had the misfortune to collide with a Presidential boom for Mr. Young, which was the last thing

her physical strength waned, but she still kept to her hours of work and study. At eighty-two she turned out one of her most delightful and revealing books, *All in the Day's Work*, a candid but reserved autobiography that gives the clue to her whole life. That title was typical of her attitude: what came her way to be done was "all in the day's work," and she gloried in it. She once asked Madame Curie what a woman's contribution to a better world should be. Madame replied that it began at home, then spread to her family, her immediate friends, and then to the community in which she lived. But the important thing was the beginning, and that beginning was in the home, the center of things.

"Work backed by such a faith makes life endurable," Ida Tarbell said. "I doubt if I could have come into my eighties with anything like the confidence I feel in the ultimate victory of freedom, the ultimate victory of man's self-respect, if I had not groped my way through work into some such faith."

Until she died she was still writing, still studying, still looking forward to new projects, still curious. It was an armchair curiosity now, she said. She thought that from an armchair she might find better answers than any she had yet found to those questions which set her at her day's work, the still unanswered question of the most fruitful life for women in civilization, the true nature of revolutions, even the mystery of God. It was the last of the three which disturbed her least—the greatest of mysteries, she said, it had become for her the greatest of realities.

"... a truly public-spirited citizen"

JOHN A. GARRATY

ONE pleasant day in the year 1894, George W. Perkins was sitting on the porch of his home in Riverdale, New York, gazing across the Hudson River at the magnificent facade of the Palisades. It was a noble view, one of the finest in the eastern part of the country, and Perkins was justifiably proud of it. Suddenly a puff of dirty brown smoke erupted from the face of the cliffs, and, moments later, a muffled rumble shook the house.

Upstairs Perkins' two-year-old daughter woke from her afternoon nap with a start and began to cry. Quarrymen were blasting trap rock for road-building material, disturbing the peace and quiet of Riverdale and incidentally destroying a famous landmark. Perkins was annoyed—he decided to do something about the blasting. "Doing something" took many years, but eventually the result was the great Palisades Interstate Park, of which Perkins was the first president. When Mr. Perkins set his mind to a project, large results were usually forthcoming.

In 1894 Perkins was thirty-two years old, but had already achieved a fabulous success in the business world. At fifteen he had quit school to work as an office boy in his father's Chicago life insurance agency, and at twenty-five was earning fifteen thousand dollars a year selling insurance. Two years later he was superintending all the agents of the great New York Life Insurance Company west of the Mississippi. In 1892, when he was thirty, the company brought him to New York as vice president in charge of its entire agency system. At the time he first took an interest in the preservation of the Palisades, Perkins was revolutionizing the whole technique of selling insurance—replacing the old system of practically independent general agents with a closely knit network of branch offices all over the world. This reduced costs and increased the volume of the company's business phenomenally.

In 1900 Governor Theodore Roosevelt appointed Perkins to head the first Palisades Park Commission. This was a turning point in his life, for besides marking the start of a long association with Roosevelt, it resulted in his leaving the insurance business for the larger world of industrial organization. The

Commission needed $125,000 to buy land controlled by the stone blasters, and Perkins called on banker J. P. Morgan in search of help. He found the titan of the financial world smoking a big black cigar in his unpretentious office, and when he began to

insurance and loved his work; but the opportunity and the large financial rewards that Morgan offered could not be refused. Soon he was deeply involved in an entirely new kind of work. Morgan was the great organizer and consolidator of American industry. As his partner, Perkins became chairman of the finance committee of the new Morgan-created United States Steel Corporation, organizer of the International Harvester Company, and a director of a dozen other large businesses. Although he represented the growing control of American industry by the bankers, Perkins was interested neither in the financial details nor the technological aspects of big business. In the insurance world he had dealt chiefly with people—with agents and policyholders—and human relations continued to dominate his attention. From the managers of large corporations he soon learned that one of their greatest problems was poor morale among their employees—the average wage earner had little loyalty for the tremendous "soulless corporation" that employed him. Great size made for impersonality and diffusion of responsibility.

Perkins had already met this problem in a less acute form when managing the agents of the New York Life Insurance Company. There he had set up a pension system, bonus plans, and other rewards to make the agents aware of the stake they had in the company's success. Now he worked out a profit-sharing scheme for the Steel and Harvester Corporations, and a plan whereby ordinary workers could buy stock in their companies on time and at prices below the market rates, with special bonuses for those who remained at their jobs for stated periods of years. His objective was to make the workers feel that they were personally involved in the success or failure of their businesses, not merely drawing their weekly wages. Money expended by the companies in this direction, he felt sure, would be returned with interest in the form of more efficient production and fewer strikes.

Like Morgan, Perkins believed that a large business was more efficient than a small one, and that competition was wasteful and frequently cruel. He considered the anti-trust laws both foolish and dangerous to the nation's economic health. The power of large corporations should be curbed, he thought, not by destroying the corporations but by government regulation. Only thus could the benefits of large scale production be obtained at the same time that the wage earner and the consumer were protected against exploitation. His advocacy of government regulation led several of his business associates to call him a socialist, while at the same time many public spirited citizens were suspicious of the motives of a man as closely connected with big business as Perkins was. In 1911, therefore, though not yet fifty, Perkins decided to retire from the House of Morgan to devote all his time to publicizing his ideas. He had, he reasoned, more money than he would ever need; instead of piling up additional millions he would devote his energies to what seemed to him the most critical problem of the modern world—the relation between business and government.

Soon he was traveling widely, explaining his theories to groups of businessmen, workers, and college students. Inevitably he became involved in politics. When his friend Roosevelt broke with the Republicans in 1912 and formed the Progressive Party, Perkins backed him heavily with his time and money, for Roosevelt's New Nationalism, with its emphasis on government regulation of business had been greatly influenced by Perkins' criticisms of the anti-trust laws. Perkins became chairman of the new party's executive committee, a post he held until the party collapsed after the 1916 election. Then, like Roosevelt, he returned to the Republican fold, but until his death in 1920 he continued to fight to "liberalize" that organization.

As a politician Perkins was less successful than as a businessman. He tended to be too headstrong, too thoughtless of the needs and opinions of his associates, too resistant to compromise. Qualities that made him an imaginative and highly creative business leader were not easily adapted to the give and take of political life. He did not hesitate to spend his own money lavishly, particularly on newspaper advertising. Once he even paid out twenty-five thousand dollars to publicize the arguments of his opponents—so convinced was he that his own position was correct. While his political associates were eager to make use of his money, they resented the tremendous publicity he obtained, and accused him of using his millions for self-glorification.

It is not, however, because of the [illegible] his particular theories that the life of George W. Perkins is worth remembering today. His memory is worth preserving, rather, as a symbol of some of the finest aspects of the American character, for Perkins was a truly public-spirited citizen. Rising from obscure origins to a position of great wealth and power, he never forgot that he owed his success to the freedom and opportunity provided by the American system of government and American social and economic institutions. He used his wealth and power not to advance himself, but to promote the welfare of his fellow men.

Louis Henry Sullivan

The effects of the new industrialism on late nineteenth-century America were truly pervasive; every aspect of man's life and thinking was influenced by the new age of the machine. Even the arts were affected, for by accomplishing tasks formerly performed by human hands, the machines made necessary a new concept of beauty and harmony in the design of everything from kitchen utensils to great public buildings.

The essence of the appeal of human craftsmanship is its individuality. No two hand-made objects are exactly alike. That is why an old, roughly carved cabinet may be beautiful even if its design is neither original nor sublime. The essence of the craft of the machine lies in its uniformity. Variations (called "seconds" and sold at sharp discounts) are distortions and are therefore ugly.

At first, designers of machine-made products failed to understand their new tools and tried with them to copy work previously done by hand. The results, seen for instance in cast-iron imitations of intricately carved woodwork on many a Victorian mantlepiece, were uniformly monstrous. Only when the simplifying function of machinery was understood and designers began to express themselves in clean lines and smooth, unadorned surfaces, could art forms natural to machine production emerge.

The architect Louis Henry Sullivan was one of the great pioneers of this new conception of art. Seizing upon the potentialities of steel construction, he erected buildings that were expressions of that construction, not mere Gothic and Romanesque facades plastered against an iron skeleton. Sullivan's story is told here by Oliver W. Larkin. Professor of Art at Smith College, Larkin is the author of the Pulitzer Prize-winning book, Art and Life in America.

". . . a new way of thinking about architecture"

the stamp of their names upon this age, Sullivan had no great family behind him, no social status to support him, and no inherited wealth on which to build an education and a career. If he loved democracy, it was because he saw how America had made possible a new life for his father and mother, who were both immigrants; an Irishman named Patrick who set up a dancing school in Boston and a young and sensitive Swiss girl with a love of music and a talent for the piano.

Out of this simple background came one of the most brilliant architects in our history, whose preparation for a complex and difficult profession was scrappy, to say the least. When he was sixteen he had one year at the Massachusetts Institute of Technology, and he had a brief discipline as a draughtsman in the office of a Philadelphia architect. At eighteen he enrolled as a student of the *Ecole des Beaux-Arts* in Paris, but he endured the backward-looking routine of that institution for less than two years.

When he came home in 1876, his idea of his chosen profession owed more to his own independent thinking than to any instruction by his elders. Sullivan gave his admiration to those bold innovators who had moulded the material of their art into new forms: to Michelangelo, to Wagner, and to Walt Whitman; and he himself was one of those rebellious spirits who were destined to change the shape of things. In Boston and Paris architectural history had been presented to him as a succession of styles—the Greek, the Roman, the Gothic, the Renaissance, and so on, as though each style were complete in itself. Louis rejected these neat classifications. The history of his art seemed to him a continuous out-pouring, never to end, from the infinite fertility of man's imagination, evoked by his changing needs. Architecture, he once wrote, is the projected life of a people.

As he looked around him in the 1870s he could not see the life of the American people projected in its buildings. Here was a nation dedicated to a new concept of society, of politics, of culture; a democratic ideal whose goal was the free and rich development of the individual. Yet our architects were content to imitate and adapt architectural themes that symbolized the ancient and the feudal way of life against which our whole country was a protest.

The spirit led Sullivan to Chicago a few years after a great fire had destroyed much of the city. He joined a group of architects who dared to make bold experiments, and whose ingenuity and courage were writing a new chapter in the story of American building. Here was a growing metropolis which demanded bigger, taller, and more intelligently planned structures; here were engineering problems to be tackled and solved; here were new materials to challenge the designer. Sullivan the poet, the dreamer, the innovator, was lucky enough to find a partner whose abilities supplemented his own. Dankmar Adler, who had been an army engineer, liked nothing better than to face a tough structural problem; at the same time he fully appreciated the artistic genius of Sullivan.

Thus began an association of fifteen years. Between 1880 and 1895 the firm of Adler and Sullivan produced more than a hundred buildings—private dwellings, churches, tombs, stores, theaters, and office structures—each unlike anything that had been seen before. When Sullivan sat down at his drawing board, he banished from his mind all recollected ancient forms. He knew every detail of the material needs of the structure to be conceived, and started from those needs to develop its interior spaces, then its main outer forms. He took as his guiding principle what he had learned from nature, the swooping eagle or the toiling work-horse, the branching oak tree or the drifting cloud. In all these he found the expression of one pervading law—that form ever follows function.

"Form follows function." That phrase has become famous. But it is important to remember that when Sullivan used the word function, he gave it more than a mechanical meaning. He meant that when buildings truly expressed democratic aspirations, religious beliefs, human hopes, and human sorrows, they achieved real beauty.

Thus inspired, Adler and Sullivan created the Chicago Auditorium. This vast masonry building which was dedicated in 1889 contained, among many other things, a theater with four arches [illegible]

without the need for thick masonry walls, which decreased inner space and required small windows. No one man can take credit for having invented the skyscraper. Leroy Buffington grasped its principle—a self-sufficient steel skeleton whose walls would only be a thin sheath. William Jenney actually built the first of them, and other Chicago men achieved similar results at almost the same time. The most advanced steel construction was used in the ten stories of the Wainwright Building. But Sullivan went beyond engineering. He once wrote concerning the tall building that its one characteristic must be loftiness. It must be a proud and soaring thing, he said, rising in sheer exultation, a unit without a dissenting line. The Wainwright embodies that vision. Its corner piers spring uninterrupted from sidewalk to cornice, while narrower piers between windows repeat this vertical movement. The only ornaments are on terra cotta panels above and below the windows, and on a frieze that runs below the simple cornice.

The versatility of Sullivan appears in the small tomb he designed a year later for the Wainwright family, a plain block of grey limestone with a low dome and bands of delicate carving along its edges. It speaks not only of the quiet dignity of death, but also of the grace and beauty of the woman whose life it symbolizes.

These extraordinary buildings, the Auditorium, the Wainwright, the tomb in Saint Louis, and others like them, provoked surprise and displeasure among the traditionalists. But their meaning for the future was not lost upon the younger men. One of the most gifted of these was to be found, during those years, in Sullivan's own office, working as an assistant to the firm. His name was Frank Lloyd Wright, and he was destined to carry far and wide the ideas he owed to long talks with the man of whom he always spoke as his beloved master. Wright left the firm and had launched his own career, soon to overshadow that of Sullivan, when the partnership of Adler and Sullivan was dissolved in 1895. The man who had given America a new idea of what architecture can be in a democracy was now to enter a period of neglect and loneliness. During the nearly thirty years that remained to Sullivan, he designed only twenty buildings, and much of his time was given to talks and articles on his philosophy.

As the years went on, Sullivan was given few opportunities to demonstrate what he called his Idea. He designed the florid store in Chicago for Carson-Pirie-Scott, and small banks in Grinnell, Iowa, in Sidney, Ohio, in Columbus, Wisconsin. He was not at home in the America of the early twentieth century. In the early 1900s he wrote his *Kindergarten Chats,* to reaffirm his principles and to blast with a sarcastic scorn the evasive practices of his more famous and successful colleagues. Tired, ill and impoverished, he summed up the visions and frustrations of a lifetime in a book he called *The Autobiography of an Idea;* he had the first copy of it at his bedside in a shabby Chicago hotel when he died on the thirteenth of April in 1924.

On the day before the end, Frank Lloyd Wright sat with his beloved master. More in anger than in sorrow, he wrote a tribute to a prophet whom America had almost forgotten. Wright had already proved himself an even greater genius, and in the years since 1924 our modern buildings were to take on forms far different from those of Sullivan. He did not bequeath a style to the future. His enduring gift to the country he loved was a new way of thinking about architecture, a way of thinking that has made it possible for our skyscrapers, our churches, and our dwellings to express, honestly and beautifully, the life of our people.

..., increasing complexity its chief characteristic, and nowhere more so than in the United States. Although this condition has led some to call our era the Age of Anxiety, it has certainly made Americans forward-looking in their general view of life. Indeed, Richard Hofstadter has aptly called the period "The Age of Reform." Acceptance of new ways and adjustment to altering conditions are well-established American habits.

However, reformers usually aim at a specific goal and have to work long and hard to achieve it. When they have won their battles it is perfectly natural for them to want to sit back and enjoy the new dispensation in peace. Yesterday's reformer is often today's conservative—and sometimes, alas, he is tomorrow's reactionary. Only a person committed generally to progress, rather than to a particular step forward, can continue to look ahead when that step has been successfully taken.

Charles Evans Hughes was never an extremist, but he was, as Dexter Perkins makes clear, a consistent supporter of an enlightened and intelligent liberalism. As a young lawyer he prosecuted grafters and corrupt businessmen; as a politician he stood for honest administration and moderate reforms; as a diplomat he worked for international cooperation in an age of isolation. Far too much has been made of his association with the conservative wing of the Republican party in 1916, when he was narrowly defeated for the Presidency by Woodrow Wilson.

Frank Murphy was, by the standards of the present day, much more liberal than Hughes. Especially where civil rights were concerned he was always in favor of freedom and the right of minorities to dissent. But he was most characteristically a true reformer in the plasticity of his mind. As was true with Hughes, neither the passage of time nor the achievement of his ambitions could alter his basic approach. He was a progressive in the literal sense of the word.

Few would question Murphy's right to be called a reformer, but some will say that men like Hughes are merely sensible conservatives who accept slight change not out of preference but to keep the rest of the social fabric intact. Perhaps this is true, but in our dynamic times only such men are consistently able to be at once comfortable, complacent, and creative. Impatient idealists may find them frustrating companions, but they make very valuable citizens when, as Hughes did, they devote their lives to public service.

Dexter Perkins, John L. Senior Professor Emeritus at Cornell University and former President of the American Historical Association, has written many works covering a wide range of American history. Among his best known are Hands Off: A History of the Monroe Doctrine, America and Two Wars, *and a life of Hughes. Madison Kuhn is Professor of History at Michigan State University and author of* Michigan State: the First Hundred Years.

". . . a statesman of the first order"

DEXTER PERKINS

Charles Evans Hughes' career divides itself into two parts. He was Governor of New York from 1907 to 1910 and Secretary of State from 1921 to 1925. This is the purely political part of his public service. He was also a judge in the highest court in the land, an Associate Justice of the Supreme Court from 1910 to 1916 and Chief Justice from 1930 to 1941. And in every office that he held he attained great distinction.

Before we examine his career we should say something about one of the big aspects of American politics, the division between the conservatives and the liberals. There are some men who are deeply conscious of the evils of the social and economic order and wish to see them remedied, and in fact devote themselves primarily to the task of reform. There are others who are aware of the great permanent values in the American scheme of things and wish to see them preserved. Both points of view have some validity. Of course the liberal view can become radicalism, if it is exaggerated. And the conservative view can become reaction, if *it* is exaggerated. The problem is to strike a balance between them.

Hughes was a happy mixture of the liberal and the conserva-tive. He was wise enough to know that you cannot preserve a social order unless you eradicate its

which one of the problems was to con-trol too powerful business interests which were abusing their strength. Theodore Roosevelt saw this and so did Hughes. At Albany he pressed for laws regulating the public utilities of the state, and his work in this regard was pioneering. He took a friendly attitude towards organized labor. He established new standards of administration. And he did it without truckling to the politicians, chiefly by his direct appeal to the people. He set an example that others were to follow.

As Secretary of State, Hughes accomplished a great deal. There are many good judges of foreign policy who would rank him as the greatest Secretary of State of the twentieth century. He came into office at a very difficult time, when the battle over the League of Nations had raised partisan temper to a high pitch and when there were many questions to be solved. Hughes never believed in the idea of collective security, and he viewed the League with no great enthusiasm—the American people, in 1921, did not be-lieve in collective security either. Hughes had to work with the tools he had, and he did a good job. He promoted and carried to successful completion by his personal force the 1921-22 Wash-ington Conference on Disarmament. The great nations of East and West agreed to limit naval armament so far as capital ships and aircraft carriers were concerned. When the conference met there was severe tension between the United States and Japan. When it closed the tension had been lessened, and it remained lessened for almost a decade. It is true that the agreements made at Washington broke down in the thirties, but at the time they seemed a substantial achievement, and Hughes's statesmanship in bringing them about was widely acclaimed. In particular, he made enormously successful use of public diplomacy and of the appeal to popular sentiment.

Hughes also helped to straighten out the reparations tangle, which arose out of the excessive demands for reparations from Germany at the end of the First World War. He brought about an agreement that gave the world a chance to recover economically. Here, too, there were later difficulties that overturned his work, but in his time he performed great services.

Finally, as Secretary of State, Hughes initiated a policy of friendship with Latin America that flowered into the good-neighbor policies of the Roosevelt administration.

As a judge Hughes was among the very greatest in our history. The Supreme Court is one of the most important agencies of our government. By its power to declare state and federal statutes unconstitutional it can powerfully affect the course of events, and it can put a brake not only on unwise measures but also on wise and necessary ones. The manner in which it uses its power is of great concern to every American. Hughes was never one of those judges who believed that the *status quo* was perfect. He saw, for example, the necessity for increasing the power of the federal government. In his service as Associate Justice from 1910 to 1916 he rendered important decisions which permitted more thoroughgoing federal regulation of the railroads. He took a sympathetic view of legislation dealing with the position of labor, and with federal and state attempts to improve that position. On the other hand he was aware of the possibility of the undue extension of federal authority. When he was Chief Justice, for instance, he spoke for a unanimous Court in striking down the National Industrial Recovery Act, which would have given the federal administration sweeping powers of control over the business life of the country. He began to fear that the power of administrative tribunals might become excessive, and on this kind of question he sometimes exhibited his conservative side and his fear that the power of regulation, which he had sponsored, might be abused and used without due regard for the rights of those concerned.

On certain questions Hughes was particularly positive. He had great sympathy for the rights of the Negro, as his decisions show, and he stood out strongly for the preservation of civil rights, free speech, freedom of assembly, and the like. He believed that the violation of these rights undermined the very basis of the American order.

As Chief Justice, Hughes had to meet the attack on the Court made by President Roosevelt in 1937. The President, dissatisfied with the opinions of the tribunal, proposed to add to the number of the judges and swamp the judicial majority that on occasion declared New Deal legislation unconstitutional. Hughes was naturally opposed to this

agree that this was a good thing, *provided* the Court took a sympathetic view of the necessity for widening national power. During and after the Supreme Court fight, some of the conservative judges resigned, and President Roosevelt appointed others who took a more liberal view. Hughes presided over the new Court with dignity, won the deep admiration of his new colleagues, and associated himself with many of their decisions.

In his balance, his wise restraint, and his understanding of the process of change, Hughes showed himself a statesman of the first order. He ranks, as we have said, amongst the very greatest Americans of his generation.

". . . the conscience of the Supreme Court"

MADISON KUHN

As Frank Murphy assumed the governorship of Michigan in January 1937, he was confronted by a threat of civil war in the sit-down strike at General Motors in Flint. For several days hundreds of workers had been barricaded inside two Fisher Body plants, eating meals carried from an emergency kitchen across the street, sleeping in relays on piles of upholstery, fashioning crude weapons, patrolling doorways, and singing "Solidarity Forever." Because the plants contained dies for the new all-steel "turret-tops," a handful of strikers were beginning to paralyze the national network of General Motors plants.

The sit-downers there and in other company plants insisted that under the Wagner Act management must bargain exclusively with their new CIO United Automobile Workers; they refused to leave until General Motors agreed to obey the law. Management, believing the Wagner Act unconstitutional, demanded that the plants be vacated.

In mid-January Flint police smashed windows at Fisher and threw tear-gas grenades, only to be driven away with firehose and car-door hinges in what the UAW called the "Battle of the Running Bulls." Governor Murphy assembled Michigan National Guardsmen in Flint to preserve order. Would they merely patrol the streets, leaving the strikers secure in their illegal seizure of private property, or would they eject the men with machine-gun and bayonet? Would the Governor decide in favor of the right of stockholders to their plants, or in favor of the worker's claim of a right to his job?

Discerning men began to trace Frank Murphy's career, seeking clues to his future action. Much of what they discovered was pertinent to the sit-down crisis.

Born in Harbor Beach, Michigan, forty-seven years before, he had been raised in the Roman Catholic Church and had decided against the priesthood because he believed that he could serve his Church better as a lawyer. His promise at confirmation to abstain from liquor and tobacco until he came of age had been extended to his whole life. When he reached the United States Supreme Court in the 1940s the red-haired justice would be called the saint with a red halo.

His father was a lawyer and stalwart Democrat who in his youth had been jailed in Canada in a Fenian (Irish) uprising against the Crown. There were stories of another ancestor hanged in Ireland by the English for similar activity. At the close of World War I, Frank Murphy, Captain, was selected for graduate law study in Europe. He chose Trinity in Dublin, where he was usually to be found in company with leaders of the Irish independence movement, an activity that led to his being shadowed by the English secret service. Out of these memories and experiences came some part of his belief, frequently expressed, that a people loses faith in any government that uses its police power to suppress human freedom.

Returning to the law in Detroit, he was shortly elected to the highest criminal court bench. There he gained attention in the murder trial of men who had resisted efforts to drive a Negro physician from a white neighborhood. The principle that a man's house is his castle, Judge Murphy remarked, applied to Negroes, too. Clarence Darrow, who defended the accused successfully, wrote in his autobiography that the young judge had "proved to be the kindliest and [illegible]

[illegible] that in any other major city. Those were years when the nation chose to buy food and clothing rather than Detroit's automobiles. And because private charity proved completely insufficient, Murphy expanded public relief, until by 1932 the city was caring for 30,000 families.

By the spring of 1932, with Detroit's credit exhausted, Murphy invited fellow mayors from leading cities to a conference which he persuaded to petition Congress for a five-billion-dollar relief program. This at a time when both Herbert Hoover and Franklin Roosevelt still hoped that cities and states could carry the load unaided.

In the midst of unemployment, the hungry and homeless listened to Communist agitators on street corners and park benches. Detroit, because of the mayor's relief work, was less susceptible than it might have been; but there were speakers and they found audiences. People who saw in such gatherings the beginnings of revolution urged Roman Catholic Frank Murphy to disperse them, with police clubs and tear gas if necessary. But the Mayor refused; instead he despatched police to maintain order tactfully, with instructions to harass neither the agitator nor the listener. Thus he deprived Communists of their traditional arguments: the twin charges of starvation and police brutality.

In the spring of 1933 President Roosevelt sent Frank Murphy to the Philippines as Governor-General to guide them along the road to freedom. There Murphy made local government honest, and pressed through a public health program, the eight-hour day, votes for women, and a reformed parole system. Reminding Filipinos that he was descended from Irish rebels who had fought for independence, he presided at the transition to Commonwealth status and his own evolution to High Commissioner, symbolized in his move from the regal Malacañang palace to a Manila hotel.

Then in 1936 President Roosevelt was faced with the threat of the Lemke party, whose best voice was that of Michigan's Radio Priest, Father Charles E. Coughlin. Roosevelt summoned Murphy home to run for governor, and thus draw Coughlin followers into the Roosevelt camp.

In January 1937 he was governor of Michigan, surrounded by forbodings of civil war. While guardsmen patrolled the streets of Flint, leaving strikers secure within the plants, Murphy assembled union and company representatives in separate rooms in Detroit, moving between them as messenger and catalyst. The red-haired governor warned GM's William S. Knudsen that further delay might lead to riot and bloodshed, which could create martyrs to haunt future negotiations. One of the Fisher brothers told Murphy: "I would rather lose our plants than lose the life of a single American workingman." And the governor, whose bristling eyebrows matched those of John L. Lewis, warned the CIO president that the courts and public opinion would soon force intervention by the guardsmen. But, he told Lewis, first he would go into the plants himself to urge strikers to leave voluntarily. Lewis knew that the men would follow Murphy. Mutual capitulation followed quickly, and a haggard governor emerged to announce that peace would come to Flint.

The only casualty was Frank Murphy. *Business Week* observed that he had been "holding the steaming red-hot potato of labor difficulties in his hands, trying to cool it off." It predicted great national prestige if he settled the strikes "without bloodshed or permanent damage." Two years later *Time* magazine concluded that "peaceful settlement of the great sit-down of 1937 remains his monument as Governor." But in November 1938, despite a fine record in building mental hospitals, in bringing the merit system to civil service, and in suppressing gambling, Murphy went down to defeat—devastating defeat.

His career seemed near its close, his ladder out of rungs.

True, President Roosevelt appointed him as Attorney-General, but the nation was not enthusiastic, recognizing it as a lame-duck appointment through which Murphy would pass quietly to private life.

But the popular estimate changed within a few months. His press conferences were drawing reporters in numbers second only to the President's. Murphy reorganized the Department of

Justice, established a Civil Rights Section, and strengthened J. Edgar Hoover's FBI. He also began to read the personal files on federal judges. A half

was appointed to the United States Supreme Court where, his red hair greying and his voice soft, he spoke for the underprivileged, the inarticulate, and the oppressed. Again and again he defended human liberties in stinging dissent or in vigorous concurrence, and sometimes as spokesman for the majority. Newsmen remarked that the Court was beginning to dispense "justice tempered with Murphy."

He became the most predictable Justice on the Court, rushing to protect not his friends but the friendless. When Jehovah's Witnesses were arrested for distributing literature that attacked his beloved Catholic Church, it was Murphy who spoke most vigorously in their behalf. The sidewalk, he explained, "no less than the cathedral or the evangelist's tent, is a proper place, under the Constitution, for the orderly worship of God." American unity and strength, he warned, would come "not by enforced orthodoxy of views, but by diversity of opinion."

Opposed to Communism, he insisted that Communists must not be deprived of constitutional rights merely because of the beliefs of an organization that they had once joined. A friend of unions, he upbraided them when they excluded Negroes. Picketing by strikers he declared to be a form of persuasion and therefore a right of free speech; but violence on the picket line should be punished. An ardent New Dealer, he decided in favor of newspaper and radio when Washington bureaucrats deprived them of the freedom of the press.

In World War II ex-Major Murphy took leave to qualify in armored warfare, but back on the bench he objected to Army policies when personal rights were at stake. The exile of Japanese from the West Coast was, he argued, based not on acts of espionage or sabotage—of which there had been none—but on an "erroneous assumption of racial guilt." When Hawaiians were tried in military rather than civil courts, he wrote that "the swift trial and punishment which the military desires is precisely what the Bill of Rights outlaws." And he condemned the summary trials of Japanese generals at the close of the war: "Either we conduct such a trial as this in the noble spirit and atmosphere of our Constitution or we abandon all pretense to justice, let the ages slip away and descend to the level of revengeful blood purges."

Frank Murphy became the conscience of the Supreme Court, reaffirming in stirring rhetoric the principles upon which America was founded and for which it had fought.

In mid-career on the Court he wrote: "The law knows no finer hour than when it cuts through formal concepts and transitory emotions to protect unpopular citizens against discrimination and persecution." When he died in 1949, his decade as a Justice had been his finest hour and, in terms of human rights, Frank Murphy had made it the Court's finest hour too.

... Slosson goes on to describe the fantastic growth of the auto industry (28,000,000 cars were in use by 1928). He tells of its tremendous impact on other industries like steel, glass, and rubber, whose products it so voraciously consumed, and explains its widespread social implications, such as the enrichment of rural life, the development of tourism, and—on the dark side—the stimulation of certain types of crime, for example, bank robbery. "The motor car," Slosson even points out, "replaced the parlor and the porch as the courting ground of the new generation."

The men who were primarily responsible for these revolutionary changes were generally unaware of the larger implications of their work. They were interested in solving the challenging problems of producing an intricate mechanism cheaply and in great numbers, and in making money. Henry Ford was the most notable (and in this respect the most typical) of the early automobile makers—a man who greatly altered the world in which he lived but who thought far more highly of the past he unwittingly destroyed than of the future he was helping to create.

Walter P. Chrysler was not as much an emotional reactionary as Ford, although he was little concerned with all the implications of the automobile for American life. But, as Thomas C. Cochran explains in the following essay, Chrysler was almost as important as Ford in the development of the industry, and after about 1920 he was much more continuously productive of new ideas and more efficient methods than Ford.

Thomas C. Cochran, Professor of History at the University of Pennsylvania, is an expert on economic history. He has written many books including The Age of Enterprise *and* Railroad Leaders.

". . . personality and good practical judgment"

THOMAS C. COCHRAN

THE making of automobiles has been the great twentieth-century American industrial development, and two of the three major companies in the field were personally created by Walter Chrysler and Henry Ford. These two men had much in common, both coming to the industry from an early life spent in working with machinery. But there were significant differences: Ford, born in 1863, entered the industry on a small scale at a relatively early date; Chrysler, not born until 1875, won a place for a brilliant new car when the industry was mature and there scarcely seemed room for more major competitors. Ford had the advantage of a father prosperous enough from farming to provide him with a good home machine shop. Chrysler had a father in the ranks of labor, and made his own way from the lowest level in the railway shops.

In his autobiography Chrysler recalled his youth in Ellis, Kansas, a railroad and cow town of the frontier. Unlike most boys, he never wanted to be a cowboy, but, he wrote: "I certainly aimed in those days to grow up tough." Toughness in Ellis did not mean delinquency, it meant being able to take whatever came along. He was fascinated by machinery. "I loved to see the engines" at the railroad shops "with their mysteries exposed. I envied the mechanics who understood their inner workings. I liked to handle tools."

His father, a locomotive engineer who did not want Walter to be a mechanic, would have sacrificed to send him to college, but Walter wanted to get into the shops. Here he showed the aggressive confidence backed up by extraordinary ability that was eventually to make him millions. He went ahead on his own, won a job as an apprentice in the Union Pacific shops, and persuaded his father to give in.

Unlike Henry Ford who, treasuring the world of his childhood, spent most of his life within a short distance of the family homestead, Chrysler was restless. He was big, friendly, and anxious to find out what challenges new places and new situations would bring, so after making a local reputation as a fine mechanic he began to move around. For four years he drifted through western railroad

without complaint the difficulties involved in raising children on a modest salary in frontier towns. By 1908, when he was thirty-three, Chrysler had reached the top of the ladder in the mechanical side of railroading. He was Superintendent of Motive Power on the Chicago, Great Western with a salary of $350 a month, a good sum for those pre-inflation days but still far from wealth.

Within the next four years he made two key moves that vitally affected his career. First he decided to leave railroading and go to the American Locomotive Company—at an initial loss of salary of $75 per month. He no doubt would have become a top executive had he stayed with American Locomotive, but in 1912, the year automobiles were adding front doors to their carriage-like bodies, he decided to shift to that industry, even though it again meant making a financial sacrifice.

This most important decision of his life came about in an interesting way. Fascinated by a red and white four-cylinder Locomobile that he saw at the Chicago Automobile Show in 1908, he bought it—not so much for the pleasure of driving this fine car as for the chance to learn how it was put together. With the endorsement of a friend, who perhaps sensed the importance of turning Chrysler's abilities loose on an automobile, he borrowed $4,300 of the $5,000 price. It was hard to meet the installments, but Della did not complain. This car gave him an enthusiasm for automobiles that led to his next major decision.

In 1912 Charles Nash, president of Buick, the biggest of the General Motors companies, needed a new manager. Although American Locomotive offered Chrysler $12,000 to stay with them, he accepted the new job at $6,000 a year. The reason he gave was that he saw so many chances to improve manufacturing efficiency that he could not resist the desire to take hold. The Buick, and most other automobile shops, were still influenced by the practice of fine carriage-making. Chrysler could introduce the method of large-scale metal-working for strictly utilitarian ends. Thus at Flint he carried out much of the same kind of reorganization of production that Ford's engineers were doing at Detroit. Although Ford's economies were more spectacular because of his greater volume of production, both shops introduced the assembly line at about the same time.

So successful were his methods that, when Nash left General Motors to make his own cars, W. C. Durant, who in partnership with the Du Ponts bought control of the company in 1917, made Chrysler president of Buick at a salary of $500,000. By 1920 when Chrysler and Durant, both excitable and imaginative, had found it too hard to work together, Chrysler was able to retire with the expectation of living on his savings.

But retirement at forty-five was impossible for Chrysler. Furthermore, the depression of 1920 and 1921 plunged many automobile companies into financial difficulties. The kind of economies for which Chrysler was famous were the order of the day, and when the Willys-Overland people came to him to save their company he set his own price—a million dollars a year for a two-year term. This was at a time when the maximum income tax was about twenty-five percent. While still working at the Willys-Overland salvage operation he took on, for allied financial interests, the reorganization of the Maxwell company.

His acceptance of the Maxwell presidency, after completing the financial reorganization, was the step that led directly to the creation of the Chrysler Corporation. From Willys-Overland he took three brilliant automotive engineers—Carl Bruer, Owen Skelton, and Frank M. Zeder—and set them to work planning a car to bear Chrysler's name that would mark a step forward in design. A high compression engine that gave new flexibility, power, and speed was the major feature of the car, but there were many other innovations, such as smaller wheels, lower lines, and four-wheel hydraulic brakes. The main difficulty was that the Maxwell company had neither the cash nor the credit to finance a new car. In January of 1924 Chrysler exhibited a pilot model in the lobby of the Hotel Commodore in New York. The public response was so enthusiastic that bankers agreed to market five million dollars worth of Maxwell bonds in order to put the Chrysler into production.

This medium-sized car became the sensational automobile of the late twenties. The initial price of $1,600 was high, but the performance was amazing for the period. It took other car manufacturers a couple of years to catch up with Chrysler's design, and by then the new car had won a secure place in the market. This outstanding success led to di...

... the most impor-
tant act of his career. A small company had swallowed a big one, and the combined organization was third in the industry.

With the company gaining on its competitors, Chrysler turned to building a skyscraper in New York City as a monument, and as a gift to his children. When this great structure in the heart of the American metropolis was completed in 1930, its long chromium spire towered higher than any building in the world.

By the time the building was finished the automobile company was facing a depression. This test found Chrysler at his best. Innovations were continued and costs were cut, so that when Chrysler retired to the chairmanship of the board in 1935, the company had no debts and, having overtaken Ford, had become second in volume of production in the industry.

However, he was granted little time to survey the results of his creative leadership. In 1938 he fell ill; later in the same year his wife died. He never regained his health, and died in 1940.

In many respects Chrysler represented one of the last of an older school of American businessmen. The key to his success was ability to increase the efficiency of production. He was relatively unschooled and unread, but he learned things by doing, and he commanded by force of personality and good practical judgment. Although loving power and unrestrained action, he was extremely sensitive about remaining a common man—he was afraid right up to the end that some workmen would think Walter Chrysler felt superior.

Like most of our early business leaders, Chrysler was preoccupied with building his own enterprises. While he enjoyed music all his life, and came to appreciate art, he did not feel it his duty to donate large sums for fellowships or foundations. Perhaps, at sixty-five, he died too young to have reached the stage where he might have turned his energies to affairs outside the circle of business.

Charles Ives, David Wark Griffith

Two more different men than Charles Ives and David Wark Griffith would be hard to imagine. Ives, an extremely successful businessman, made his artistic reputation as a composer of esoteric music. Griffith, an indifferent actor, became famous when he was caught up suddenly in a new, easily commercialized art form, the motion picture. But aside from the obvious fact that both were artists, there was something else about their careers that merits uniting them here in this collection of Unforgettable Americans. Each developed a new way of dealing with an old form of expression. Ives, turning to early New England hymns for inspiration, produced a strange music at once reflective of the past and yet perfectly in keeping with the tensions and discords of the present. Griffith, dealing with the simplest and most obvious stories, used the magic hidden in the motion picture camera to convert trite and childish drama into a new art.

The work of each, in this sense, was a response to the machine age. Ives expressed the artist's reaction to the new dispensation in strange sounds; Griffith employed machinery itself to expand and amplify a conventional art and bring it to the masses with a force and impact never before known.

In quite dissimilar ways the experiences of these men give the lie to the oft-expressed argument that modern life, with its assembly-line standardization and its glorification of material production, must stifle artistic expression. Ives managed to be a successful businessman without either exhausting or corrupting his muse. Griffith worked in the most commercial of media and reached a huge audience of ordinary people without sacrificing his integrity or limiting his creative imagination. Their careers are evidence that there is room in our society for many kinds of artistic expression, and further demonstration of the well-known truth that men of talent can find beauty in the simplest and most unpromising materials.

Alfred Frankenstein, art and music critic for the San Francisco Chronicle *and for many years program editor of the San Francisco Symphony Orchestra, has written widely on musical sub-*

jects. Jay Leyda, of Yale University, is the author of Kino: A History of the Russian and Soviet Film, The Years and Hours of

THE history of Charles Ives' third symphony is the history in brief of that composer's entire career. Begun in 1901 and finished in 1904, it was first performed in 1946, won the Pulitzer Prize in 1947, was published in 1948, and recorded in 1950. Observe the time lag between the completion of this symphony and its first presentation: forty-two years. Observe also the remarkable speed with which it was accorded every form or recognition as soon as it had been placed before the public. This sort of thing happened over and over again with works of Ives in those last years of his life, and by the time he died, in 1954, he had become a famous man.

This looks like the conventional artistic success story, but it has some highly unconventional features. For one thing, Ives was largely responsible for his own obscurity. He did nothing to put his music forward, and indeed often placed obstacles in the way of those who expressed interest in it. He had a violent horror of musical commerce, of playing the game with conductors, publishers, and patrons, and he retired from the profession of music almost as soon as he embarked upon it.

For fifty years Charles Ives sold insurance, and the agency he founded was for many years the largest in the world. Because he was a power in Wall Street, his music, with its extreme and extraordinary features, was long written off as the work of an amateur, but he was an amateur only in the literal sense of that word: he composed for the love of music and for no other reason.

It is, of course, common knowledge that many of the most advanced and iconoclastic musical practices of the twentieth century appeared in the compositions of Ives before they appeared anywhere else. He was writing atonally before Schoenberg, had mastered polytonality long before that term was invented, and knew all about polyrhythms well in advance of

Stravinsky. To say this, however, is to miss the essential point. Ives did not experiment with these things in an abstract, laboratory frame of mind. The source of his experiments lies in American life as he had lived it—first as a boy organist and son of the town bandmaster of Danbury, Connecticut, later as a student at Yale, still later as a resident of New York City. Ives took seriously aspects of American life that the rest of intellectual America did not even know existed. That is the real story of Ives in a nutshell.

He loved the old hymns that were sung in the New England churches, and unlike other musicians he also loved the way people sang them. The congregational singing of New England has not changed much since 1740, when the Reverend Doctor Thomas Walter of Boston observed that "one man will be upon one note and another man upon another note, and the result is beyond description bad." Charles Ives did not think this was bad at all; on the contrary, he delighted in it, and it was one of the principal sources of his style.

Ives' prose is as revealing as his music, and it provides us with a convenient avenue of approach to the man. Highly characteristic is the essay he wrote as preface to his fourth violin sonata, composed in 1915. This work, he tells us, is

> . . . a kind of reflection, remembrance, expression, etc., of the children's services at the outdoor summer camp meetings held around Danbury and in many of the farm towns of Connecticut in the '70s, '80s, and '90s.
>
> The first movement was suggested by an actual happening at one of these services. The children, especially the boys, liked to get up and join the marching kind of hymns. And as these meetings were outdoor, the "march" sometimes became a real one. One day Lowell Mason's "Work for the Night Is Coming" got the boys going and keeping on between services, when the boy who played the melodeon was practicing his "organicks of canonicks, fugaticks, harmonicks, and melodicks." In this movement, as is remembered, they—the postlude organ practice (real and improvised, sometimes both) and the boys' fast march—got to going together, even joining in each other's sounds, and the loudest singers and also those with the best voices, as is often the case, would sing most of the wrong notes. They started this tune on ME, so the boy organist's father made him play SOH hard, even if sometimes it was not in a key that the postlude was in just then. The boys sometimes got as far off from Lowell M. as they did from the melodeon. The organ would be uncovering "covered 5ths," breaking "good resolutions" faster and faster and

the boys' march reaching almost a "Main Street Quickstep" when Parson Hubbell would beat the gong on the oak tree for the next

with two quite separate things—the now-existing sonata and the remembered incident of the camp meeting—and in its intermingling of past and present it scrambles tenses in a fashion calculated to drive any grammarian out of his mind. Ives scrambled the conventional grammar of music in the same way, and to the same ends: past and present, music and reminiscence, all flow together in his work in a fashion not unlike that which the stream-of-consciousness school of fiction was ultimately to perfect for purely literary purposes.

In addition to Congregationalist hymns, Ives loved the popular songs and the fiddle tunes of his youth and the interpretative practices associated with them. He was a northerner, and there is a certain New England austerity in his handling of this material. The folk tunes of the Southern Appalachian region, which so many American composers have used, had no appeal for him at all, but a catalogue of the popular themes he employed would reveal very richly what people were whistling on the streets of Connecticut villages in the latter part of the nineteenth century. It is characteristic of Ives that when he wrote a piano piece for the left hand alone he called it "Some Southpaw Pitching." Only he would have written an orchestral work entitled "The Hook and Ladder on Main Street," and another called "Central Park in the Dark Some Forty Years Ago." One of his major symphonic compositions is called "Holidays," and its individual movements are "Decoration Day," "Washington's Birthday," "Fourth of July," and "Thanksgiving." These flavorsome and provocative titles afford some sense of the color of the man, but they should not be over-emphasized.

The New England organist in his quiet organ loft can, if he is sensitive and creative and knowing, accomplish remarkable things. Ives conjured wonders from the old hymn books; some of the most profound expressions of religious feeling ever set down in music are to be found in the slow movements of his symphonies, which are largely derived from the organ improvisations of his youth. In works of this kind he rises far above the picturesque and parochial to attain a musical transcendentalism not at all unlike that of the New England philosophers on whom he was raised.

It is no accident that Charles Ives wrote a "Concord Sonata," with movements about Emerson, Thoreau, Hawthorne, and the Alcotts. This he preceded with a long essay from which I extract some significant lines:

> There are communities now, partly vanished, but cherished and sacred, scattered through this world of ours, in which freedom of thought and soul, and even of body, have been fought for. And we believe that there ever lives in that part of the over-soul, native to them, the thoughts which these freedom-struggles have inspired. America is not too young to have its divinities and its place legends. Many of those "transcendent thoughts" and "visions" which had their birth beneath our Concord elms—messages that have brought salvation to many listening souls throughout the world—are still growing, day by day, to greater beauty, are still showing clearer and clearer man's way to God.

Translate that into music, and you will have something very like the symphonies and sonatas of Charles Edward Ives.

" . . . meaning and artistic courage"

JAY LEYDA

It is granted to few individuals to determine the nature and use of a completely new medium of art. Our century has witnessed one such rare opportunity, seized so recently by an extraordinary artist that we have not yet fully realized the scope of his achievement. There is little critical attention to his work and there is no full-length biography of him, although 1958 marked the tenth anniversary of his death. Perhaps his work is too recent, too close for perspective—his medium, too, is one that we have very confused notions about.

No precedent exists for this situation: there was a mere decade

complished through the trials and errors of many inventors, representing most of the industrial nations at the end of the nineteenth century. Without those first technical steps Griffith could not, of course, have taken his artistic step, but his was the great step that generally lacks acknowledgment. If we enjoy films today, it is largely because D. W. Griffith took a commercial toy and showed it how to express emotions, ideas, states of mind, feelings. He turned a device into an art that changed the development of all dramatic arts.

Griffith is credited with a large number of introductions, such as the close-up, the moving camera, the lengthened film, bold lighting, the fadeout, and other expressive devices. Yet with the high premium placed on novelty in this industry, in its early years as well as today, it is possible that many of the essential devices used by Griffith had previously appeared on screens somewhere in the world. But the important difference between invention and creation is wide, and what Griffith did with these devices was to manipulate them for dramatic and expressive purposes. Earlier films had included an occasional close-up, for example, but no one had before used it for emphasis, climax, characterization. In Griffith's hands it was always further heightened by shots from other viewpoints to gain maximum effect. For a comparable situation imagine some remote prehistorical period after the invention of words, when one man found that poems and songs could be made of them. Griffith did something more fundamental, too: he put the primitive words of film invention into coherent and dynamic sentences. There were, however, two subtle inventions of far-reaching significance for which Griffith should be given full credit: he discovered that the new medium could fix its own relationship in space and in time. Film-space could be freer than stage-space, and film-time could be compressed or extended in any way the subject required. When

Griffith discovered that this flexibility could be achieved on the film cutting-table, the future was opened.

The end of Griffith's career and the end of his life, for he outlived his working career, had a bitterness not to be equalled among American artists of comparable stature, though possibly the ends of Herman Melville's career and life were as bitter. His earliest, most obscure, most anonymous work in films had been so clearly marked with meaning and artistic courage. He had sent out from the New York studio of the Biograph Company to the nation's nickelodeons, month after month, films that were amazingly fresh strides forward in film expressiveness. He broke down all commercial and cultural barriers erected around the young medium with one overwhelming big film. He had carved some of the star-pillars that held up the industrial structure. His most casual work seemed to embody the highest ideals circulating in American films. How, then, could such a man have been allowed to sit for years in the lobby of the Hollywood-Knickerbocker Hotel, talking of past and future dreams to anyone who would listen, while seven of the most splendid studios of the world, all within local bus distance, remained closed to him?

Part of the answer can be found in the shifting film worlds of taste and commerce, but a deeper answer—one that is harder to face—may be sought in the artist himself. What equipment did Griffith bring to films in 1907 when he offered himself as employee, actor, writer, and finally as controlling artist? The one art in which he had practical and excitingly uncertain experience was the theater; and no theatrical period in history has been more colorful or less substantial than the American theater that sprawled over into our century. From ten years of acting, young Griffith brought to films a surer sense of dramatic presentation than they had known, and in films he found himself, for the first time, among people who knew less and had had less experience than he.

His spare-time love and dream was literature: plays, verse, stories, all were tried and some even reached the stage or print before he directed his first film. With this love he brought enthusiasm and some half-formed artistic ideals to his film work. From his Biograph films to his last sad effort, "The Struggle," one sees this literary luggage as mixed, offering a fullness and breadth of thematic ambition unsupported by real knowledge of the nature of literature, or of any art, but reinforced by instincts that were exactly what was needed by the new medium.

[illegible] himself to any old or fixed art, we

Griffith found his medium gradually, taking on more jobs as they appeared, and finally he knew what he had, and what his relationship to it had to be. This new business needed all the arts he had touched, and all those incomparable waiting instincts. It was *the* opportunity for both business and man. Opportunity is not enough, though chance has much to do with it—the chance of the right temperament and talent at the right historical moment.

From what we prefer to think a sophisticated viewpoint, Griffith's dramatic material may now seem old-fashioned and naive. But examined objectively, the Griffith subject matter appears so far ahead of its time that in many respects we have not yet caught up with it. In regard to his historical subjects alone we must feel ashamed that he gave a broader treatment to both the American and French Revolutions than we have seen on any screen since the production of "America" and "Orphans of the Storm."

Despite the bias of "The Birth of a Nation" and the free-for-all logic of "Intolerance," no one can deny that their powerful artistic embodiment probably influenced the historical attitudes of every viewer exposed to them. When we summon a pictorial image for the Civil War, most of us recall the first half of "The Birth of a Nation" rather than Brady's photographs, though they, too, contributed to this film's power. Any mention of Babylon always brings to my mind the fantastic Babylonian scenes of "Intolerance." In the final two reels of the latter film, the medium and its new master take over your attention completely, as "history itself seems to pour like a cataract across the screen," to quote the admirable monograph on Griffith written by Iris Barry and published by the Museum of Modern Art. If there is anything naive about "Broken Blossoms," you are not aware of it while that intense, perfect work is on the screen. The simple pathos of "Isn't Life Wonderful," a film about Germany after the first World War, is rarely touched by German films on the same subject.

All Griffith films had a *personal* quality that is now almost totally absent from the American film. It took a large number of people then, too, to make a film, but a Griffith film always showed one person's dominant idea to the world; and when he could no longer be sure of that, he and the increasingly impersonal film machinery had to part company. Griffith's one-man rule of film should not imply any artistic inadequacy among his cast and crew, for he developed a group of our best actors and actresses, and his assistants became the leading film-makers of the next two generations. Growing alongside Griffith's incredibly swift development was the first imaginative cameraman of film history —Billy Bitzer. In speaking with any associate of Griffith, whether Lillian Gish or Mary Pickford or Bessie Love or Mae Marsh or Lionel Barrymore or Mack Sennett or W. S. Van Dyke, one heard the secret of that dominance over and over: to get what he wanted from the people who worked with him, Griffith used only the power of conviction—a convinced, sure artist swaying others to see as he did.

The "others" always included audiences, for he was constantly aware of this chief reason for making films. Once he called the motion picture theater "the workingman's college." This was certainly true whenever a theater showed a film by Griffith, even the poorest, for he rarely lost sight of his moral responsibility to that audience.

His films were the world's college, too; no American since Walt Whitman has had such influence on European audiences and European artists. There his work and name are more often recalled than in his native country. In the evolution of film art, Griffith is responsible beyond his own films and even beyond his own country, for no one anywhere in the world made a contribution to that evolution outside the influence of D. W. Griffith.

INDEX